50 STRATEGIES THAT CHANGED HISTORY

50

STRATEGIES THAT CHANGED HISTORY

DANIEL SMITH

METRO BOOKS
New York

METRO BOOKS
New York

An Imprint of Sterling Publishing
1166 Avenue of the Americas
New York, NY 10036

This book was designed, conceived, and produced by
Quantum Books Ltd
6 Blundell Street
London N7 9BH
United Kingdom

Publisher: Kerry Enzor
Managing Editor: Sorrel Wood
Senior Editor: Philippa Davis
Copyeditor: Donna Gregory
Proofreader: Josh Ireland
Indexer: Diana Le Core
Production Manager: Rohana Yusof
Design: Gareth Butterworth, Jason Anscomb, Guy Croton

ISBN: 978-1-4351-6009-5

For information about custom editions, special sales, and premium and
corporate purchases, please contact Sterling Special Sales at 800-805-
5489 or specialsales@sterlingpublishing.com.

Printed in China by Toppan Leefung

2 4 6 8 10 9 7 5 3 1

www.sterlingpublishing.com

CONTENTS

INTRODUCTION

"WHAT'S THE USE OF RUNNING IF YOU ARE NOT ON THE RIGHT ROAD"—GERMAN PROVERB

"TACTICS WITHOUT STRATEGY IS THE NOISE BEFORE DEFEAT"—SUN TZU

While occasionally the fate of an individual, or even the world as a whole, might turn on a moment of chance or some freakish alignment of circumstances, the majority of human history has been defined by the results of strategy. Strategy—which is to say, a plan of action designed to achieve an overarching aim—is the means by which individuals attempt to bring order to a disordered world. Take, for instance the words of one of the greatest strategic thinkers of all time, Napoleon Bonaparte: "The battlefield is a scene of constant chaos. The winner will be the one who controls that chaos—both his own and the enemy's."

In the pages that follow, we will analyze 50 strategies that shaped the world we live in today. In each case, we will consider the character and ambitions of the person (or, now and again, people) behind it, how they went about executing it, and how effective it was. Examples are drawn from the disparate arenas of warfare, commerce, and politics. It probably comes as little surprise that there is significant overlap between all three areas. The modern business tycoon or political operator can doubtless learn as much from the ruthless battlefield techniques of a Julius Caesar or a Napoleon as they can from more obvious forerunners such as a John D. Rockefeller or a Karl Marx. Similarly, the modern military general may pick up just as much about empire building from Rupert Murdoch as from Lenin, or garner as many tips on leadership from Mark Zuckerberg as Joan of Arc.

OUTCOMES OF SUCCESSFUL STRATEGY

All of them reside within this book, providing case studies as to how we might seek to take advantage of our own strengths and exploit the weaknesses of rivals and opponents. Almost all the examples gathered here offer at least some positive lessons. However, in a handful of instances—notably the Nazis's Final Solution strategy—it may be seen that strategic thinking can sometimes lead to disaster.

US troops disembark at Omaha beach on D-Day, World War II. Operation Overlord was a triumph of minutely detailed military planning by the combined Allied forces to gain the initiative against Nazi Germany.

Again, this was a lesson Napoleon learned long ago, as when he observed that he made it a rule never to interrupt an enemy while he was making a mistake. Or as Winston Churchill would have it: "However beautiful the strategy, you should occasionally look at the results."

All of the strategies here have had a lasting influence, whether in setting the standard for other strategists to follow, such as Robespierre's rule by terror or Gandhi's highly influential discourse of nonviolent protest, or in bringing about lasting change as a result of that strategy.

A BROAD SPECTRUM

The full gamut of human history is covered here, from ancient stories of the Trojan horse and the deadly battle between David and Goliath, through the birth of banking in the medieval age, the emergence of modern marketing strategies in the eighteenth century, the exploits of the Red Baron in World War I, and on to up-to-the-moment analysis of Jeff Bezos's approach to internet commerce and Barack Obama's tactical engagement with social media.

Even across centuries there are remarkable similarities between successful strategic approaches. For example, leaders in all ages need to be able to communicate their ideas to as wide an audience as possible. The method of delivery may have changed from Ashoka the Great to US President Barack Obama, but the core strategy remains the same: Exploiting the latest medium of mass communication to broadcast their message to as wide an audience as possible. The designation of key strategical types for each of the 50 chapters highlights the similarities between each example, drawing comparisons throughout the book.

Many of the strategies in this book were driven by brilliant individuals who implemented tactics to further their own vision of the future and secure success. But there are also examples of seminal strategies adopted by broader groups. The elite order of warrior monks, the Knights Templar, from 1119 to 1314 successfully capitalized on their unique position of trust and power to establish a system that would become the blueprint for modern banking. The wars of the twentieth century also have many examples of strategies adopted by forces as a whole to win advantage over the enemy, from the Q-boat tactics of the allied forces to the terrible industrialization of mass murder introduced under the Nazi regime.

While of course such a book as this can never claim to be comprehensive, these fifty studies open a window onto a fascinating array of strategic approaches. Most are driven by individual force of will rooted in a desire to leave a real mark on the world. Even if your own goals do not include writing your name into history, these stories of personal endeavor, ambition, and forethought provide myriad hints and tips that may be applied to everyday life. For instance, you need not be intent on besieging a city to benefit from Caesar's insight that you are at risk of being knocked off-balance, even when you appear to be on the front foot!

LEARNING BY EXAMPLE

It is worth remembering too that the great strategic thinkers discussed here were just that because they absorbed lessons from the experiences of others and adapted them to suit the peculiar circumstances they themselves faced. Any truly great strategist is prepared to mold and adjust his tactics as the situation requires. The ancient Chinese military theorist, Sun Tzu, emphasized the importance of constantly evolving strategy: "Do not repeat the tactics which have gained you one victory, but let your methods be regulated by the infinite variety of circumstances." Charles de Gaulle would make much the same point some two-and-a-half millennia later: "You have to be fast on your feet and adaptive or else a strategy is useless."

As well as offering valuable lessons, these are also fifty fascinating stories in their own rights. Each tells how key players have coped, adapted, and thrived at crucial moments in time. If nothing else, enjoy them as gripping snapshots of life through the ages, charting great moments of progress, crisis, and hope.

HOW TO USE THIS BOOK

Organized by date, the chapters in this book have been carefully designed for ease of reference. Each of the chapters in the book is color-coded according to the type of strategy being discussed (see key right). An information panel at the start of each article provides a quick summary of the key details, and a strategy analysis panel sums up the take-away lessons from each story—including the strategy type typified by that example also indicated by the icon at the top of each panel (see key right). Time lines with key events are also featured with the key turning-points indicated by the larger circle next to that specific entry.

KEY TO SECTIONS

POLITICS AND SOCIETY

COMMERCE

MILITARY

KEY TO STRATEGY ICONS

 TACTICAL DECEPTION

 DEFENSIVE

 STRATEGIC THINKING

 MARKETING

 COMMUNICATION

 LEADERSHIP

 PERSEVERANCE

 PREPARATION

 ATTACK TACTICS

 INNOVATION

 DOMINANCE

1

INFILTRATE THE ENEMY

GREEK GENERAL **ODYSSEUS** DEVISED A FIENDISH TRICK TO FINALLY PENETRATE THE CITY WALLS OF TROY

KEY PLAYER: *Odysseus*
NATIONALITY: *Greek*
STRATEGY IMPLEMENTED:
Between the eleventh and fourteenth centuries BC
CONTEXT: *After ten years of failed attempts to break down Troy's walls, the Greeks used cunning deception to achieve their ends*

The phrase "beware Greeks bearing gifts"—meaning to be on your guard if an enemy offers an apparent hand of friendship—is a staple of the modern vernacular but its roots lie in the Trojan War of antiquity. In a cunning plan devised by Odysseus, Greek forces broke the resistance of the Trojans by pretending to abandon the conflict, when in fact troops were hiding in a giant wooden horse—an object they correctly guessed would intrigue their foes. Sure enough, the Trojans willingly wheeled the curiosity and its deadly contents into their city.

Detailed in classical literature, the dispute between the Greeks and the city state of Troy arose after the Trojan prince, Paris, eloped with (or perhaps abducted) Helen, reputedly the world's most beautiful woman and wife of the Spartan king Menelaus. There followed years of bloody conflict during which the Greeks tried desperately to conquer Troy and return Helen to Menelaus.

After a decade or so a Greek general called Odysseus had a brainwave. Rather than continuing with their fruitless onslaught, why didn't the Greeks pretend to return home, so leaving their enemy off-guard? Meanwhile, a crack troop of men (numbering some thirty or so) would hide in a giant wooden horse outside the city walls. Celebrated by the Greek poet Homer as a man of great wisdom and resourcefulness, this cunning ploy was a perfect example of Odysseus's strategic intelligence.

A man called Sinon, who would tell the Trojans that he had been left behind during the Greek retreat, would explain that the horse was an offering to the goddess Athena, given by the Greeks in the hope of safe passage back across the seas and to atone for the earlier sacking of her temple in Troy. According to Virgil, he would also tell them that it had been made just too large for the Trojans to bring it inside their city walls, a precaution so that they should not benefit from the offering. A narrative designed to pique Trojan interest, it worked like a dream.

NEVER LOOK A GIFT HORSE IN THE MOUTH
Whether the Trojans regarded the horse as booty or whether they were intent on hijacking the good will of the goddess, they of course brought the giant equine statue

▲ *Giovanni Domenico Tiepolo depicts the horse being hauled into the city by citizens unaware of the terrible surprise that awaits.*

inside the city walls, even breaking down ramparts to ease access according to some accounts. The jubilant Trojans then spent the night in celebration before returning to their dwellings to rest their weary heads.

Once their enemies were asleep, the Greeks emerged from their hiding place inside the horse and silently dispatched the Trojans keeping guard on the city walls. They then gave a signal to the mass of Greek forces, who had not started out for home but had merely set up camp on a nearby island. Troy was soon flooded with enemy troops who set about the Trojans mercilessly, killing many men and seizing women and children to take as slaves. Odysseus's carefully planned deception had succeeded in breaking the stalemate and Troy was brought to its knees.

It is difficult to say whether the tale of the Trojan horse as it has come down to us is historically accurate. Indeed, the narrative of the entire Trojan War and even the existence of Troy itself is highly contentious. The ancient Greeks and Romans certainly treated the events detailed by authors including Homer, Ovid, and Virgil as historical reality. However, for many centuries afterward it was widely accepted that the story of Troy was merely myth until, in the 1860s and 1870s, archeologists Frank Calvert and Heinrich Schliemann discovered a lost city in northwest Turkey that many now believe was the real Troy. And if the city existed, so the argument goes, there is surely a good chance that parts of its history as they are recorded happened too.

TIME LINE

Given the disputed nature of the Trojan War, below is a time line that offers a broad chronology of events without attributing specific dates to them. The date of the fall of Troy has traditionally been put at somewhere between 1135 and 1334 BC, although modern archeological evidence suggests some time in the 1180s as the most likely candidate.

From a wide array of suitors, King Menelaus is chosen as husband of Helen, a renowned Greek beauty.

Paris, Prince of Troy, believes the goddess Aphrodite has promised Helen to him. He duly kidnaps her and brings her to Troy.

Menelaus raises an army to get his bride back.

Greek forces arrive at Troy. Inconclusive fighting continues for several years.

Odysseus comes up with the "Trojan horse" scheme.

The Trojans, believing the Greeks have left, wheel the giant horse inside the city walls.

As the Trojans sleep, Greek soldiers emerge from the horse and open the city gates to let in further reinforcements.

Troy's population is massacred as they sleep and the city falls.

800-700 BC
Our main sources of knowledge for the Trojan War are Homer's Iliad *and* Odyssey, *and the* Epic Cycle, *a collection of poems by assorted Ancient Greek poets that only survives in fragments.*

1865
Archeologist Frank Calvert began excavating ruins in northwest Turkey (formerly Anatolia) that many now believe are those of Troy.

So what of the Trojan horse? Maybe it occurred just as the ancients described. Alternatively, modern historians have posited that the horse was actually some sort of battering ram or perhaps even a ship ostensibly carrying a Greek peace envoy but actually containing troops intent on assault. Regardless, the Trojan horse serves as a powerful cypher for a certain type of confidence trickery and provides a model for dishonest and fraudulent behaviour through to the modern day.

TRICKS OF THE TRADE

If a tale of such outlandish deception seems dubious to the modern reader,

AN OFFER YOU CAN'T REFUSE

The tale of the Trojan Horse has become so absorbed into the popular consciousness that the phrase itself has become shorthand for any ruse or strategy to gain entry into a prohibited space. It has found particular resonance in the twenty-first century in the context of malicious computer programs, known as "Trojans," that infiltrate users's machines without their knowledge. It is a term also used in the world of commerce for an offer of such apparent generosity that customers are sucked in only to be charged a much greater sum in order to take up the offer. An example of such may include the offer of a free mobile phone, but only on condition the consumer signs up to a long contract at above market-rate cost.

it is worth remembering that modern warfare has witnessed its fair share of outrageous subterfuge. Consider, for instance, Operation Mincemeat, a feat of extraordinary misdirection perpetrated by the British during World War II.

In 1943, the British planned to launch an attack on Italy from North Africa, landing in Sicily. However, fearful that the Germans would get wind of the invasion, it was decided to plant misinformation that Berlin would believe it had fortuitously stumbled upon. A team of intelligence officers, including James Bond creator Ian Fleming, came up with an audacious scheme. They procured the body of a vagrant who had been found dead in London and created an entirely new identity for the cadaver. They dressed the dead man in military garb and created fake identity papers, even placing used ticket stubs among his personal possessions to create the illusion that this was a "real" person. They then filled a suitcase with papers that suggested the Allies were planning an invasion of Greece.

Finally, in complete secrecy, they deposited the corpse in waters off the Spanish coast. When it washed up on the beach, it looked for all the world like a high-ranking officer had drowned after some catastrophe. Just as the British hoped, his papers fell into the hands of Spanish spies who dutifully passed on the intelligence to Berlin. Hitler amassed troops in Greece to await the hypothetical Allied attack, only for the Allies to hit Sicily, taking the island in a month and helping to turn the war's tide decisively.

▲ Identity papers for "William Martin" the persona created by British intelligence during WWII to deceive the Germans.

TAKE YOUR ENEMY BY SURPRISE

The Trojan horse (and modern variations thereon, such as that described above) is such an effective tactic because it exploits the element of surprise. The enemy's lines are breached and its defenses infiltrated before it has time to realize. It is, then, perhaps the ultimate strategy for taking an enemy off-guard, allowing a strike just as they are at their most relaxed and vulnerable. Odysseus's cunning set the bar for the many tactics of deception that have been employed by strategists in all fields ever since. Today, tellingly, it is rather more often used in commerce than warfare (see panel opposite).

STRATEGY ANALYSIS

STRATEGY TYPE: *Tactical deception*
KEY STRATEGY: *Infiltrating enemy lines by proffering an apparent enticement*
OUTCOME: *Troy is sacked*
ALSO USED BY: *Sultan Baibars at Krac des Chevaliers, 1271; Operation Mincemeat, World War II; and in the modern world of commerce.*

2

A WINNING MINDSET

IN ONE OF THE GREATEST APPARENT MISMATCHES DAVID USED SHARP THINKING TO OVERTURN THE ODDS

KEY PLAYER: *David*
NATIONALITY: *Israelite*
STRATEGY IMPLEMENTED:
c.1024 BC
CONTEXT: *For forty days, the Israelites and Philistines lined up against each other in the Valley of Elah. Each day Goliath, challenged his enemies to send down a single man to face him in a winner-takes-all battle to the death*

It is the ultimate tale of the underdog triumphing and has become the shorthand phrase to describe any fight between an established "giant" and a plucky minnow. It is a term that recurs throughout history not only in a military context, but in the spheres of politics, sport, and commerce too. So how did David, an Israelite shepherd boy, upset the odds? While physically underpowered compared to his opponent, he was quicker of mind and action.

The Philistines were regarded as among the most dangerous enemies of the ancient Israelites, who at the time of David and Goliath were led by Saul. When the two armies met around the middle of the 1020s BC, their very sovereignty was at stake. If the Israelites lost, they would become subjects of the Philistines, and if the result went the other way, the Philistines would serve the Israelites.

It was therefore little wonder that the stand-off was so tense. Remarkably, David—the teenage boy who would change everything—was not even part of the Israelite army. As the youngest of eight sons, he had stayed behind in Bethlehem. Every now and again, his aging father would send David to check on how his brothers were doing on the front line and to bring them supplies. David was in no way groomed for military greatness, which made his subsequent actions all the more notable.

Goliath, on the other hand, was the archetypal fighting machine. Hailing from the city of Gath, he is said to have stood somewhere between 6 feet 9 inches and 9 feet 9 inches tall. His armor consisted of a helmet, long coat, and leg guards, all made from bronze, and he carried a long bronze spear that was slung across his back. Each day, he came down into the Valley of Elah that separated the two armies and harangued his enemy: "This day I defy the armies of Israel! Give me a man and let us fight each other." According to the Book of Samuel, his words struck fear into the hearts of Saul and his men.

Caravaggio's striking image, painted in 1600, of David severing the head of his giant nemesis, so providing the blueprint for underdog victories. ▶

TIME LINE

c. 1040 BC
David, son of Jesse, is born in Bethlehem.

c. 1030 BC
David is annointed as the future king of Israel.

c. 1024 BC
He meets and kills Goliath in one-on-one battle after the Philistine and Israelite armies draw up battle lines at the Valley of Elah.

c. 1020 BC
David is by now a respected warrior in King Saul's army. However, the two soon fall out.

c.1010 BC
David becomes king of Judah.

c.1002 BC
His rule extends to all the kingdoms of Israel. He plans to build a temple to God.

c. 990 BC
He begins an affair with Bathsheba.

c. 988 BC
David's son, Absalom, conspires against him. David flees Jerusalem but Absalom is later killed in battle.

c. 982 BC
David returns to Jerusalem.

c.970 BC
David dies in Jerusalem. His son, Solomon, succeeds him.

Around this time, the Israelites and Philistines were engaged in a long war. The Bible records seven battles: Shephelah, Aphek (where Israel was defeated and the Philistines captured the Ark); Eben-Ezer (Israelite victory); Michmash, (Israelite victory); Elah (Israelite victory); Mount Gilboa (Philistine victory, during which Saul and his three sons were killed); and Hezekiah (Israelite victory).

One day David was at the front to speak with his brothers when he heard a rumor that Saul would richly reward anyone who killed Goliath. Whether it was these enticements or simply youthful bravura that spurred him on, David volunteered himself to Saul to take on the giant. It was an act of extraordinary, even reckless, courage. However, his bravery was also rooted in profound faith. He described how in his role as a shepherd he had to fight off lions and bears which attacked the flock. "The Lord who rescued me from the paw of lion and the paw of bear," he said, "will rescue me from the hands of the Philistine." As the story is told, David could not have succeeded without utter confidence that victory was his destiny—a "winner's attitude" of a type that modern, elite sportsmen regularly evoke in search of the small margins that separate victor and vanquished.

THE CHALLENGER

Sometimes it can seem like the modern commercial world is dominated by lumbering behemoths, relying on their sheer size for market dominance. Yet technological advances have ensured that there has rarely been a better time to be a "David" in business. So-called "challenger brands" have taken on established giants, taking advantage of their greater ability to respond to changing market conditions and emerging opportunities. Apple, for instance, blossomed by playing David to the Goliath of IBM, while Avis did much the same with Hertz in the hire-car market.

THE BIGGER THEY ARE, THE HARDER THEY FALL

Having agreed to take up the challenge, David was rigged out in the best armor the Israelites could find. However, he was less concerned with its ability to protect him than with the restrictions it put on his movement. He recognized there was no point in trying to match his enemy in strength and weight. Instead he would need to take advantage of those attributes that he possessed which Goliath could not call upon. Specifically, he could move much quicker than the giant and that would prove key to his success. But weighed down by heavy armor, he would be even slower than Goliath. The armor had to go.

So David made his way to the fateful encounter armed only with a sling and five rounded stones. When Goliath saw the fresh-faced boy, he treated him with disdain but David, fueled by utter self-belief, announced to the giant that he would fell him and cut off his head. As Goliath advanced toward him, David saw his chance. Wise enough to know that he could never win in close combat, he rushed to a point in sufficient range of his foe, inserted a stone into his slingshot, aimed and fired. It hit Goliath in the temple, embedding itself as the great warrior crumpled. David then unsheathed Goliath's own sword and, true to his word, decapitated him. The lightly armed teen had achieved one of history's most unlikely victories by exhibiting skill, self-belief, and quick-thinking.

THE QUICK AND THE DEAD

David and Goliath is arguably the earliest "giant-killing" story—a paradigm that recurs throughout history. Indeed, such tales are pivotal in everything from the construction of national identity to corporate branding and instilling sportspeople with a winning mentality.

Take the example of the great American athlete, Michael Johnson, who dominated the world of 200- and 400-metre sprinting in the 1990s. With an ungainly, upright running style and a short stride, few experts considered his technique to be up there with the best of them but he used psychology to enable him to overcome perceived finer physical exponents year in and year out. By visualizing races unfolding in triumph, he dismissed negative thoughts and gave himself the best chance of success—just as David's faith in God's support allowed him to overcome apparently insurmountable odds.

In addition, David knew to capitalize on his particular strengths. He could not hope to overpower Goliath bodily, but with the vision to know when to strike, and the dexterity and agility to perfectly execute the attack, he gave Goliath no chance. There is little as satisfying as when the little guy wins by using his brains and a bit of nimble-footedness. David provided the perfect template for all such victories and the tale of his defeat of Goliath has given succour to every underdog since.

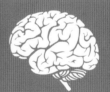

STRATEGY ANALYSIS

STRATEGY TYPE: *Strategic thinking*
KEY STRATEGY: *David used quick wits and speed to defeat his formidable opponent*
OUTCOME: *The Israelites were victorious and David set on the path to kingship*
ALSO USED BY: *Apple against IBM, and Richard Branson's Virgin Atlantic Airways against British Airways.*

3

FEIGN RETREAT

THEMISTOCLES'S PLAN TO LURE THE PERSIANS INTO DANGEROUS WATERS WON THE GREEKS VICTORY AT SALAMIS

KEY PLAYER: *Themistocles (c.524 BC–459 BC)*
NATIONALITY: *Greek*
STRATEGY IMPLEMENTED: *480 BC*
CONTEXT: *With Athens abandoned, the Persians seemed in reach of conquering all Greece until Thermistocles convinced his Greek allies to engage the Persians in a do-or-die naval battle in the sea around the island of Salamis*

After the Persians inflicted a crushing defeat on the alliance of Greek city-states at the Battle of Thermopylae in 480 BC, it appeared only a matter of time until the Persian king, Xerxes, ruled over all Greece. However, Themistocles, a military commander from Athens, persuaded the disparate alliance that their best chance lay in bringing the Persians to battle near Salamis. He then employed cunning to induce Xerxes into a confrontation that ended with victory for the Greeks.

Following the Greek collapse at Thermopylae and stalemate in the accompanying naval Battle of Artemisium, Athens was evacuated to Salamis and the Persians moved in, looting and burning the great city down. The Greek cause was further hampered by distrust and rivalry between its constituent states. As Athens fell, the Spartans were intent on returning to the Peloponnese, with a plan to build a wall across the Isthmus of Corinth to counter any Persian land attack. However, with the Greek fleet having also withdrawn to the island of Salamis, the Athenian Themistocles used all his political skills to talk his compatriots into remaining where they were. His reason was a belief that the Persians could be defeated in the surrounding waters.

Themistocles was a divisive figure over the length of his career but ahead of the Battle of Salamis he was at his most persuasive. He argued that a wall would only hold back the Persians for so long, not least because their naval dominance meant that the army could be continually resupplied with essential resources. To return to the Peloponnese was merely to delay the inevitable, he suggested. However, if the Persians could be beaten once and for all on the water, their entire mission in Greece would be severely compromised. The Greeks, he contended, had a genuine chance of victory if the Persians's much larger fleet was led up a blind alley in the straits between Salamis and the port city of Piraeus. Such was the restricted space that the Persians's larger force would actually prove a disadvantage and the Greeks's knowledge of the terrain would give them the edge over their numerically superior foe.

It was an undeniably sound tactical argument but Themistocles realized that a sign of good faith was required on his part. He had long proclaimed the importance of naval

This view of the Battle of Salamis, painted by Wilhelm von Kaulbach in 1858, gives an impression of the utter confusion that faced the Persians.

strength and had spent years persuading the Athenian authorities to invest in building ships and training first-rate crews. In fact, Athens supplied more than half the vessels of the entire Greek navy. Themistocles was, then, the natural choice to command the force. However, given the political delicacy of the situation, he sacrificed his own ambitions

TIME LINE

c.524 BC
Themistocles is born in Athens.

493 BC
He is elected an archon (a senior official) of the city-state.

492–490 BC
The first Persian invasion of Greece ends with Athens' victory at the Battle of Marathon.

483 BC
Themistocles is responsible for a major re-strengthening of the Athenian navy.

480 BC
Xerxes leads the second Persian invasion of Greece. After success at the Battle of Thermopylae in August, his forces are roundly defeated the following month at the Battle of Salamis.

479 BC
The Persian invasion ends with defeat in June at the Battle of Plataea.

459 BC
Themistocles dies, having been forced into exile from Greece on charges of treachery.

so that a Spartan, Eurybiades, was given nominal command. Themistocles thus secured backing for his plan and ensured relations within the alliance were as strong as possible ahead of the potentially crucial engagement. Long before Ludwig von Rochau coined the phrase in the nineteenth century, Themistocles was proving himself an arch exponent of realpolitik—politics based on practical and material considerations rather than ideological or personal concerns.

SETTING THE BAIT

Now came the trickier task of convincing Xerxes that his ambitions were best served by joining battle at Salamis. Few historians doubt that he would have been wiser to steer well clear. However, Themistocles used all his powers of deception to entice him there. He sent a slave called Sicinnus to Xerxes, pretending to be serving as an informer. Sicinnus fed Xerxes the story that the Greek naval forces could not decide on a suitable battle location so were instead planning a stealthy night-time retreat.

Xerxes, hungry to complete his Greek campaign as quickly as possible, fell for the story and sent out his ships to block any potential escape route from the narrow channel. Furthermore, he ordered his fleet to fruitlessly scour the area for evidence of the purported retreat. On the day of the actual battle, the Persian crews were thus already tired after a hard night's work, while the Greeks were well rested. Nonetheless, defeat does not seem to have crossed Xerxes's mind. It is said that he had a throne set up on the shores of the battle scene so that he might survey his forces's expected triumph.

While it was still morning, the Persians received the signal to attack. They sailed into the straits, where they first met a contingent of Corinthian vessels. The Corinthian commander, Adeimantus, gave the signal for his boats to retreat. As they did so, a great cat-and-mouse game began, with the Persians following the Greek ships into ever narrowing waters. While some contemporary sources suggested the Corinthians showed cowardice, it is likely they were simply following the wily orders of Themistocles, who was running the show even though Eurybiades was officially in charge.

THE BATTLE COMMENCES

In terms of simple numbers, the Greeks should have been no match for the Persians. Themistocles could call upon 368 ships, while Xerxes's force boasted over 1,300, including the masterful naval forces of the Phoenicians. But just as at the Battle of Artemisium a few weeks earlier against the same opponents, the Persians allowed themselves to be drawn into a narrow strait where their vast numbers were least effective. The Greeks carried on retreating until they were at risk of running aground. Then all of a sudden, one of the Athenian ships drove forward and rammed its Persian counterpart. So the fighting began in earnest.

As more and more Persian vessels piled into an ever-decreasing space, confusion overtook them. Such was their density that they struggled to turn, often finding themselves caught sideways-on as Greek ships rammed them. Their difficulties were compounded because many of the Persians, unlike their Greek opponents, were unable to swim. As the ancient historian Herodotus described it: "The Greek fleet worked together as a whole, while the Persians had lost formation and were no longer fighting to any plan."

By nightfall, the Persians had lost perhaps a third of their fleet. Xerxes, earlier so confident of victory, was forced to concede that the game was up. He ordered his navy to retreat and, without logistical support from the sea, his army was compelled to withdraw too. His invasion plan had lost its momentum and a year later his forces were defeated at the Battle of Plataea, marking the end of Persia's attempt to wrestle control of Greece. Had it succeeded, classical Greek culture would have been stymied and the whole of Western history would have taken a different course. As it was, Themistocles masterminded an unlikely victory by inducing Xerxes to fight an unnecessary battle.

THE ART OF DECEPTION

The feigned retreat would be a strategy employed many times in the future. William the Conqueror used the ruse during the Battle of Hastings, while the Mongols were also skillful exponents. World War II, meanwhile, was littered with examples of deception designed to draw the enemy into an unadvantageous location. Most famously, Operation Bodyguard sought to persuade Hitler that the Allies's planned 1944 landings at Normandy were a cover and that the real attack would be elsewhere.

STRATEGY ANALYSIS

STRATEGY TYPE: *Tactical deception*
KEY STRATEGY: *Luring the enemy navy into waters where they cannot maneuver*
OUTCOME: *The Second Persian War turned irrevocably in Greece's favor*
ALSO USED BY: *William the Conqueror at the Battle of Hastings, 1066; Mongol warriors, and Operation Bodyguard, World War II.*

4 PLAY THE PERCENTAGES

ALEXANDER THE GREAT DEFEATED DARIUS'S VAST PERSIAN FORCE AT GAUGAMELA USING TACTICAL NOUS

Alexander died aged just 32 but by then he had established himself as the greatest leader of the ancient world and arguably the most brilliant military tactician in history. During a career that saw him become king of Macedonia, Persia, and Asia, as well as pharaoh of Egypt, he never lost a military engagement. In most cases, he defeated armies far larger than his own. His triumph at Gaugamela epitomized his strategic genius that maximized every possible advantage.

KEY PLAYER: *Alexander the Great (356 BC–323 BC)*
NATIONALITY: *Macedonian*
STRATEGY IMPLEMENTED: *October 1 331 BC*
CONTEXT: *Having secured dominance of the Greek city states, the Mediterranean coast, Syria, and Egypt, Alexander set his sights on the Persian Empire*

Alexander succeeded his assassinated father, Philip II, as King of Macedonia in 336 BC when he was just twenty. Three years later he oversaw a crushing defeat of Darius III, king of Persia, at the Battle of Issus, taking advantage of Darius's poor intelligence network to bring the enemy to battle at a site far better suited to the Macedonians than the Persians. After fierce fighting, Alexander captured several members of Darius's family, while Darius himself fled.

After Issus, Alexander turned his attention to extending his rule throughout the Mediterranean and in Egypt and Syria. Then he determined to vanquish Darius once and for all and claim his crown. In 331 BC he marched over the rivers Euphrates and Tigris unopposed but Darius was intent on stemming Alexander's advance. He plundered the full extent of his realm for men and resources, building a vast (if slightly rough-and-ready) force numbering somewhere between 90,000 and 250,000 (sources contemporary to the event are not clear on the exact figure).

Darius was determined to fight Alexander on his own terms this time, so opted for a plain near the village of Gaugamela on the Bermodus River (not far from the city of Arbela, now modern-day Erbil in Iraq). This setting, he hoped, would favor his vast forces, which included chariots (complete with scythes fixed to their wheels) and elephants. Darius even had the land further leveled to maximize his advantage.

NEVER DO THE EXPECTED

Alexander led a force of some 47,000 and was well aware that his army was greatly outnumbered. However, he had already been wily in extracting any possible edge. He had

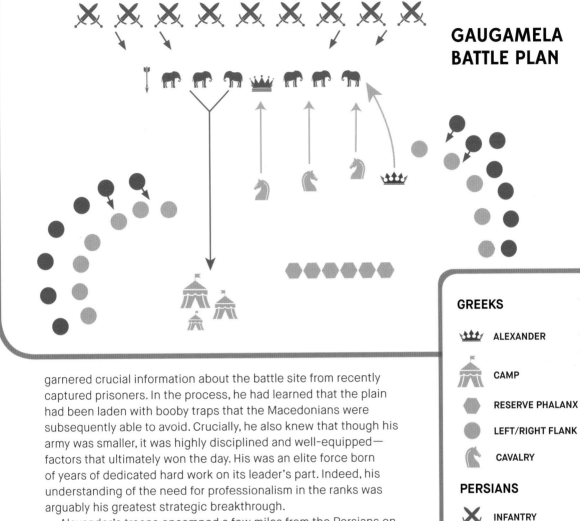

GREEKS

♕	ALEXANDER
⛺	CAMP
⬡	RESERVE PHALANX
●	LEFT/RIGHT FLANK
♞	CAVALRY

PERSIANS

⚔	INFANTRY
🐘	MERCENARIES
♕	DARIUS
●	CAVALRY LEFT/RIGHT
↓	ARCHERS

garnered crucial information about the battle site from recently captured prisoners. In the process, he had learned that the plain had been laden with booby traps that the Macedonians were subsequently able to avoid. Crucially, he also knew that though his army was smaller, it was highly disciplined and well-equipped—factors that ultimately won the day. His was an elite force born of years of dedicated hard work on its leader's part. Indeed, his understanding of the need for professionalism in the ranks was arguably his greatest strategic breakthrough.

Alexander's troops encamped a few miles from the Persians on the night of September 30 331 BC and he held a war council after sending out a patrol to spy on the enemy. His right-hand man, Parmenion, argued that they should launch a night-time attack but Alexander dismissed the idea out of hand. It proved to be his first tactical masterstroke of the engagement, for Darius had anticipated an attack under cover of dark and so kept his troops up all night on high alert. By the time the armies met the following day, Darius's men were already exhausted.

When Alexander arrived at the battlefield, he was faced by an awesome sight. Darius's forces seemed to stretch across the whole horizon, vast banks of cavalry on either flank sandwiching the infantry. In front of them were banks of scythed chariots and a platoon of elephants. Yet he did not panic. Instead, Alexander commanded his own men to take up a formation that offered the greatest protection against the most obvious threat: That Darius's great line of men would simply envelop their much smaller enemy. He

356 BC

Alexander is born in July at Pella, Macedonia, the son of King Philip II and Olympias.

336 BC

Alexander succeeds his father as ruler of Macedonia.

334 BC

Alexander defeats Darius III at the Battle of the Granicus River.

333 BC

Alexander is again victorious against Darius, this time at Issus.

331 BC

Alexander routs Darius's forces at Gaugemela. In the same year, he founds the city of Alexandria in Egypt.

323 BC

Alexander dies on June 10 at the palace of Nebuchadnezzar II in Babylon.

TRUE GREATNESS

Perhaps the most remarkable feature of Alexander's incredible success on the battlefield is that his military prowess was put to such lasting political effect. In establishing an empire that stretched from Europe to Asia, Alexander united East and West. He oversaw the spread of Greek culture, built numerous great cities, and proved an inspiration to the leaders of the Roman Empire that followed his own. Alexander, then, combined strategic genius with true statesmanship in a way perhaps only Napoleon (see page 96) has ever come close to emulating.

lined his army up in two compact phalanxes, with the cavalry on either flank angled back at 45 degrees to hinder any attempt at encirclement. Having taken care of defence, Alexander now looked to get on the front foot.

OPTIMIZE EVERY ADVANTAGE

Alexander's men were confident despite being outnumbered. His personal charisma inspired great loyalty and his army had the wind in its sails after a succession of victories. Alexander, meanwhile, had complete faith in its ability to follow orders quickly and efficiently, allowing for sophisticated maneuvers that no other army of the age could envisage. Furthermore, his troops had an edge over the Persians in terms of hardware. The Macedonians had heavy-duty armor where the Persians relied on little more than wicker shields, and they could also call on formidable weaponry. The infantry, for instance, were armed with pikes some eighteen feet in length, which gave them a huge advantage in hand-to-hand combat against enemies bearing much shorter weapons. Similarly, the cavalry carried fearsome double-headed lances that were literally at the cutting edge of ancient armory. Despite the mismatch in troop numbers, Alexander's thoroughness in preparation meant that he did not feel like the underdog.

He was also masterful at reading the battlefield, drawing up plans that he could adapt to changing circumstances. He saw that the plain favored the enemy so he decided to try and draw the Persian line away from the flat ground to rougher territory. Alexander led his cavalry out to the right and Darius's left flank went to meet them. Fighting was ferocious and losses heavy on both sides but Alexander's few held their own against the Persian many. Wary of losing the advantage of the plain, Darius refocused his attack via his infantry and chariots in the middle. But Alexander had drilled his men to cope with such an eventuality. They disrupted the attack by grabbing the reins of the chariots, throwing spears at the elephants which promptly panicked, and by opening their lines to let some infantry harmlessly through, only for the Macedonian rearguard to deal with them.

Now Alexander went in for the kill. He suddenly redirected the troops who had been stretching the right flank to assume a wedge shape and go left, into the Persian middle, which had become disconnected from its left flank. It required utter discipline from the Macedonians but they executed the move perfectly, completely wrong-footing their foe. Darius saw the writing on the wall and, just as at Issus, fled the scene. Alexander abandoned his pursuit only to come to the aid of Parmenion's struggling troops. In short order, the Persians were vanquished and Alexander had clocked up arguably the most astounding victory of an astonishing career. The Persian crown was his.

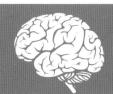

▲ *Alexander's enduring impact is reflected in this first-century AD mosaic illustrating his triumph over Darius III at Issus in 335 BC.*

MASTER STRATEGIST

Throughout a glittering military career Alexander perfected a military strategy based on the principles of properly training and resourcing his troops, accumulating and analyzing intelligence, forming a sound battlefield plan, and responding quickly to changing conditions. Few argue that he not merely provided the template for great military commanders of the future—from "Stonewall" Jackson to Erwin Rommel and George S. Patton—but surpassed them all.

Alexander demanded a level of preparation unequalled by any other war leader of his time. Leaving nothing to chance, he worked on both long- and short-term timescales. On the one hand, he devoted years to ensuring his army was a model fighting force. On the other, he undertook intelligence analysis right until the last minute. By such thorough preparation, he could confidently rely on his forces to be responsive and adaptable in the face of changing circumstances, setting the benchmark by which all later military commanders would be judged.

STRATEGY ANALYSIS

STRATEGY TYPE: *Strategic thinking*
KEY STRATEGY: *Stole every advantage to overwhelm a numerically stronger opponent*
OUTCOME: *Alexander routed the forces of Darius, extending his dominion deep into Asia*
ALSO USED BY: *Napoleon at the Battle of Rivoli, 1797, and Finnish army at the Battle of Tolvajärvi, 1939.*

5 MASS COMMUNICATION

ASHOKA THE GREAT DICTATED HIS EDICTS FAR AND WIDE

KEY PLAYER: *Ashoka the Great (304 BC–232 BC)*
NATIONALITY: *Indian*
STRATEGY IMPLEMENTED: *c.260s BC–232 BC*
CONTEXT: *Ashoka's ascent to power and the early years of his rule were characterized by bloodshed. However, after his conversion to Buddhism he spread his ethos of justice and goodliness far and wide*

For a long while, Ashoka seemed to be one of those apocryphal rulers of the ancient world, perhaps better treated as a symbolic rather than a real historical figure. Then in the nineteenth century a number of giant stone pillars were discovered across the Indian subcontinent, each carved with an edict in his name. Together they indicate that the stories of the Buddhist convert devoted to peaceful coexistence were true after all. His appeal for social cohesion was underpinned by a remarkably effective program of mass communication.

Ancient texts including the *Divyāvadāna*, *Dipavamsa*, and *Mahavamsa* all relate that Ashoka's conversion to enlightened rule was particularly remarkable for its contrast to the early part of his life. Ashoka was born in 304 BC, the son of the Mauryan emperor Bindusara and one of his lower-status wives. When his father died, there seems to have been a power struggle before Ashoka claimed the throne.

Known as a ruthless military man, the new emperor's fearsome reputation only grew in the first few years of his rule. He is said to have designed what looked like a beautiful palace on the outside but which in reality was a torture chamber that became known as Ashoka's Hell. He also set about expanding the territories of his empire. Most notably, he conquered Kalinga (the modern Indian state of Odisha) and some 100,000 of the enemy were killed and 150,000 deported. This shockingly brutal campaign proved the turning point of his life and the warrior undertook a gradual conversion to Buddhism.

The cold killer became concerned instead with Dharma (the natural laws that underpin Buddhism, key aspects of which are shared by other ancient Indian religions). It was a message he communicated in edicts inscribed on huge rock edifices as far afield as India, Pakistan, Afghanistan, and Nepal. Edict XIII, for instance, details his remorse at what occurred in Kalinga and his calls for an end to war and the embracing of a deep-rooted compassion for one another. It was a remarkable about-turn and by inscribing his ideas on monumental stones, he was attempting to propagate his directives as widely as possible. Today, he would doubtless have tweeted his commandments or made a YouTube video in the hope that it would go viral (see Barack Obama on page 215).

▲ Shown here is the Great Stupa that Ashoka had built at Sanchi in India's Madhya Pradesh province. Such works helped spread his Buddhist beliefs.

SEEING THE LIGHT

Although only a few of his edicts survive to the present day, it is reasonable to assume that he was a prodigious inscriber of pillars. He set out a moral code for his subjects that included showing kindness to one another (even prisoners—a notable statement from the builder of Ashoka's Hell) and which prized purity, generosity, and honesty. Tellingly, he referred to his subjects as his "children" and spoke of his fatherly concern for their well-being. In line with Buddhist teachings, he promoted respect for all animal life and demanded animal sacrifice be kept to a minimum. It was a thoroughly modern agenda.

Along with the edicts, Ashoka also commissioned the erection of tens of thousands of Buddhist shrines, which are widely believed to have played an important role in the global spread of the religion. However, he was no zealot, instead pleading for peaceful coexistence between religions. He also pledged to curb his empire's formerly expansionist foreign policy. Together the edicts amount to a remarkably liberal, all-embracing constitution that sets out the responsibilities of the state and of each individual within it. They set Ashoka apart as an enlightened ruler far ahead of his time.

A MAN FOR ALL SEASONS

Until the rediscovery of the edicts in the nineteenth century, tales of Ashoka's life had long been read almost as if they were parables. The ancient texts that tell of his reign raised him up as an example to other rulers. Indeed, he became virtually too good to be true. In the absence of hard historical evidence to corroborate the stories told about

304 BC

Ashoka is born. He is said to have been a fearless fighter and hunter, once killing a lion with a wooden rod as a child. With such a reputation, he was considered a natural choice to quell riots in the Avanti region of his father's empire when still just a young man. He is also reputed to have put down a rebellion by his father's ministers.

272 BC

His father, the Emperor Bindusara, dies, creating a power vacuum.

269 BC

After a bitter battle for the throne, Ashoka is crowned king. He is accused of killing as many as 99 of his brothers to secure power. He builds a notorious torture chamber, Ashoka's Hell, and sets about expanding the empire.

262 BC

Ashoka's Mauryan forces conquer Kalinga.

c.260 BC

Ashoka undergoes a spiritual conversion in the aftermath of the brutal Kalinga expedition. Over almost three decades he issues a number of edicts promoting good rule and citizenship, all of which are inscribed on giant stone pillars.

232 BC

Ashoka dies.

16th century

An English traveler in India, Thomas Coryat, discovers what will turn out to be one of Ashoka's pillars. However, it is not until the 1830s that they begin to be accurately translated.

1851

Large numbers of inscriptions are unearthed by the excavations by Sir Alexander Cunningham, head of the Archaeological Survey of India.

1904-1905

Further inscriptions are discovered in excavations led by F.O. Oertel.

OPPORTUNITY

The Ashoka Chakra is the 24-spoke wheel that appeared on a number of the emperor's edicts and which was adopted for the flag of the modern Indian state in 1947. Imbued with deep spiritual significance, its inclusion reflects the influence Ashoka had on members of the independence movement and continues to wield today. These included, of course, Gandhi—the great twentieth-century voice for religious tolerance and social cohesion—as well as India's first prime minister, Jawaharlal Nehru.

him, he became first mythologized and then all but forgotten, not only in the West but in the East too. But the appearance of his edicts breathed new life into the old emperor. His philosophy of social cohesion and enlightened rule looks ever less like a curiosity of the ancient past than a template for modern governance.

In an age when whole swathes of the world are being carved up amid internecine religious rivalries and when religious radicalism casts a shadow over us all, Ashoka's message of tolerance is one that we would do well to heed. Meanwhile, his belief in social justice, egalitarianism, and large-scale public infrastructure projects has echoes in the "Third Way" politics that took root in the 1990s, the "Big Society" ethos of community action, and even the rebuttal of traditional "dog-eat-dog" capitalism espoused by the Occupy protest movement.

Furthermore, just as every leader knows, refining your philosophy is one thing, but

LEADERS AND COMMUNICATION METHODS

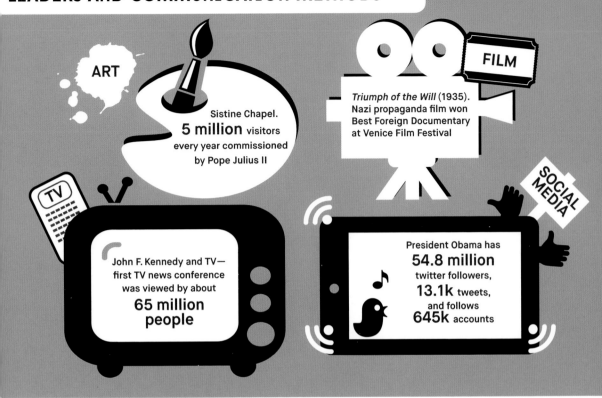

ART

Sistine Chapel.
5 million visitors
every year commissioned
by Pope Julius II

FILM

Triumph of the Will (1935).
Nazi propaganda film won
Best Foreign Documentary
at Venice Film Festival

TV

John F. Kennedy and TV—
first TV news conference
was viewed by about
**65 million
people**

SOCIAL MEDIA

President Obama has
54.8 million
twitter followers,
13.1k tweets,
and follows
645k accounts

getting the message out is quite another.
Ashoka was a master communicator,
employing the mass media of his time as
effectively as he could. The author H.G.
Wells memorably summed up his talents:

"Amidst the tens of thousands of names
of monarchs that crowd the columns of
history, their majesties and graciousnesses
and serenities and royal highnesses and
the like, the name of Ashoka shines, and
shines, almost alone, a star."

It is a lesson that has been learned by
virtually every significant leader who has
followed Ashoka. Whether brilliant wartime
leader (Napoleon), grisly dictator (Stalin),
or champion of democracy (Obama), those
with a serious interest in wielding authority
understand that power relies on the
cooperation of the masses, and the masses
need to be convinced to cooperate.

STRATEGY ANALYSIS

STRATEGY TYPE: *Communication*
KEY STRATEGY: *Used ancient "mass media" to
spread a message of peaceful coexistence*
OUTCOME: *One of the most revered reigns of
any monarch in history*
ALSO USED BY: *Martin Luther King for the US
civil rights movement, 1950s–60s, and Barack
Obama in his 2008 election campaign.*

6 THE PERFECT PINCER

FACING A NUMERICALLY SUPERIOR FORCE **HANNIBAL** USED CUNNING TO SECURE VICTORY

KEY PLAYER: *Hannibal (247 BC–c.182 BC)*

NATIONALITY: *Carthaginian (in modern-day Tunisia)*

STRATEGY IMPLEMENTED: *2 August 216 BC*

CONTEXT: *Rome was intent on driving Hannibal from Italy after he had wrestled control of much of the north of the country. The Romans were relying on their greater manpower at the Battle of Cannae. Instead, they fell for a wily Carthaginian trick and were all but annihilated*

After famously leading his army across the Alps in 218 BC, Hannibal gave the Romans bloody noses at the battles of Trebia and Lake Trasimene. Rome was incensed and gathered together a huge army (between 50,000 and 90,000 men) to evict the Carthaginians, who hailed from North Africa, once and for all. However, Hannibal took advantage of their reliance on brute force to outmaneuver them and secure a famous victory with far fewer men.

Until their engagements with Hannibal, the Romans had secured most of their military victories by going into battle with larger forces than their enemies. While this had hitherto proved highly effective, it had done little to foster a culture of sophisticated tactical thinking. Hannibal, on the other hand, was all about using cunning and strategy to outwit his opponents, whatever their size.

At Trebia and Lake Trasimene he had taken advantage of the landscape to hide troops, who then emerged to ambush their Roman foes. When Hannibal took control of a provisions depot at Cannae, Rome decided the time had come to act. Furthermore, the land there was flat and featureless, giving Hannibal less opportunity to use his trickery. Rome duly assembled a huge force of men under the joint leadership of two consuls, Lucius Aemilius Paulus and Gaius Terentius Varro. However, Hannibal's one head full of tactical nous was far better than their two heads, which did not always see eye to eye and mostly relied, as ever, on the numerical superiority of their armies.

Not only did Hannibal have fewer men, but he had something of a mongrel force consisting not just of Carthaginians but also Gauls, Spaniards, and Numidians. He lined them up so that his light infantry were front and center, hiding the heavier infantry, who had assumed a crescent formation behind them. On the right flank were his heavy cavalry, and on the left the light cavalry. However, as battle commenced, Hannibal gave a signal so that his light infantry fell back and went to the wings of the crescent behind them to form a reserve force. Hannibal was shaking things up and, just as he suspected, the Romans were too set in their ways to respond.

1

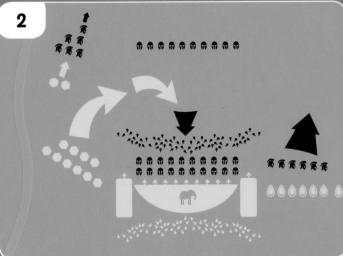

2

Roman infantry

Roman skirmishers

Roman cavalry

Carthaginian infantry

Carthaginian skirmishers

Carthaginian cavalry

Carthaginian light cavalry

Hannibal

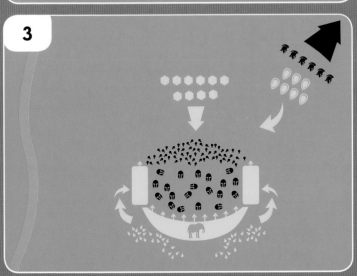

3

TIME LINE

247 BC
Hannibal is born in the North African state of Carthage, son of an esteemed army general.

221 BC
He becomes commander-in-chief of Carthage's military forces.

220 BC
Rome forges an alliance with the city state of Saguntum.

218 BC
The Second Punic War begins between Rome and Carthage when Hannibal besieges Saguntum. Hannibal marches his army across the Alps into northern Italy and defeats a Roman force at the Battle of Trebia.

217 BC
Hannibal defeats the Romans again, this time at Lake Trasimene.

216 BC
He is victorious at the Battle of Cannae on August 2.

202 BC
Scipio leads Roman forces to victory against Hannibal at the Battle of Zama, marking the end of the Second Punic War. Carthage sues for peace.

200–196 BC
Hannibal pursues a political career in his homeland.

195 BC
Under pressure to surrender himself to Rome, Hannibal goes into exile, first in Tyre and then Ephesus.

c.190–182
Hannibal commits suicide by drinking poison to avoid capture.

THE BOOBY TRAP

The numerically superior Roman infantry advanced in columns in its customary fashion and found itself making easy headway into the enemy ranks. Buoyed by this apparent success, they continued to plough onward, those at the back of the advancing columns pushing those at the front ever further forward. Meanwhile, the cavalry on each wing was engaged in much more finely-balanced fighting. Eventually the Carthaginian heavy cavalry succeeded in getting the better of their opponents, freeing them up to sweep across the field to help the light cavalry gain the upper hand by attacking their Roman counterparts from the rear. The Roman infantry thus found itself stranded. Hannibal had masterminded a breach in the enemy lines.

Meanwhile, the Roman infantry continued to press on. However, the arms of the Carthaginian crescent realigned to form a narrow alley in which the Romans suddenly found themselves trapped. The Carthaginian cavalry then rode in to completely encircle them. The Romans found themselves under attack from heavy infantry at the front, light infantry at the sides, and cavalry at the rear. They stood no chance. Hannibal had used imagination while the Roman generals called only upon raw physicality, executing a strategy (it might even be called a non-strategy) with little justification other than it was what they had always done before. Hannibal had coaxed his foe into blindly advancing to their own annihilation.

PUT TO THE SWORD

It is difficult to establish exact casualty numbers given between contemporary sources, but it is fair to say the Romans lost somewhere between 30,000 and 70,000 men at Cannae. Hannibal's losses, meanwhile, were closer to 8,000. Suffice to say, the Roman army was left in utter disarray and morale was at its lowest ebb. Hannibal had not merely secured victory but he had utterly decimated the opposition.

Maharbal, his commander of the Numidian cavalry, urged him to promptly advance on Rome. But Hannibal was aware that his own troop numbers were depleted and opted for a more cautious approach. In the event, he never captured Rome, with Maharbal reputedly exclaiming that Hannibal knew how to conquer but not how to make use of his victory.

The truth of that statement has been debated by historians ever since. Beyond doubt, though, is Hannibal's strategic know-how. The devastation he wrought at Cannae made a huge mark on the Roman psyche. Before Hannibal, Rome used force to beat its opponents. After him, they used tactics, becoming the greatest military strategists of the ancient world. Indeed, Hannibal would himself succumb to the Romans at the Battle of Zama in 202 BC. On that occasion, the Roman general Scipio led a force lesser in number than the Carthaginians. However, he exploited a weakness in the enemy, sounding horns to disorientate the Carthaginian elephants, which stampeded and caused a breach in Hannibal's defenses. Scipio prevailed using tactics of which Hannibal himself would have been proud, and the Carthaginians were never the same force again.

At Cannae, by adopting the pincer movement strategy, Hannibal was able to encircle a much larger foe and render it not only impotent but defenseless. It is a tactic that military generals have been wedded too ever since. For instance, the German army proved particularly adept exponents in World War II, when the pincer formed a crucial part of the Blitzkrieg strategy (see page 166). As the historian Will Durant would note in the twentieth century, at Cannae Hannibal "set the lines of military tactics for 2,000 years."

▲ *An eighteenth-century sculpture of Hannibal counting the rings of Romans felled during the Battle of Cannae.*

STRATEGY ANALYSIS

STRATEGY TYPE: *Tactical deception*
KEY STRATEGY: *Disguising battlefield formation to lull the enemy into a trap, Hannibal executed a devastating pincer movement*
OUTCOME: *The worst defeat in Roman history*
ALSO USED BY: *Suleiman the Magnificent at the Battle of Mohács, 1526, and General Patton at the Battle of the Bulge, 1944.*

7 SET FIRM BOUNDARIES

TO DEFINE THE BORDERS OF HIS NEW EMPIRE QIN SHI HUANG ORDERED CONSTRUCTION OF THE GREAT WALL

KEY PLAYER: *Qin Shi Huang (260-210 BC)*
NATIONALITY: *Chinese*
STRATEGY IMPLEMENTED: *221-210 BC*
CONTEXT: *Qin Shi Huang united the disparate kingdoms of China into a single empire. He ordered the construction of the Great Wall, both as a defensive measure and to impose his authority on those residing within his realm*

The Great Wall of China as we know it today evolved over the course of millennia. The stretches of brick wall familiar to us largely date from the Ming Dynasty (1368–1644). However, it was China's first emperor, Qin Shi Huang in the third century BC who first commanded that existing ad hoc defensive fortifications be joined into a single identifiable edifice. It remains one of the greatest engineering achievements in history.

When the First Emperor came to power, he brought to an end the destructive era of Chinese history known as the Warring States period. For over 250 years, a number of smaller kingdoms had jockeyed for power in what was essentially a prolonged civil war. But Qin Shi Huang was able to subjugate his rivals and impose his rule on a unified entity, which evolved into what we now think of as China.

Fortified walls had been constructed in China as long ago as 4000 BC. The first cities emerged around 1500 BC with still more sophisticated walls, while the Warring States period saw an upsurge in construction of defenses as each kingdom looked to fend off hostile neighbors. The result was a mish-mash of defenses of varying quality scattered throughout the country. The First Emperor recognized their potential but also realized that much work was required if they were to be converted into a useful, contiguous defensive system. In particular, he wanted to fend off invasion by nomadic Hun tribes to the north. So he commissioned a wall to demarcate his northern frontier.

AN ENGINEERING MEGA-PROJECT

If the challenge seemed a mighty one, then the First Emperor was just the man to rise to it. In fact, having emerged as head of a vast empire, his ego was rampant and he believed nothing was beyond his grasp. He was, for instance, convinced that he could make himself immortal by drinking an elixir of life (which, ironically, probably contained mercury compounds that ultimately killed him) and spent a large part of his reign preparing for the afterlife. Specifically, this meant the commission of another mega-building project—a vast mausoleum complex near the city of Xi'an. Though much of it remains hidden to archeologists, we know that the complex took up a large geographical area and comprised an underground version of his royal court and its environs that he could enjoy post-mortem. There were, reputedly, rivers of mercury and a sky adorned with golden stars. And the emperor himself was provided with a vast personal bodyguard made up of some 8,000 individually modeled soldiers, more than 100 chariots, and some 700 horses—the famous Terracotta Army that today ranks as one of China's premier tourist attractions, along with the Great Wall.

Qin Shi Huang had no intention of holding back on his ambitions for the Great Wall, any more than he expected to compromise on his eternal prospects. Having brought relative peace to China, he had a vast army of soldiers who needed to be occupied, along with prisons full of convicts. He put his trusted commander, General Meng Tien, in control of the works. In a surge of activity that was mostly completed by 212 BC, existing defenses were adapted and joined together to repel invasion, while those that had divided the Warring States were torn down. In the First Emperor's realm, there was to be no suggestion of division. Most of the wall at this stage was constructed by rammed earth, augmented with stones and wood. It wended its way through inhospitable territory, including mountains and regions of unforgiving aridness. It is thought that up to 400,000 people perished in this building phase, many of the corpses being contained within the wall itself.

In his short reign, Qin Shi Huang oversaw other large infrastructure projects, including the development of a sophisticated road network to aid trade. Yet nothing matched the wall (which rose many meters into the air) for ambition, architectural sophistication, and, let it also be said, artistry. It may have been primarily a strategic, defensive edifice, but almost instantly it served as a cultural monument too. It was a symbol of strength, not only repelling aggressors but also emphasizing the emperor's control over his own citizens. He had redefined the borders of his realm, removing internal barriers and keeping—as he saw it—the bad out and the good in.

A SYMBOL FOR THE AGES

Just as remarkably, Qin Shi Huang's work on the Wall was in many senses only the beginning. Its development and evolution continues to the present day, making

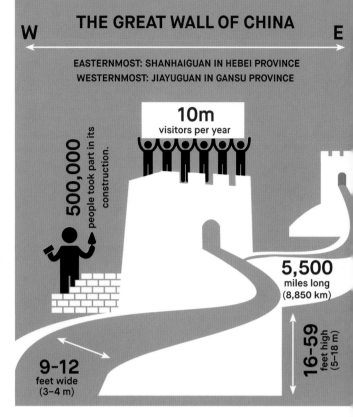

THE GREAT WALL OF CHINA

W ← → E

EASTERNMOST: SHANHAIGUAN IN HEBEI PROVINCE
WESTERNMOST: JIAYUGUAN IN GANSU PROVINCE

10m visitors per year

500,000 people took part in its construction.

5,500 miles long (8,850 km)

16-59 feet high (5-18 m)

9-12 feet wide (3-4 m)

TIME LINE

his legacy all the more impressive. Construction has progressed in fits and starts throughout its long history, reflecting changing political climates. Built initially with defense in mind, the Great Wall has had little to do in that direction for much of its life. It has, however, been variously used to regulate migration and trade.

Although several of the dynasties between the Qin and the Ming developed the Wall for their own purposes, it was the Ming who brought it into the modern age. Having expelled the Mongols from China, they were keen to improve their fortifications and so began reconstructing long stretches of wall using brick and building new fortresses and gun emplacements. In Chinese the wall is known as "Wan-Li Qang-Qeng" ("10,000-Li Long Wall"; 10,000 Li equating to about 3,100 miles [5,000 km]). Yet this actually downplays its magnificence. Over 200 years, the Ming extended it so that modern estimates suggest that it twisted and turned over some 13,000 miles (20,000 km). The walls were so thick that mounted cavalry could move with ease along their tops. By the end of the Ming period, it was the largest military structure in the world.

Today, the Wall stretches from Shanhaiguan in Hebei province in the east to Jiayuguan in Gansu province in the west, and it still remains a potent political symbol. Under Chairman Mao Zedong and his Cultural Revolution, it was regarded as a remnant of the old China. Parts of it were thus destroyed while the rest was left to fall into a state of disrepair. However, in 1982 the Chinese premier Deng Xiaoping took a new approach, ordering its restoration as a symbol of Chinese greatness. UNESCO gave it World Heritage Site status in 1987 and today it attracts tens of millions of visitors each year. Throughout it all, it has retained the power to dazzle, its sturdy expanse keeping outsiders in, preserving China's culture and territorial integrity, and speaking of the nation's strength. The First Emperor made a lasting impression indeed.

POWERFUL SYMBOLS

Walls have always served as potent symbols, from the one that surrounded Jericho in the Bible to that built by the Roman Emperor Hadrian between England and Scotland. The most notorious example of the last century was that which divided East and West Berlin between 1961 and 1989. Meanwhile, since the 1990s, the Separation Barrier—ostensibly built to defend Israel against attacks from the West Bank—has come to denote the bleak reality of the Israeli-Palestinian conflict.

STRATEGY ANALYSIS

STRATEGY TYPE: *Defensive strategy*
KEY STRATEGY: *Defining territorial borders with a frontier wall*
OUTCOME: *An enduring symbol of the Chinese nation*
ALSO USED BY: *Roman Emperor Hadrian, AD 122, and the East German government at Berlin, 1961–89.*

8 SIEGE WARFARE

AT ALESIA **CAESAR** ESTABLISHED THE TEXTBOOK STRATEGY FOR SIEGE WARFARE AND BROUGHT GAUL TO HEEL

KEY PLAYER: *Julius Caesar (100-44 BC)*
NATIONALITY: *Roman*
STRATEGY IMPLEMENTED: *52 BC*
CONTEXT: *Beginning in 58 BC, Caesar spent several years bringing Gaul under Roman control. In 52 BC he and his forces faced a serious revolt from a united Gallic force led by Vercingetorix*

Military historians celebrate the strategy Julius Caesar used at the town of Alesia in 52 BC as the textbook example of siege warfare—using an army to pin the enemy into a fortress or town. Caesar's great innovation was to build two encircling walls—one to hold the defenders of Alesia in, and the second to keep out Gallic relief forces.

Caesar had arrived in Gaul (roughly, modern France) in 58 BC and by 54 BC had subjugated most of the region. However, a rebellion by local tribes in the winter of 54–53 BC saw Caesar's Fourteenth Legion wiped out. He suddenly found himself shorn of about a quarter of his troops, with little hope of replacing them as a result of political machinations in Rome.

Although Caesar succeeded in putting down the rebellion, the Gauls had the scent of battle in their nostrils. In 52 BC various tribes held a war council in which they agreed to unite under the leadership of Vercingetorix of the Arverni. The Gauls unleashed a tsunami of violence against any Romans they could reach, whether soldiers, traders, or settlers. On hearing of this Gallic resurgence, Caesar began a new campaign to crush them. However, after victories in a few minor skirmishes, he was defeated by Vercingetorix in September 52 BC at the Battle of Gergovia, suffering heavy losses in the process.

Caesar then regrouped and used his cavalry to scatter the Gallic army, forcing Vercingetorix to take refuge with an 80,000-strong force in the hilltop fort of Alesia (probably on Mont Auxois near Dijon in Burgundy). Caesar, whose army was

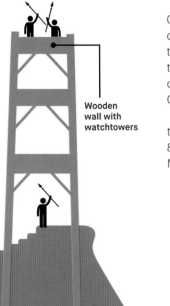

Wooden wall with watchtowers

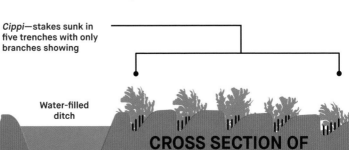

Cippi—stakes sunk in five trenches with only branches showing

Water-filled ditch

Ditch

CROSS SECTION OF SIEGE DEFENCES

numerically smaller, decided on a strategy of starving the enemy out. It was hardly a new tactic, having been employed in civilizations far older than the Romans, but no-one had yet conducted it with such ruthless efficiency as Caesar was about to demonstrate.

THE INS AND OUTS OF VICTORY

To enforce his blockade, the Roman general first built a wooden wall enclosing the fortress. In just three weeks his troops raised an enclosing wall 11 miles (18 km) long and 13 feet (4 m) tall, complete with watchtowers to be manned by Roman artillery. On its inner side two ditches were dug, each 16 feet (5 m) wide and 16 feet (5 m) deep. The Romans filled the inner one with water from a diverted stretch of the nearby river, a feat achieved despite regular attack from units of Vercingetorix's cavalry.

When one group of Gallic cavalry managed to burst through the wall, Caesar knew they would probably ride off in search of reinforcements, resulting in him having to face a relief army. Therefore, he ordered the construction of a second wall, this time to defend his own troops from possible attack. The second wall was even longer at 13 miles (21 km) and included no fewer than four cavalry forts.

Meanwhile, conditions were becoming desperate for the Gauls trapped within Alesia. In a bid to make supplies go further, Vercingetorix expelled the women and children from the fortress, on the assumption that Caesar would allow them safe passage. However, Caesar knew that his siege strategy would work only if ruthlessly executed. If he allowed the women and children free passage, he would have to break his defensive lines, leaving his own men open to attack. He issued orders that the women and children be kept herded within the inner siege wall. Exposed to the elements and without food, they were left to die. Caesar would let nothing get in the way of victory.

FIGHT TO THE DEATH

At this point, the Gauls's relief army arrived under the command of Commius, king of the Atrebates tribe. Vercingetorix ordered a simultaneous attack by Commius's army and his own troops but the Romans held firm. However, a second night-time attack by Commius broke through the outer wall. Another attack on the inner wall by the Gauls trapped in Alesia also hit home. In response, Caesar sent his cavalry under the command of Mark Antony, and they saved the situation, for the time being.

Nonetheless, events hung in the balance. Just as the trapped Gauls were suffering, so Caesar's supplies were running low and his men were living on reduced rations. They were exhausted when on October 2 they faced renewed attack. Gallic leader Vercassivellaunus led an onslaught of some 60,000 men, focusing on gaps in the Roman defenses where natural obstructions prevented the construction of a continuous barrier.

Lily—series of pits containing disguised tapering stakes

Spurs—stakes with iron hooks attached, sunk into the ground at intervals

TIME LINE

100 BC
Gaius Julius Caesar is born around July 13 in Rome.

73 BC
Having established a military career, he is elected as a Pontifex (a priestly position), his first major post within Rome's political system.

61 BC
He becomes governor of Further Spain.

60 BC
He is elected a consul in Rome and forms an unofficial ruling triumvirate with Crassus and Pompey.

58 BC
Caesar leaves Rome for Gaul and does not return for nine years. In this time he conquers much of central Europe.

55 BC
He crosses the Rhine and invades Britain.

52 BC
Caesar defeats Vercingetorix at Alesia, consolidating Roman control in Gaul.

49 BC
Civil war begins in Rome between the supporters of Caesar and Pompey.

48 BC
Pompey is murdered.

45 BC
Caesar is declared dictator for life.

44 BC
He is murdered on the Ides of March.

Part of Caesar's leadership strategy was to ensure that his men loved and admired him. He could see how his troops were unnerved by the shouts of the approaching Gallic warriors, so he rode along the perimeter of the outer wall, imploring his men to hold the line, safe in the knowledge that he could rely on these battle-weary but fiercely loyal soldiers to do just that.

Calmly tackling each new challenge as it emerged, Caesar sent some of his cavalry to plug gaps in the defenses and personally spearheaded several counter-attacks against Vercingetorix and his forces along the inner wall. Then he came up with a new strategic masterstroke—breaking out from his camp with a select band of cavalry to attack the Gallic relief army from the rear. Cornered, the relieving Gauls began to flee and were cut down in the process. Meanwhile, Vercingetorix was left trapped within the city and concluded he had no option but to surrender. The Romans counted some 13,000 dead and wounded from the engagement. The Gauls lost perhaps 100,000 men, with a further 40,000 captured. The siege marked the end of serious Gallic opposition to Roman rule and is considered a crowning achievement in Caesar's military career.

TEXTBOOK STRATEGY
It is often said that defense is the best form of attack, and that is just what Caesar proved at Alesia. He realized that the besieger could so easily become the besieged—an apparently simple lesson but one often ignored by later generals.

The Crusades, for instance, were regularly punctuated by episodes of fortresses and cities changing hands as one besieging force after another found themselves incapable of defending the territories they had won. Even into World War II, the German forces succumbed to a similar oversight at the Siege of Leningrad, when their besieging forces themselves fell vulnerable to attack. Most modern sieges are in truth won or lost according to numerical advantage, but Caesar proved that by careful planning and ruthless execution, that need not be the case.

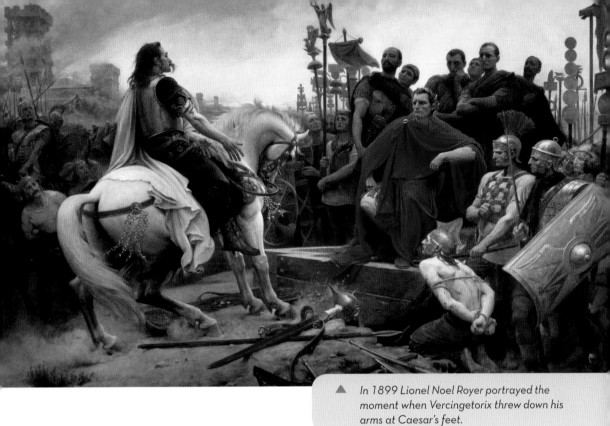

In 1899 Lionel Noel Royer portrayed the moment when Vercingetorix threw down his arms at Caesar's feet.

MASTER STRATEGIST

Caesar described, in vivid detail, the engagement at Alesia in book seven of his history The Gallic Wars. The work covers the great general's tactics in the wars, which lasted from 58-50 BC and opened the way for Caesar to become ruler of the Roman Republic. Again and again, Caesar showed himself master of effective strategy. Perhaps Caesar's greatest quality was that he was always ready to learn from mistakes. Many later generals—above all, Napoleon Bonaparte—studied and learned from Caesar's strategy.

STRATEGY ANALYSIS

STRATEGY TYPE: Strategy of attack
KEY STRATEGY: Siege warfare
OUTCOME: Defeat of the Gallic tribes, ensured Caesar's victory in the Gallic Wars
ALSO USED BY: The Axis Powers at the Siege of Sevastopol, 1941-42, and The Viet Minh at the Battle of Dien Bien Phu ,1954.

9 MISINFORMATION

TIRED OF ROMAN RULE **ARMINIUS** EMPLOYED A CLASSIC DOUBLE CROSS TO SPRING HIS TRAP

In AD 6 the authorities in Rome charged an imperial legate, Publius Quinctilius Varus, with consolidating the Empire's power in Germania. Varus pursued alliances with local chieftains—among them Arminius, who in AD 9 persuaded him to re-route his troops via the Teutoburg Forest to deal with reported local uprisings. In fact, Arminius had arranged for a tribal army to ambush the Romans, wreaking such damage that Rome was forced to curtail its ambitions in the region.

KEY PLAYER: *Arminius (c.18 BC–AD 21)*
NATIONALITY: *Cherusci (in modern-day Germany)*
STRATEGY IMPLEMENTED: *AD 9*
CONTEXT: *Rome looked to impose its hegemony over the disparate tribes of Germania. Arminius, chieftain of the Germanic Cherusci people, was considered a trusted ally but by AD 9 he had grown tired of the excesses of Roman rule*

The Emperor Augustus had long had an eye on conquering the Germanic tribes who lived east of the River Rhine, regarding them as savages to be brought to heel. Over the course of the last decade BC and first decade AD, Roman forces made incursions into Germanic territory, setting up a string of bases, cultivating trade, and establishing alliances. Varus—a relation of Augustus through marriage and a noted administrator who had overseen Roman rule in Syria—was put in charge of extending Rome's influence. However, he did not have much in the way of military experience and soon made himself unpopular in Germania by imposing heavy taxes and suppressing the local culture. Several tribes that had earlier thrown their lot in with the Romans started to regret their decision, among them the Cherusci of Arminius. Arminius reached the conclusion that the benefits of alliance had waned and the time had come to fight back.

Arminius had been held captive in Rome as a youth, during which time he had received a Roman-style education (he spoke Latin fluently) and become versed in the empire's military tactics. This made him highly useful as an ally of Rome, but even more dangerous as an enemy. For a while, the young man had proven a faithful servant to Rome, providing local intelligence and assisting its forces in making headway into territory held by far less friendly tribes. But as his discontent with Roman rule grew, he set about establishing an alliance among the Germanic tribes and used his insider knowledge of Rome's workings to devise an ingenious plan.

THE DOUBLE CROSS

(44 BC)

BRUTUS TURNS AGAINST JULIUS CAESAR

(1780)

AMERICAN GENERAL, BENEDICT ARNOLD, PLOTS TO SURRENDER WEST POINT, NEW YORK, TO THE BRITISH

(1903–1913)

ALFRED REDL, THE AUSTRO-HUNGARIAN HEAD OF COUNTER-INTELLIGENCE, IS HIMSELF A RUSSIAN SPY.

FRIEND OR FOE?

Come the fall of AD 9, Varus was looking to lead his troops to their winter quarters on the River Rhine. His force numbered perhaps as many as 35,000 men, including cavalry and three legions (XII, XVIII, and XIX). While they were en route, Varus received news from Arminius—whom he considered a trusted advisor—that hostile tribes were rising up against Roman rule. He strongly argued that Varus ought to change his plans, detouring for what should be no longer than a day or two to put down these rebellions before they gained a momentum of their own.

Segestes, a chieftain of another Germanic clan and a rival to Arminius, told Varus that Arminius was a traitor and that there were no such uprisings. Varus, though, had faith in the old ally and did not want to take the risk that Segestes was hoodwinking him. Furthermore, such was his arrogance—a trait upon which Arminius played beautifully—that he could see no harm in going off track for a couple of days to crush a little local trouble. What could possibly go wrong?

So Arminius led Varus and his three legions into territory entirely unknown to the Romans, plotting a course that took in inhospitable farmland, bogs, and the dense Teutoburg Forest. The legions soon found the going heavy, all the more so given terrible weather conditions. The ground was treacherously slippery and littered with fallen trees, so that in places they were forced to clear and rebuild paths as well as construct makeshift bridges. With no choice but to travel in a long column, the Roman forces (which included a mule-pulled luggage train) extended for as long as 12 miles (20 km). It was dangerously over-extended, but at least they had a friendly local to show them the way—didn't they?

LAMBS TO THE SLAUGHTER

It was as the going in the forest reached its toughest that the Germanic troops struck, launching hit-and-run attacks on pockets of legionaries before using their local knowledge to dart off back to safety. Unable to get into anything like a battle formation given the natural impediments of the forest, the Romans had little choice but to suffer the slings and arrows of outrageous fortune. On day two of the trek, Varus decided to head for the nearest major Roman base about 60 miles (100 km) away. With the weather

TIME LINE

DOUBLE-AGENTS

As illustrated elsewhere in this book (see the Trojan horse, page 10, Napoleon at Austerlitz, page 96, and Q-boats, page 146), trickery has a proud heritage in the history of warfare. And there are fewer better methods to sow a lie than through a double-agent. If Arminius was the archetypal double-agent of ancient times, the conflicts of the twentieth century raised this mode of espionage to an art form. For instance, the British ran a double-agent in World War II known as Garbo (real name: Joan Pujol Garcia), who so successfully hoodwinked the Nazis that he received both an MBE from the British government and also an Iron Cross from Berlin. Come the Cold War, meanwhile, the British found themselves victims when the so-called Cambridge Spy Ring saw apparent pillars of British society feeding secrets to the Soviet Union.

no better, they suffered further onslaughts from the Germanic tribes, such that Varus decided his best option was to press on through the night in the hope of reaching safety.

On the third day, Varus and his men found themselves on a narrow passage with forest on one side and a vast swamp on the other. To further hinder their progress, Arminius had ordered his troops to dig ditches and construct road blocks. As the Romans inched along, a mass of Germanic fighters appeared from the forest and from behind barriers. The already edgy Romans descended into panic, realizing they had nowhere to go. In desperation they launched an attack but to no avail. With Arminius's men overrunning them, the Roman cavalry fled, leaving the legionaries to their grisly fate.

Varus took what Rome would have considered was the honorable way out, committing suicide by falling on his sword. Others of his senior officers followed suit, with the result that the Roman army no longer had any leadership. In the ensuing slaughter, as many as 20,000 of their number perished, with many more being taken prisoner. Hardly any escaped unscathed. By contrast, losses for the Germanic forces were minimal.

Back in Rome the impact of this inglorious defeat was seismic. Augustus is supposed to have repeatedly screamed, "Quinctilius Varus, give me back my legions!" In practical terms, ten percent of the imperial army had been destroyed at a stroke and its aura of invincibility smashed. The historian Suetonius would claim a century later that the defeat

▲ *Freidrich Gun's take on the bloody carnage wrought in the Teutoburg Forest—the handiwork of Arminius's exploitation of Rome's trust in him.*

almost led to the collapse of the empire. Certainly, Rome never managed to extend its power beyond the Rhine. All thanks to Arminius, a master double-agent.

By securing the trust of his enemy and feeding them misinformation, he left his foe utterly vulnerable. Surreptitiously supplying your rivals with lies and half-truths is a tactic that remains in widespread use today, in contexts as disparate as warfare, commerce, and politics. Untruths by their nature restrict the facility for informed decision-making, so providing the misinformant with the all-important competitive edge.

STRATEGY ANALYSIS

STRATEGY TYPE: *Tactical deception*
KEY STRATEGY: *Fed misinformation to the armed forces of Rome*
OUTCOME: *A crushing defeat for Rome's forces that stalled the further Latinization of Germania*
ALSO USED BY: *Mata Hari, Dutch-born exotic dancer, spied for Germany in World War I, and agent Garbo in World War II.*

10

THE KNOCKOUT COUNTER-PUNCH

STRIKING BACK DECISIVELY AT THE BATTLE OF ARSUF **RICHARD I** DEFEATED HIS NEMESIS SALADIN

KEY PLAYER: *Richard I, "the Lionheart" (1157-99)*
NATIONALITY: *English*
STRATEGY IMPLEMENTED: *September 7 1191*
CONTEXT: *Richard, a leading figure in the Third Crusade when Christian forces sought to reconquer Jerusalem, inflicted a stunning reverse against the great Muslim general, Saladin*

At Arsuf in 1191, Richard proved himself the great warrior-king by vanquishing the Ayyubid forces of Saladin. The legendary Muslim leader had inflicted several major defeats against the Crusaders as he attempted to drive them from the Holy Land but here Richard hit back with a decisive counter-attack, unleashing a "shock and awe" strategy of a type favored by modern war leaders.

Richard I is one of a select band of English monarchs known better by a complimentary soubriquet ("the Lionheart") than by their regnal number. He is remembered as a great military leader—a reputation in no small part secured by his success at the Battle of Arsuf. In a piece of tactical mastery that has been oft repeated, he goaded his enemies into attacking until they tired and then unleashed an unstoppable counter-offensive.

Richard was born and raised in England but spent a large part of his adulthood in France, where he ruled over an assortment of dukedoms. After an unsuccessful attempt to overthrow his father, Henry II, he was finally crowned king of England in September 1189. Richard, however, was more intent on putting in place plans for his great Crusader adventure, setting off for the Middle East in the summer of 1190.

Meanwhile, in 1187 Saladin had captured Jerusalem—the unrivaled jewel in the crown of the Holy Land—after annihilating the Crusader armies at the Battle of Hattin. It was a particularly devastating experience for the Christian fighters, who had become separated from their water supplies amid searing heat. By the time he led his troops against Richard four years later, Saladin had a reputation for both personal bravery and battlefield mastery. As such, his troops did not lack for confidence.

After a difficult journey to the Holy Land, Richard landed at Acre, a city on the Mediterranean coast north of Jerusalem, in July 1191. Acre had fallen to Saladin in 1187 but had been besieged by a Crusader army led by Guy of Lusignan since 1189, only for the Crusader besiegers to find themselves besieged by relieving Ayyubid forces. When Richard arrived, he joined forces with Philip II of France to break the siege and take the city.

LEARNING FROM PAST MISTAKES
From there, he planned to travel down the coast accompanied by a flotilla of supply

vessels in the hope of capturing first Jaffa and, ultimately, Jerusalem itself. Having learned the terrible lessons of Hattin (where the Crusaders had allowed themselves to be cut off from vital provisions under pressure from the enemy), he instilled in his men the need for complete discipline. They proceeded on their march at a leisurely pace so as to avoid heat exhaustion, focusing efforts in the morning when the sun was at its least debilitating and stopping regularly to rehydrate.

Saladin was thus presented with the tempting target of a long, slow-moving column consisting of mounted knights and infantry, all tightly hugging the coastline. This was, he saw, an ideal opportunity to drive his enemies into the sea, potentially bringing the crusade to a decisive end. He ordered his soldiers to get in range of Richard's troops and rain arrows down upon them. Despite intensive harassment, Richard demanded his men stay focused. He rotated his infantry regiments—who marched furthest inland to provide a layer of protection for the Crusaders' baggage train and cavalry—so as to keep them as fresh as possible.

Nonetheless, Saladin's tactics had a wearing effect and his bowmen killed many horses belonging to the corpus of Knights Hospitaller (an elite knightly order that rose to prominence during the First Crusade and which provided care in Jerusalem for ailing pilgrims). Richard, though, insisted his forces keep their shape. While he knew the Ayyubid attacks were taking their toll, he believed the enemy was tiring too and hoped that they might expose their own flank, at which point he would order a cavalry charge. Holding one's nerve was the order of the day.

However, the Hospitallers feared that by waiting, they would lose so many horses that they would be incapable of launching an effective offensive. They repeatedly appealed to their commander to give the attack order but each time he refused. Finally, the desperate Hospitallers turned on their attackers. Adapting to these new circumstances with admirable speed, Richard wisely judged that he must now send in the highly skilled Knights Templar (another knightly order, see page 50) to support the Hospitallers.

SHOCK AND AWE

Saladin's men, having tried to provoke a battle all day, were totally unprepared for the sudden onslaught. The knights unleashed a savage torrent of built-up aggression but

1069–99
First crusade ends with the Crusaders capturing Jerusalem.

1145–49
Second Crusade ends with defeat of King Louis VII's forces at Damascus.

July 4 1187
Saladin takes most of the Crusader-held Kingdom of Jerusalem after victory at the Battle of Hattin.

September 30 1187
Saladin takes the city of Jerusalem.

October 29 1187
Pope Gregory VIII calls the Third Crusade.

September 3 1189
Richard is crowned King of England.

June 24 1190
Richard sets out on Crusade.

October 4 1190
Richard takes Messina on Sicily.

May 6 1191
Richard arrives on Cyprus, which he duly conquers.

May 12 1191
Richard marries Berengaria of Navarre.

June 5 1191
Richard leaves Cyprus for the Holy Land.

July 12 1191
The city of Acre falls to Richard and Philip II Augustus of France.

September 7 1191
Richard defeats Saladin at the Battle of Arsuf.

September 2 1192
Richard and Saladin reach a peace, bringing the Third Crusade to an end.

Richard, keenly aware of the need for discipline now more than ever after the initial attack, commanded his troops to regroup. They then undertook a second and a conclusive third wave of charges. Had the Hospitallers been able to hold their nerve a little longer, the result may have been even more decisive but Richard had played his hand masterfully and claimed a resounding success.

Saladin's armies were at a low ebb after this reversal and Richard went on to conquer Jaffa. However, infighting within the Crusader ranks meant that Jerusalem remained out of reach. Just short of a year after his great triumph, Richard agreed a peace with Saladin amid an atmosphere of mutual respect. While Richard's track record as king was mixed to say the least (in his ten-year reign, he spent little more than six months actually in England and left behind a legacy of political instability and unpopular taxes), Arsuf would secure his legendary status.

If the result at Arsuf had gone the other way, it is difficult to see how the Third Crusade (or any of the subsequent Crusader forays that lasted into the fourteenth century) could have proceeded. It proved the necessity of discipline to a successful counter-attack and illustrates how the enemy may be caught off-guard just as they appear on the brink of success. As no lesser light than Napoleon (see page 96) would note in due course, "the greatest danger occurs at the moment of victory."

No wonder that the counter-attack has been a strategy others have so often striven to emulate. The vital Battle of the Bulge, for instance, that took place in Ardennes in 1944 during World War II was virtually a succession of counter-attacks, first by an ailing Germany and then by the American-led Allies. Just as one side

SIEGE OF LENINGRAD

Among history's numerous counter-attacks, there has perhaps been none more spectacular than that engineered by Joseph Stalin against the German forces that besieged Leningrad (modern-day Saint Petersburg) during World War II. Hitler's troops invaded Russia in June 1941 and surrounded the city on September 8, beginning a siege that lasted 872 days. In late 1943 Stalin flooded the area with reinforcements and General Zhukov launched a counter-offensive involving some 500,000 men. Within a few days, the Germans—already suffering from the long Russian winter—were on the retreat and suffered huge casualties. The dramatic end of the siege marked a decisive turn in the tide of the war.

▲ *A rueful scene of Leningrad natives trudging along Nevsky Prospect, the city's main thoroughfare, during the siege.*

seemed to be getting the upper hand, so the other side hit back.

The legacy of Arsuf is even evident in the sporting world, never more so than when Muhammad Ali adopted a "rope-a-dope" strategy (putting oneself in an apparently losing position in order to gain eventual victory) in his legendary 1974 "Rumble in the Jungle" bout against George Foreman. Ali set out to absorb Foreman's attacks and waited for his opponent to tire. Beginning his counter-offensive in the eighth round, Ali was champion again before the round was up. Foreman, meanwhile, was left to ruefully note that "I was the dope."

STRATEGY ANALYSIS

STRATEGY TYPE: *Defensive strategy*
KEY STRATEGY: *Devastating counter-attack*
OUTCOME: *Richard revitalized Crusader hopes of seizing Jerusalem*
ALSO USED BY: *The Russians at Stalingrad, 1943, and Muhammad Ali against George Foreman in 1974.*

11 PROTECT YOUR INTERESTS

EXPLOITING THEIR POSITION OF TRUST AND POWER, **THE KNIGHTS TEMPLAR** ESTABLISHED MODERN BANKING

KEY PLAYERS: *The Knights Templar (c.1118-1314)*
NATIONALITY: *French*
STRATEGY IMPLEMENTED: *Twelfth-fourteenth centuries*
CONTEXT: *Christian pilgrims to the Holy Land were wary of carrying their worldy wealth with them on their dangerous journey, so the Knights Templar gave them a different option*

It is a curiosity that the secular world of modern banking has its roots in the activities of a group of devout, medieval Christians famed as elite warriors. The Knights Templar were born out of the crusades that pitched medieval Christianity against Islam. The Knights were initially intent on protecting the physical well-being of Christian pilgrims but before long the desire to protect their earthly wealth too gave rise to the first "chain" of modern banks.

The Knights Templar emerged in 1119 when a French nobleman, Hugues de Payens, approached eight of his relatives to form an elite fighting force. His intention was that the group would ensure the physical well-being of Christian pilgrims to the Holy Land. The route from western Europe to the Middle East had long been a dangerous one, beset with bandits and militia. Since the First Crusade (1096–99), which culminated in Christian Crusaders wrestling Jerusalem from its Islamic occupiers, the journey had become only more risky. The Knights thus began life not as bankers but as top-grade bodyguards.

De Payens won permission from Baldwin II (king of Jerusalem) to base his knights at the Aqsa Mosque on the city's Temple Mount. The Christians believed this was the site of the erstwhile Temple of Solomon, so the knightly order became known as the Poor Fellow-Soldiers of Christ and of the Temple of Solomon—or the Knights Templar, for short. It was a formidable headquarters from which to launch their operations and, however selfless his reasons for establishing the order, de Payens carefully nurtured his organization to have major influence.

Its power only increased after the Vatican officially sanctioned the Templars in 1129. Although members swore various oaths of self-denial (including vows of chastity, obedience, and poverty), the Templars now had license to raise serious funding. They asked the great and the good of Europe for donations of money and land, as well as signing up the sons of prominent noble families as knights (who were then expected to sign over their personal wealth to the order). For Europe's great families, having a son who was a Templar became highly prestigious. As the French abbot Bernard of Clairvaux put it, a Templar was "a fearless knight, and secure on every side, for his soul is protected by the armor of faith, just as his body is protected by the armor of steel." The Knights had, it might be said, secured public trust.

SHOW ME THE MONEY

In 1139, Pope Innocent II issued a papal bull granting the Templars free passage across borders, exempted them from taxes, and stated they were subject to no sovereign authority but only to the papacy itself. By mid-century, du Payens's little band of fighters had become hugely wealthy, owning vast swathes of land (including Cyprus in its entirety for a while) and answering only to the pope. The Knights were still elite warriors but they were also firmly rooted in the material world. As pillars of society with a keen understanding of the economic reality of pilgrimage, it was a natural progression to become guardians not only of pilgrims themselves but of their property too.

Anyone going on a Crusade was making an enormous commitment, not least of time. There was every chance they would be leaving behind their lives in Europe for years at a time so safeguarding their worldly wealth until their return became a priority. Few, meanwhile, dared carry their riches with them on the perilous road to the Holy Land. Who better, then, to leave their assets with than the Templars?

TOOK VOWS OF RELIGIOUS DEVOTION AND SELF-DENIAL

SONS OF ELITE FAMILIES HAD TO PROVE THEMSELVES OF GOOD CHARACTER

WARRIOR MONKS

PROTECTORS OF PILGRIMS AND CRUSADERS

LANDOWNERS

RICHEST ORDER

Furthermore, the Templars offered unprecedented "customer-service." As guardians of a vast chain of castle vaults that stretched from England to the Middle East, they agreed to take deposits at various of these locations (there were few safer places than a Templar-guarded vault) and issued the depositor with what was essentially a credit note. This could be "cashed in" at any of the other Templar strongholds (bank branches, if you like) along the way. So a Crusader could leave his gold in Paris and reclaim enough of it to pay his way once he was in Jerusalem. This is the essence of modern banking and the first time in history such a system was put into operation.

While the Bible does not look well upon usury (the charging of interest), the Templars got round this knotty problem by stealthy wording of contracts that effectively meant they charged a "rent" on deposits rather than interest. All the while, the order increased its supplementary interests, buying farms and vineyards and taking part in trade (the Knights famously had their own fleet of ships). It was also the Christian world's foremost lender. Here was a multi-faceted business that many modern private equity firms might wonder at.

TIME LINE

1119
Hugues de Payens founds the Templars, who are granted a base in Jerusalem.

1129
The order receives official recognition from the Vatican at the Council of Troyes.

1139
The Papal Bull, Omne Datum Optimum, greatly expands the power of the Templars.

c.1150
The order is by now heavily involved in wealth accumulation. It offers "banking services" to Crusaders wishing to deposit their valuables for safekeeping.

1291
Defeat at the Siege of Acre forces the Templars to relocate their headquarters to Cyprus.

1307
Hundreds of French Templars are rounded up and executed for alleged crimes including apostasy and spitting on the cross.

1312
In March, Pope Clement V dissolves the Templars. In May, the Vatican orders the Templars' land and financial holdings be transferred to another elite order, the Knights Hospitaller.

1314
The last Templar grand master, Jacques de Molay, is burned at the stake on March 18.

CAN'T BUY ME LOVE

However, the Templars ultimately became victims of their own success. By the end of the twelfth century their potency as a militia unit was diminishing. Meanwhile, prominent individuals within Europe's ruling classes were increasingly wary of this elite army that answered to no-one outside of the Vatican, that could travel across the continent at will, and which, it was rumored, was interested in establishing a state of its own. Even more dangerously, there were assorted kings and dukes who had mortgaged themselves to the Templars and resented the fact. The Templars had overplayed their hand.

Their most fearsome enemy was, predictably, one of their biggest debtors, Philip IV of France. Focusing on the Templars in his native France, he accused them of grievous crimes including acts of sacrilege and sexual deviancy. In 1307 hundreds of Templars were rounded up and confessions tortured out of them. Most were killed and in 1312 Pope Clement V, under pressure from Philip, dissolved the order. In 1314 the remaining Templars in France were executed. It was a dismal end for the first great banking dynasty who grew too powerful for their own good. Nonetheless, they established a basic banking model that has underpinned the modern banking world from the Medicis (see page 58) to the modern day.

A POSITION OF TRUST

While the Templars did not set out to increase their personal wealth as bankers to the Crusaders, they nonetheless exploited their privileged role to swell the order's coffers even as they provided a valuable service. It was a strategy that secured the group phenomenal influence from 1118–1314. As defenders of the faithful and with a name for religious devotion and self-discipline, the Knights were figures of power and trust to whom others aspired. They harnessed this high public standing to establish a system of banking hitherto unknown, reaping rich rewards in the process. It was an innovation they developed with aplomb but their story is also a cautionary one for the modern reader—that trust is hard earned and valuable but easy to lose.

▲ The imposing Château Royal de Collioure in France was built by the Templars in 1207. Such fortresses were used to store Crusader riches.

BANKING CRISES

We can see echoes of the rise and fall of the Templars in the experience of modern banks following the global economic crisis that struck in 2008. The Templar banking system surely seemed too big to fail, but after a very long period of "boom" the order found itself in charge of a teetering house of cards. When the desire to go on crusade to the Holy Land waned, the Templars were left with myriad borrowers threatening to default and increasingly resentful at the order's obvious wealth (just as the banks faced when the US housing bubble burst in 2007).

STRATEGY ANALYSIS

STRATEGY TYPE: *Innovative*
KEY STRATEGY: *Leveraging the order's military and moral authority to grow its wealth*
OUTCOME: *The development of a network of banks using "paper money," and the birth of banking as we know it*
ALSO USED BY: *HSBC, Bank of America, Deutsche Bank et al today.*

12 THE SCIENCE OF WAR

BY INNOVATIVE USE OF TECHNOLOGY MONGOL GENERAL **SUBUTAI** SUBDUED THE HUNGARIAN ARMY

KEY PLAYER: *Subutai (1175-1248)*

NATIONALITY: *Mongolian*

STRATEGY IMPLEMENTED: *1241*

CONTEXT: *Ögedei Khan accuses the Hungarians of protecting the Cumans, a nomadic Turkic race that the Mongols had defeated in 1223 and whom they considered to be their slaves. Subutai is Ögedei's chief strategist in the subsequent invasion*

Subutai was the most brilliant military strategist that the Mongols boasted in the first half of the fifteenth century. His life coincided with a golden age of Mongol expansion. He eventually claimed some 60 battlefield victories but his triumph at the Battle of Mohi was undoubtedly his greatest achievement, relying on inspired use of siege engines and brilliant responsiveness to unpredictable circumstances.

Subutai's family had long been close with that of Genghis Khan but he was nonetheless a commoner who could expect no favors from his esteemed friend. His elevation through the military ranks was purely the result of his acumen and tactical perceptiveness, which he repeatedly proved on the battlefield. Subutai was what Genghis Khan described as one of his "dogs of war." He combined personal courage and a steeliness redolent of Genghis himself, with a strategic sophistication unrivaled among his fellow commanders.

Among his many talents was an ability to coordinate the movements of armies operating hundreds of miles apart. Under Genghis Khan, he proved himself in campaigns stretching across China, Central Asia, and Persia. He notched up a series of triumphs against numerically superior opponents using a deft combination of rapid maneuvers, cunning deceptions, and diplomacy. Yet it would be Ögedei Khan who most benefited from his expertise when he ordered a series of Western campaigns in the late 1230s. By 1241, the Mongols had overrun the Russian principalities and now Ögedei cast his eye to the heart of Europe. Batu Khan, a grandson of Genghis and a senior Mongol ruler, was nominally in charge, but it was Subutai who pulled the strings.

DICTATING TERMS

Subutai was famous for the thoroughness of his approach, carefully analyzing the strengths and weaknesses of the enemy as well as taking into consideration the terrain and likely climactic conditions. He was also a masterful gatherer of intelligence, employing a network of spies. Before the Battle of Mohi, he had done his research on what to expect in Austria, Hungary, and Poland for more than a year.

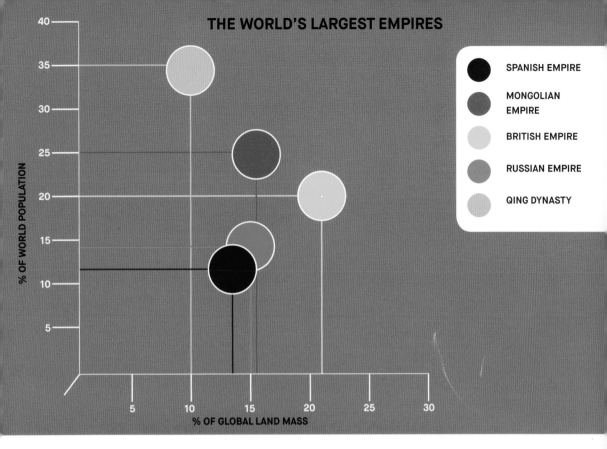

THE WORLD'S LARGEST EMPIRES

% OF WORLD POPULATION (vertical axis): 40, 35, 30, 25, 20, 15, 10, 5

% OF GLOBAL LAND MASS (horizontal axis): 5, 10, 15, 20, 25, 30

Legend:
- SPANISH EMPIRE
- MONGOLIAN EMPIRE
- BRITISH EMPIRE
- RUSSIAN EMPIRE
- QING DYNASTY

His battlefield approach was brilliant in its simplicity. He was intent on keeping his opponents where he wanted them, maneuvering them into a position of weakness before unleashing a deadly assault. Subutai was also careful to disguise his own strategies so as to keep the enemy guessing.

Meanwhile, he prepared his own men to be ready for any eventuality. He insisted that his army keep its luggage train to a minimum in order that it could move quickly and to ensure that protecting supplies did not demand the effort of too many men. Instead he trained his troops to fend for themselves. In so doing, he created soldiers who were hardy and self-reliant. He was also keen to exploit technological advantages wherever they existed—after every victory, he would force members of the vanquished enemy to serve in his army and plundered them for any specialist knowledge they might have.

By the time the Mongols advanced into Hungary in April 1241, Subutai was as ready as he could be for what lay ahead. Meanwhile, Hungary's ruler, Béla IV, had decided to consolidate his forces around Pest (part of modern-day Budapest), from where they would move north to meet the invaders. Subutai promptly withdrew his troops to the River Sajo, where he discreetly set up camp. There were woods there that offered his men protection and allowed for secretive scouting missions, while Béla's army were exposed on the Mohi plain on the opposite side of the river. Unaware of the massed ranks of Mongols on the other bank, the Hungarians were lulled into a false sense of security. Subutai had succeeded in securing a battlefield of his choosing.

TIME LINE

GOING IN FOR THE KILL

With Mongol forces having achieved victory in Poland just a day earlier, the Battle of Mohi began on the evening of April 10 1241. A small Mongol contingent crossed the recently flooded river under cover of darkness in preparation to launch an attack from the south. Subutai, meanwhile, was to lead a second, larger force across the river. However, a defector informed Béla of the plan and the Hungarians sent troops to intercept the Mongols somewhere around midnight.

Subutai and his men were taken by surprise and found Hungarian crossbowmen hurling bolts down upon them. Amidst the chaos, Subutai—illustrating his love of technological innovation—called for the Mongol siege engines to be turned upon the Hungarians. Seven of the engines launched stones at the crossbowmen, quickly dispersing them and so giving Subutai's troops the time required to cross the river. It was almost certainly the first time that such machinery had been used like this in open battle.

By the following morning, the Mongols had secured their path to Mohi, leaving the Hungarians in panic-stricken disarray. Subutai gave the order to surround them but, fearing the desperate foe would fight to the death, he left a gap in the encirclement. The Hungarians mistakenly believed they had a way out but in fact the gap led on to swampy marshland (the river had recently flooded). Men and horses struggled on the boggy land only to discover they were being chased down in small groups and killed by the Mongols. The Hungarians lost some 40,000 men at Mohi. Estimates of Mongol losses vary considerably but some put them as low as a thousand. Having offered the enemy hope of escape, Subutai annihilated them.

He was all ready to capitalize on his

triumph by advancing further into Europe and attacking the core of the Holy Roman Empire. However, Ögedei Khan died, leaving a power vacuum back at home. Subutai and his troops were duly called back for the election of a new leader, and Europe breathed a sigh of relief.

Subutai epitomizes much that is good in a military leader, from a cool head to personal bravery. But it was his openness to using technology in wholly unexpected ways that made the real difference at Mohi. Warfare has always driven technological advancement, but it is rarer to find leaders with the vision to adapt existing technology to military advantage. While Subutai is among the most notable exponents, he is not alone. For instance, troops in Iraq and Afghanistan used Apple iPhones for tasks such as running translation software, while games controllers were adapted for use with drone aircraft. What Subutai would have made of the technology may only be guessed at, but he would have approved of the principle.

▲ *This Persian manuscript from 1258 shows Baghdad under Mongol siege. Subutai was the master Mongol general.*

IMPERIAL GAINS

Subutai's efforts saw the Mongol Empire expand as far west as it ever reached. Stretching across continents it was the largest contiguous land-based empire the world has ever known. Today the Mongols have a reputation as barbarians, raping and pillaging wherever they went. While there is some truth in this, they were also a highly sophisticated military force who consolidated territorial gains by imposing strong rule and encouraging trade.

STRATEGY ANALYSIS

STRATEGY TYPE: *Strategic thinking*
KEY STRATEGY: *Adapted existing technology for innovative battlefield use*
OUTCOME: *The annihilation of one of Europe's premier armies*
ALSO USED BY: *British forces at Gibraltar, 1779, and troops in Iraq and Afghanistan, 2003–2011.*

13

MONEY BRINGS POWER

COSIMO DE MEDICI BUILDS A POLITICAL EMPIRE ON THE BACK OF BANKING

KEY PLAYER: *The Medici family*
NATIONALITY: *Italian*
STRATEGY IMPLEMENTED:
1397-1494
CONTEXT: *The Medici family runs its banking business from the Italian city-state of Florence. As chief bankers to the Vatican, they come to dominate Europe's financial sector*

The Medici Bank was founded by Giovanni di Bicci de Medici in 1397 but enjoyed its golden age under the leadership of his son, Cosimo, who took over in 1429. Using his vast banking wealth to leverage cultural and political influence, he became the de facto ruler of Florence, building his family's social position so that it thrived even after its banking interests folding in 1494.

By the start of the fifteenth century, the Italian city-states were well established as the capitals of European banking, spearheaded by families such as the Bardi and Peruzzi. The Medici family, meanwhile, had done perfectly well for themselves, principally through the wool trade. By the fourteenth century they were one of several notable families in the Florentine Republic, but were far from being the most powerful. However, the establishment of the Medici Bank in 1397 saw a rapid upturn in their economic fortunes so that when Cosimo the Elder took control of the business 32 years later, he was among the city's richest individuals. Furthermore, his father had already enhanced the family reputation by championing popular tax reforms.

But Cosimo was not a man content to be just one of Florence's leading men. He wanted to be the out-and-out man at the top. So he set about refining the bank's operations to maximize profitability. He then plowed his riches back into the city, establishing himself as the leading cultural patron of an artistic golden age as well as a populist political figure. Within five years, he was effectively the uncrowned monarch of Florence and held the position for the rest of his life. His family would reap the reward of his political and cultural acumen for centuries to come. As such, his life serves as an exemplar of how to turn private capital into public influence.

THE NUMBERS GAME

From the outset, Cosimo understood that his ambitions could only be achieved if his bank thrived. His father had left him a prosperous business but Cosimo ruthlessly looked to grow it in every way possible. He became notorious for ruling his commercial empire with an iron fist. His greatest advantage was that the Medici family were already established as the bankers to the Papacy in Rome. Not only was this a hugely profitable

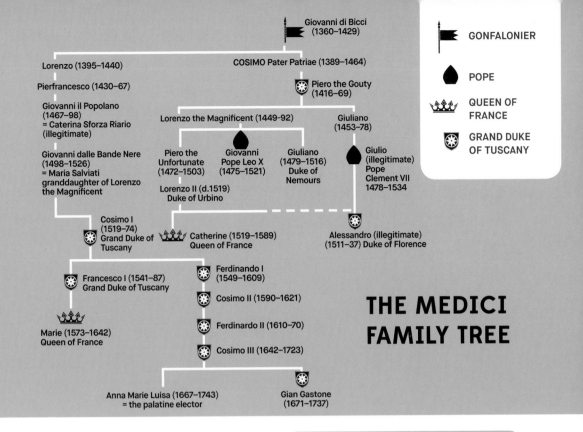

Family tree labels:

Giovanni di Bicci (1360–1429) — GONFALONIER

Lorenzo (1395–1440)

COSIMO Pater Patriae (1389–1464)

Pierfrancesco (1430–67)

Piero the Gouty (1416–69) — GRAND DUKE OF TUSCANY

Giovanni il Popolano (1467–98) = Caterina Sforza Riario (illegitimate)

Lorenzo the Magnificent (1449–92)

Giuliano (1453–78)

Giovanni dalle Bande Nere (1498–1526) = Maria Salviati granddaughter of Lorenzo the Magnificent

Piero the Unfortunate (1472–1503)

Lorenzo II (d.1519) Duke of Urbino

Giovanni Pope Leo X (1475–1521) — POPE

Giuliano (1479–1516) Duke of Nemours

Giulio (illegitimate) Pope Clement VII 1478–1534 — POPE

Cosimo I (1519–74) Grand Duke of Tuscany — GRAND DUKE OF TUSCANY

Catherine (1519–1589) Queen of France — QUEEN OF FRANCE

Alessandro (illegitimate) (1511–37) Duke of Florence — GRAND DUKE OF TUSCANY

Francesco I (1541–87) Grand Duke of Tuscany — GRAND DUKE OF TUSCANY

Ferdinando I (1549–1609) — GRAND DUKE OF TUSCANY

Cosimo II (1590–1621) — GRAND DUKE OF TUSCANY

Marie (1573–1642) Queen of France — QUEEN OF FRANCE

Ferdinardo II (1610–70) — GRAND DUKE OF TUSCANY

Cosimo III (1642–1723) — GRAND DUKE OF TUSCANY

Anna Marie Luisa (1667–1743) = the palatine elector

Gian Gastone (1671–1737) — GRAND DUKE OF TUSCANY

Legend:

GONFALONIER

POPE

QUEEN OF FRANCE

GRAND DUKE OF TUSCANY

---

enterprise in its own right, accounting for over half the bank's business until 1434, but having insider knowledge of the Vatican's finances gave Cosimo significant clout. It was also a powerful marketing tool. Where the pope was happy to bank, members of royal families and the aristocracy were not far behind. So Cosimo used this platform to undertake a phase of dramatic international expansion. Before long, he had bank branches as far afield as Belgium, England, France, and Switzerland, and throughout the Italian city-states. His customers included many of the most powerful families on the continent.

With access to vast deposits of gold and cash, he was able to authorize ever-larger loans and investments. Because usury (the charging of interest on loans) was not permitted by the Catholic Church, he was also innovative in devising methods of

FAMILY BUSINESS

The modern world has also thrown up its fair share of political dynasties based on personal wealth. The United States boasts perhaps the most famous example in the shape of the Kennedy family. Already well established, Joe Kennedy took them to new heights on the back of wily business deals in the first half of the twentieth century. He thus provided the foundations for his son John to claim the White House, and John's brother Bobby was another prospective president until an assassin's bullet ended that dream. Meanwhile, only personal scandal put an end to the chances of presidency for a third sibling, Teddy.

1389
Cosimo de Medici ("the Elder") is born on September 27 in Florence.

1397
Giovanni de Bicci de Medici establishes the Medici Bank.

1429
Cosimo takes over running of the bank and builds it into the leading financial institution in Europe.

1434
He wins election as Florence's gran maestro.

1464
Cosimo dies on August 1 in Florence. His son, Piero, takes over the bank.

1494
The bank closes after years of mismanagement.

1513–21
The first of the Medici family popes, Leo X.

1523-34
Pope Clement VII.

1531
The family become hereditary dukes of Florence.

1547–59
Catherine de Medici is queen of France.

1559–65
Pius IV is pope.

1600–10
Marie de Medici is queen of France.

1605
The last of the Medici popes, Leo XI

1737
The last Medici Duke, Gian Gastone, dies without issue.

making profit. For instance, the bank was at the forefront of developing currency exchange and issuing bills of exchange, which allowed the bank to charge interest-like fees that did not contravene church law. Furthermore, he pushed for greater efficiency from his employees and championed the emerging discipline of double-entry book-keeping (i.e. keeping a record of all incomings and outgoings). He also evolved the concept of the "holding company," structuring the bank so that the institution as a whole wouldn't suffer contagion from any struggling branch. Cosimo thus turned a successful bank into an absolute powerhouse of finance—the biggest international bank on the planet.

BUYING POWER

The Medicis emerged at a time when several families throughout Italy were establishing long-lasting and powerful dynasties. Among them were the notorious Borgias (who originally hailed from Spain but came to dominate Rome and the Vatican) and the Sforzas in Milan. With unimaginable wealth at his disposal, Cosimo next looked to consolidate his political power and establish his family as a powerful dynasty alongside the Borgias and Sforzas.

Although Florence was nominally a democratic state, if you wanted to progress up the hierarchy you were expected to pay your way. A populist politician by nature, he spent hard cash to win election in 1434 as Florence's gran maestro (unofficial head of state)—a post he retained for the rest of his life. Having used his financial muscle to secure political power, his political power now ensured the ongoing success of his business.

He also used his position of influence and wealth to fund patronage of some of the greatest artists of the Renaissance.

Again, Cosimo turned it into a win-win situation for himself. As gran maestro he commissioned buildings and works of art from the likes of Brunelleschi, Ghiberti, Donatello, and Fra Angelico. In return, as Florence grew into the undisputed cultural capital of the Renaissance world, so its grandeur ensured Cosimo's ongoing popularity and pre-eminent position in society.

When Cosimo died in 1464, the bank's best days were behind it. Control of the business went first to his son, the stricken Piero the Gouty, and then to Piero's son, Lorenzo. Neither of them rivaled Cosimo for banking acumen. Immersing themselves in Florence's political life at the expense of their business, their failure only highlighted Cosimo's strategic brilliance in balancing those two spheres. By 1494, the bank was on its knees.

Yet so effective had Cosimo been at building Medici influence, the family remained one of Europe's great political forces well beyond the bank's decline. His descendants were made hereditary grand dukes of Tuscany from 1531, a lineage that continued until 1737 and the absence of a male heir. Furthermore, the family provided no less than four popes and two queens of France in the sixteenth and seventeenth centuries, wielding incredible influence in international politics. It represented a remarkable legacy for a man who understood perhaps better than anyone the mutual co-dependence between money and power.

▲ *The Medici's influence lasted centuries after Cosimo's death. Namesake Cosimo I, above, was created Grand Duke of Tuscany in 1569.*

STRATEGY ANALYSIS

STRATEGY TYPE: *Dominance*
KEY STRATEGY: *Using wealth generated by banking to win political power*
OUTCOME: *Influence over Italian and European politics even after the bank's collapse*
ALSO USED BY: *The House of Sforza in Milan, 15th–16th centuries, and the Kennedy family in the United States.*

14

LEADING BY EXAMPLE

JOAN OF ARC TAKES THE BATTLE TO THE ENGLISH DURING THE SIEGE OF ORLÉANS

KEY PLAYER: *Joan of Arc*
NATIONALITY: *French*
STRATEGY IMPLEMENTED:
May 1429
CONTEXT: *Joan, a girl of lowly birth, is an unlikely military hero but, guided by "divine voices," she turned the tide of the Hundred Years' War*

A peasant girl who claimed to hear divine voices, Joan of Arc went on an incredible journey to become a national hero of France. Her role in lifting the English siege at Orléans during the Hundred Years' War provides a classic example of how an individual can use their personality to galvanize those around them and so change the course of history.

Joan was around thirteen years old when, she claimed, she began to hear voices belonging to the Saints Michael, Catherine, and Margaret, which would guide her for the rest of her life. In the centuries since, there has been much debate as to how to interpret these "voices" (which were accompanied by visions too). Some believe they should be taken as genuine manifestations of divine intervention, while others suggest they indicate hallucinations brought on by stress (perhaps caused by the sacking of her home town in 1425, the year they began to appear to her). Few, though, believe Joan thought them anything other than real.

In late 1428, the voices told her that she had a crucial two-part job to fulfil: Firstly, to remove the English forces that had been besieging the city of Orléans since October 1428; and, secondly, to accompany the dauphin, Charles, to Reims that he might be crowned king of France. In February 1429 she traveled to the French town of Vaucouleurs in the hope of persuading a prominent army captain, Robert de Baudricourt, to supply her with troops. He was impressed by her piety and agreed to help her after she correctly predicted that the French would be defeated at the Battle of the Herrings. That he acceded to the wishes of an unknown peasant girl is evidence of her powerful personality.

With his backing, and dressed as a male soldier, she then made the dangerous journey through enemy territory to the city of Chinon to offer her services to Charles VII, the uncrowned son of Charles VI—who had died in 1422—whose legitimacy as monarch was challenged by Henry VI of England. Joan told Charles what the voices had commanded her to do but he was understandably cautious about accepting the word of an unknown peasant girl. He subjected her to weeks of testing to assess her claims of purity and piety and in the end was convinced that she was all that she purported to be. He thus accepted her offer of service. Again, Joan had broken the "glass ceiling" by force of will and strength of character alone.

JOAN'S JOURNEY

- Executed at Rouen
- Captured at Compiegne
- Paris
- Reims
- Blois
- Tours
- Battle of Patay
- Orléans and St Loup
- Vaucouleurs
- Chinon
- Domrémy

Legend:
- Meets Charles VII
- Crowning of Charles VII
- Major battle
- Joan's birthplace
- Capital city
- Location of key events

TURNING THE TIDE

At the end of April, Joan set out to relieve the French forces at Orléans, which had been in an English stranglehold for some six months by then. Maintaining the dress of a male soldier, against expectations she quickly earned the devotion of the doughty men under her command. When she got to Orléans, she was frustrated by the conservative tactics of the French war council. Although she was not a great military tactician in the classical sense, she inspired in her men a belief that they were destined for victory. She sent goading missives to the enemy and demonstrated great self-discipline in her personal conduct that resonated with those on her own side. Assisted by a little good luck, she went against the war council's defined strategy and launched an attack on an English garrison at St Loup, outside the city, on May 4. Guided as ever by her voices, she persuaded those around her that God was with them in the fight. Within a few hours, St Loup had indeed fallen.

Two days later, the French began an assault on the English complex of Boulevart-Tourelles-Augustines. Initially, things went against them as rumors that English reinforcements were on the way caused an outbreak of panic. Yet Joan again managed to rally her forces, supposedly halting the English advance with a cry of "Au nom de Dieu" ("in the name of God"). Despite an injured foot, she reappeared for action the following day after a period of prayer and quiet reflection. Before long, she was struck on the shoulder by a crossbow bolt but still she refused to turn away from

TIME LINE

1337
The Hundred Years' War begins between England and France.

1412
Joan of Arc is born in Domrémy in the Lorraine region of France around January 6.

1428
English forces besiege Orléans in October.

1429 March 22
Joan has her offer to serve the dauphin, Charles, accepted.

April 27
Joan and her small force of troops set out from Blois to assist the French forces at Orléans.

May 4
Joan launches a sudden attack on the English.

May 7
Despite an arrow wound, she leads her men into battle at Les Tourelles.

May 8
The siege is decisively broken.

June 18
Joan achieves a stunning victory at the Battle of Patay, paving the way for the capture of Reims.

July 17
Charles is crowned king of France at Reims.

1430
In May Joan is captured at Compiègne.

1431
Joan's trial for witchcraft begins on January 13. After she is convicted, the English burn her at the stake on May 30.

1920
The Roman Catholic Church declare Joan a saint on May 16.

the battlefield. After some basic medical attention (some historians say she pulled the bolt out herself), she returned to the crucible of fighting, inspiring her men on to ever greater deeds by her own show of valour. By nightfall on May 7, the English siege of Orléans was over.

THE PRICE OF SUCCESS
Having established legendary status within the French ranks in just a few months, Joan enjoyed her greatest military triumph in June at the Battle of Patay. There she crushed English relief forces that had been rushed to the scene from Paris. It was a victory that the French believed made up for the ignominious defeat against the army of Henry V at Agincourt some fourteen

DESTINED FOR VICTORY

History is littered with individuals whose personal qualities spurred their armies to great efforts and achievements—Alexander the Great, Napoleon, even Henry V at Agincourt to name but a few. Into the twentieth century, arguably the greatest of all wartime leaders was Winston Churchill. Although he did not see front-line action in World War II, he had more than you might think in common with the Maid of Orléans. Having proven his battlefield courage as a young man in the Boer War, by the time he faced Hitler he had the unerring knack of making his people feel that their fight was a just one and that by exhibiting courage and self-discipline, they too would fulfil their destiny: Victory.

years earlier. A month later and the French had secured Reims, so allowing for Charles's coronation there and the fulfilment of Joan's apparently divinely-appointed mission.

That all of this could be achieved by a teenage girl of humble birth and no real military experience provides us with one of history's greatest tales. It is a narrative that highlights the importance of personal faith, determination, self-discipline, and charisma. Yet, as we know, it is a story with a twist in the tale.

While Joan was a godly figure to those on her own side, the English believed (or at least propagandized) that her powers came from witchcraft. She fell into English hands at the end of 1430 and was put on trial the following year. Her captors treated her with scant respect and despite her agreement to abjure, burned her as a witch on May 30 1431. A little under 500 years later the Vatican declared her a saint instead. She was indubitably a great captain of men who understood the importance of leading by personal example.

STRATEGY ANALYSIS

STRATEGY TYPE: *Leadership*
KEY STRATEGY: *Demonstrated personal bravery and confidence to inspire her troops*
OUTCOME: *Joan was key to stifling progress of the English forces and securing the French crown for Charles VII*
ALSO USED BY: *Napoleon Bonaparte throughout his military career, 1785–1821, and Winston Churchill, World War I.*

TAKE ON YOUR CRITICS

POPE PAUL III INSTIGATES THE CATHOLIC CHURCH'S COUNTER-REFORMATION

KEY PLAYER: *Pope Paul III (1468–1549)*

NATIONALITY: *Italian*

STRATEGY IMPLEMENTED: *1534-49*

CONTEXT: *In the early sixteenth century, the German clergyman Martin Luther spearheaded the Reformation that challenged the authority of the Roman Catholic Church. Paul III was the first pope to address the critics*

By the sixteenth century, the Roman Catholic Church had garnered many critics angered by its spiritual malaise and worldly excesses. A number of states in northern Europe broke with Rome for religious and political reasons, leaving the Vatican facing a serious crisis.

The Protestant Reformation is considered to have begun in 1517 in Wittenberg when a clergyman named Martin Luther pinned a document that became known as the 95 Theses to the doors of a local church. It listed a litany of complaints against the church, including charges of nepotism, the trading of church offices, and the selling of indulgences (a dispensation against time in Purgatory for one's Earthly sins). Martin Luther was joined by other Reformation leaders throughout Europe, including John Calvin, John Knox, and Huldrych Zwingli, in his condemnation of the Vatican and its church. Before long there were powerful Protestant churches throughout the princely states of Germany, in Switzerland and Scandinavia, England, Scotland, and beyond.

In many ways, Alessandro Farnese (as Pope Paul III was born) represented much that was wrong with the Catholic Church in this period. He hailed from a wealthy family and was widely thought to have leveraged influence to secure his position as a cardinal. Indeed, it was a role to which he was appointed some quarter of a century before he was even ordained as a priest. He also had affairs that produced children, practiced nepotism, and indulged a taste for the finer things in life. Yet when he was made pope in 1534, he exhibited a desire for reform that reflected not only political pragmatism (he recognized the rise of Protestantism posed a real threat to papal authority) but also a genuine desire for spiritual renewal within the church. Paul understood the time had come to act: To accept reform where he believed it necessary and to fight back against criticisms he deemed unjustified.

Pasquale Cati's depiction of the Council of Trent, the brainchild of Pope Paul III and a vital component of his fight-back against the Protestant Reformation.

TIME LINE

1468
Allesandro Farnese is born on February 29.

1493
He becomes a cardinal.

1517
Martin Luther posts his 95 Theses on the doors of a church in Wittenberg, Germany, marking the start of the Reformation.

1534
Farnese becomes Pope Paul III.

1537
A committee of nine cardinals reports to Paul on the state of the church.

1540
He recognizes the Society of Jesus (Jesuits).

1542
Paul established the Roman Inquisition.

1545
First session of the Council of Trent opens and lasts until 1547. There are further sessions from 1555–59 and 1562–63.

1549
Paul III dies on November 10.

1648
The culmination of the Thirty Years' War marks the end of the Counter-Reformation.

LOOKING INWARD

In 1536 he established a committee of nine cardinals to investigate and report on the affairs of the church. In a remarkably frank document, it condemned such abuses as the selling of offices and highlighted the inadequacies of many priests, a large number of whom never visited the dioceses they were meant to be serving. In 1542, Paul invited senior church figures from around Europe to the Great Church Council at Trent (in northern Italy), which held its first session in 1545 and met for the last time in 1562–63 (during the tenure of Paul's successor, Paul IV). As Paul III hoped, the Council became a fundamental driver of the Counter-Reformation.

On the one hand, it reaffirmed basic Catholic doctrine and the supreme authority of the papacy. On the other, it demanded an end to many of the most obvious abuses that so offended the Reformers. Priests were to be carefully selected and properly trained so as to better engage with the laity. Clergy and bishops were to regularly visit their dioceses and bishoprics if they were not resident there. Meanwhile, the selling of relics and indulgences was expressly forbidden, as were priestly affairs. Paul had shown a real appetite to make right those things that had gone wrong with the church. In so doing he won back at least some of those who had been drawn towards Protestantism.

GOING ON THE ATTACK

However, he knew that the rise of Protestantism was such that Catholicism needed to come out fighting too. To this end he adopted a multipronged approach. He recognized numerous new religious orders that he hoped would bring energy and vitality to the fight. These included the Capuchins, the Barnabites, and, most famously, the Jesuits. Formed by Ignatius of Loyola along military lines, the Jesuits were officially sanctioned by Paul in 1540. The order's numbers quickly swelled and its missionaries became vital in winning back many Protestant converts throughout Europe. Furthermore, their later ventures into Africa and the New World gave Catholicism a foothold in those continents, establishing church strongholds that have lasted to the present day. Paul also established the Roman Inquisition in 1542 to forcefully counter heresy, following in the footsteps of the much-feared Spanish Inquisition.

He also believed that commissioning buildings and artworks from the greatest Renaissance artists added to the glory not only of Rome itself but the church as a whole. For instance, he oversaw completion of Michelangelo's *Last Judgment* in the Sistine Chapel and hired the same artist to paint several other frescoes in the Vatican, while Titian was brought in to paint his portrait. The church had long used art as a medium to communicate its religious and spiritual messages and Paul was intent on keeping up the tradition. The Reformers could have their bare churches, but he knew such austerity was not to everybody's taste.

Given the peculiar challenges thrown up by the Reformation, Paul was very much the right man at the right time. He exhibited a desire for reform that won over many of those who might otherwise have turned to Protestantism, but maintained a bold belief in the essential "rightness" of his church. He was at once responsive to criticism but not a slave to it. His strategy of eliminating the most obvious abuses of church law, aggressively promoting its fundamental doctrines and using art as a weapon of propaganda laid the foundations for the Counter-Reformation, which extended well into the seventeenth century. Had he not put the basics in place at an early stage, it may well have been the case that Protestantism would have entirely overwhelmed the Catholic Church. Instead, it maintained its spiritual domination across large swathes of Europe and was left well-set to spread its influence into the rest of the world. The Counter-Reformation showed how a complex organisation can pull itself back from the brink with a mixture of internal reform and an aggressive response to its critics.

FIGHT BACK

In the 1990s, many left-of-center parties launched a political "Counter-Reformation" as they strived to marry their liberal ideals with the laissez-faire capitalism dominating the global economy. The result was the so-called "Third Way," spearheaded by the US Democratic Party under Bill Clinton, the UK Labour Party, Gerhard Schröder's German Social Democrats, and the Labor Party in Australia. All trod a path between internal reform and defense of their established principles to reinvigorate their parties.

STRATEGY ANALYSIS

STRATEGY TYPE: *Defensive strategy*
KEY STRATEGY: *Answered criticism by undertaking necessary reform*
OUTCOME: *The Counter-Reformation bolstered Catholicism in its existing heartlands and prompted its emergence in new territories*
ALSO USED BY: *1990s Third Way exponents— Bill Clinton, Tony Blair, and Gerhard Schröder.*

16

MARKET YOUR BRAND

JOSIAH WEDGWOOD CREATES THE FIRST "MUST-HAVE" BRAND

KEY PLAYER: *Josiah Wedgwood (1730-95)*
NATIONALITY: *English*
STRATEGY IMPLEMENTED: *Second half of the eighteenth century*
CONTEXT: *Wedgwood identified a growing hunger among the aristocracy and middle classes for quality chinaware traditionally imported from the Far East*

The eighteenth century was a time of great social change in Britain. Rapid improvements in industrial and agricultural production saw the population become increasingly urban, while the middle class was ever expanding. Where once fine porcelain had been a status symbol that only the very rich could afford, it was now within the grasp of many more people. If only someone could supply it...

Born in 1730 in the great pottery center of Staffordshire, Wedgwood was the youngest of twelve children in a family of potters. Never short of ambition (he once described how "I want to astonish the world all at once"), he had established his own workshop by 1759 in Burslem, not far from the burgeoning industrial metropolis of Manchester.

At this stage in history, British-produced chinaware tended to be functional, basic, and cheap enough so that the masses could afford it. Those with money, meanwhile, purchased fine porcelain from China. Not only was it manufactured using advanced techniques that remained shrouded in mystery to their counterparts in the West, its exoticism was much prized too. Only those who had "made it" had the buying power to purchase china from China.

But Wedgwood noticed that society was changing. More and more people of the "middling sort" were appearing, hungry to emulate their "social betters" even if they could not rival them for wealth. So Wedgwood, a brilliant autodidact with a penchant for technical innovation, set about developing new techniques to produce high-quality china for the domestic market. He sourced fine clay, developed new glazes, and focused on winning designs to create must-have goods.

BY ROYAL APPROVAL

As master of a factory that could produce consistently first-rate products that people lusted after, Wedgwood realized he now needed to build his brand. He wanted to be the "go-to china guy" for the British, and ultimately European, markets. To this end he set about first wooing the aristocracy, whom he knew had money to splash on such luxuries. He was greatly assisted in this process by his extremely well-connected business partner, a Liverpool merchant called Thomas Bentley. Once he had gained a foothold in

CELEBRITY ENDORSEMENTS THROUGH THE AGES

Lily Langtry and Pears Soap

Kylie Minogue & Agent Provocateur

Queen Victoria and Cadbury's Cocoa

Al Jolson and Lucky Strike cigarettes

Babe Ruth and Red Rock Cola

the high-end market, Wedgwood knew that the emerging middle classes would be keen to buy their own versions of his goods.

It was an enormously successful marketing strategy. His greatest breakthrough came in 1765 when Queen Charlotte, wife of George III, commissioned a tea service from him. All those earls and dukes and duchesses who supped from its sumptuous cups inevitably wanted their own Wedgwood services. As did Catherine II of Russia, for whom he created a 952–item dinner service. Furthermore, he persuaded Charlotte to allow him to name the particular style of cream porcelain he used "Queen's Ware," thus establishing a direct association between his name and royalty. His letterhead and advertising material soon read "Potter to Her Majesty." Sure enough, not only did he become the favored purveyor of china to the social elite, but the middle class developed an insatiable taste of their own for his work.

SPORTING ICONS

If the high-born were most likely to become popular heroes in Wedgwood's time, these days such adulation is more frequently reserved for sportsmen. Where Wedgwood leveraged aristocratic and royal patronage to secure gigantic sales, sportswear giants such as Nike and Adidas have spent decades doing much the same thing but using sporting heroes. It is well reported that icons including Michael Jordan, Lionel Messi, and David Beckham have received head-spinning figures to wear particular brands—investment that has reaped obvious rewards in increased profile and, ultimately, profit.

1730
Born Josiah Wedgwood at Burslem in Stoke-on-Trent.

1744
Wedgwood is an apprentice to his elder brother, Thomas.

1754
Forms a commercial partnership with Thomas Whieldon, a leading potter of the day.

1759
Wedgwood goes it alone, opening the Ivy House factory in Burslem.

c. 1760
Develops an improved method for producing creamware.

1762
Meets Thomas Bentley, who becomes his life-long business partner.

1765
Wedgwood trademarks his Queen's Ware.

1768
Introduces his patented black basaltes ware.

1769
He opens his giant new factory at Etruria.

1770s
He develops techniques to produce pearlware and, Jasperware, much of it in the trademark Wedgwood Blue.

1774
The company manufactures a near thousand-piece service for Catherine II of Russia.

1789
Landmark reproduction of the Portland Vase.

1795
Wedgwood dies at Etruria on January 3.

19th century
The company begins producing colored earthenware, as well as bone china. In 1895 it becomes Josiah Wedgwood and Sons Ltd.

KEEPING UP MOMENTUM

Wedgwood was early in the uptake of an extraordinary number of sales strategies. For instance, he advertized widely in newspapers and magazines and created colorful catalogs for potential customers. He also timed the arrival of new designs to coincide with the latest fashion season and befriended high-profile artists including George Stubbs and George Romney, gifting them pieces of his work that would subsequently crop up in their pictures.

Furthermore, he used direct mailing techniques and employed a small army of traveling salesman to get his goods out "into the field," offering free delivery in many cases. Having come to utterly dominate the British market, he turned his attention to conquering Europe. In this aim, he was greatly assisted by having access to people of influence and standing. He called in his contacts so that before long British ambassadors across the continent were singing his praises and showing off his wares as they entertained their colleagues in the diplomatic ranks.

Wedgwood is also believed to be the first commercial figure to promise "satisfaction guaranteed or your money back." Meanwhile, he understood the great publicity value in producing "one-off" pieces that might not in themselves be large revenue earners. The most notable example of this is his recreation of the Portland Vase (a beautiful cameo-glass, Illyrian antiquity) that Wedgwood labored over for three years.

TECHNICAL INNOVATION

Yet it would be wrong to consider Wedgwood merely as a great salesman. All the while, he kept up with technical innovations (indeed, his invention of a thermometer for use inside kilns earned him membership of the Royal Society) and ensured his products remained the best quality on the market. He was also an enlightened employer, paying his workers a fair wage (and demanding high standards in return), and a social reformer dedicated to the abolition of slavery.

Committed to the abolitionist cause, he produced the Wedgwood medallion—featuring the most famous image of a black person in all eighteenth-century art. The medallions' inscription "Am I not a Man and a Brother?" became a catchphrase of the abolitionist movement, and Benjamin Franklin declared that the medallion had been "equal to the best-written pamphlet." As in his business endeavors Wedgwood in creating this medallion demonstrated his understanding of the importance of brand: The medallion was a clear and powerful public statement of the abolitionist cause.

Ever on the look out for development opportunities, he pushed for improvements to the social infrastructure, particularly upgraded roads and the construction of canals, with an eye to giving his own business a competitive advantage.

Wedgwood was a commercial visionary. His desire to couple brilliant products with imaginative ways of selling remains an example to all those working in the retail field. Today perhaps more than ever, given that all too rarely do companies manage that complex balance of desirable object and effective marketing.

▲ Above, Josiah Wedgwood by Joshua Reynolds; and opposite, a Wedgwood design in Jasperware. This finish was also used for the Portland vase.

STRATEGY ANALYSIS

STRATEGY TYPE: *Marketing*
KEY STRATEGY: *Use of innovative marketing techniques to build a recognizable brand*
OUTCOME: *His firm came to dominate the market for decades and he remains the most famous potter of all time*
ALSO USED BY: *Nike, Adidas, and other leading sports brands since the 1970s.*

17

KEEP IT IN THE FAMILY

MAYER AMSCHEL ROTHSCHILD
ESTABLISHED AN INTERNATIONAL BANKING DYNASTY

KEY PLAYER: *Mayer Amschel Rothschild (1744-1812)*
NATIONALITY: *German*
STRATEGY IMPLEMENTED: *From the 1760s to present*
CONTEXT: *Rothschild graduated from dealing in rare coins to providing financial services to Europe's leaders. He capitalized on political instability to earn a personal fortune before sending out his sons to develop the business*

Mayer Amschel Rothschild developed his connections with prominent members of European society to further his banking interests. He introduced a number of innovations including high-volume dealing, an extremely effective communications network, and diversified investments. Having become one of the wealthiest men in the world, he brought his five sons into the business and made provision in his will so that their accumulated wealth remained within the Rothschild family.

Rothschild was born in the Jewish quarter of Frankfurt am Main in Germany into a family involved in the textile trade and money-lending. However, they were far from wealthy. When he was twelve, his father died and Rothschild traveled to Hannover to undertake an apprenticeship with the Oppenheim banking family. Rothschild was a quick learner, schooling himself in the fine arts of foreign trade and currency exchange. He also quickly realized that money begets money and made sure to ingratiate himself with people of wealth.

On returning to Frankfurt, he started dealing in rare coins and other antiquities, showing himself to have a good eye and making consistently sound investments that soon granted him complete financial security. Furthermore, he was operating in a world full of wealthy patrons eager to splash their cash with those who provided them with what they desired. Increasingly, Rothchild offered credit lines until he was less a trader and more a financier.

In particular, he forged a close alliance with Crown Prince Wilhelm, who in 1785 became Wilhelm IX, Landgrave (equivalent to a count in the Holy Roman Empire) of Hesse-Kassel. On succeeding his father, Frederick II, Wilhelm inherited one of the largest fortunes in Europe. Rothschild became his chief financial advisor and provided an array of commercial services. He also assisted the landgrave in finalizing a deal that saw Hessian mercenaries hired out to a Britain made nervous by the fall-out of the French revolution. He then used money from the British to provide the Austrian army with supplies, rapidly increasing his own wealth in the process.

RICH LIST

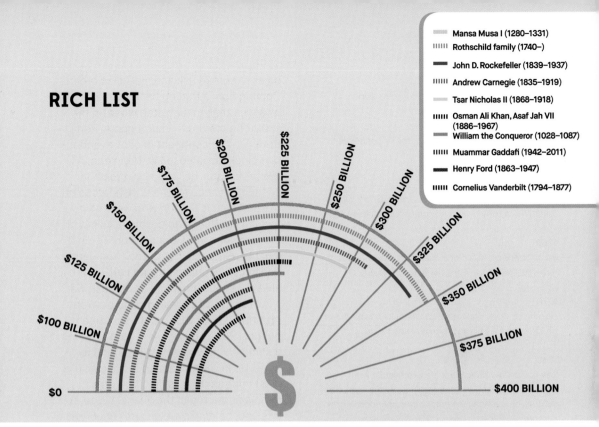

$0
$100 BILLION
$125 BILLION
$150 BILLION
$175 BILLION
$200 BILLION
$225 BILLION
$250 BILLION
$300 BILLION
$325 BILLION
$350 BILLION
$375 BILLION
$400 BILLION

That experience opened up his eyes to the possibilities inherent in doing business with governments. There was good money to be made in providing loans and other services to individuals and businesses, but it paled when set against the riches on offer from national administrations.

PROFIT IN MISFORTUNE

By the 1790s Rothschild was firmly established as an international financier. He made increasingly significant international loans, often using capital provided by the Landgrave. Furthermore, he prospered as Europe teetered on the brink of war. Where there was political instability, he saw opportunity: Governments fearing war or revolution required loans to pay for their armies and to fund other essential outlays.

In addition, Rothschild was keen to expand his portfolio of financial activities

POLITICS AND MONEY

The Rothschilds utterly dominated European finance throughout the nineteenth century. In his role as a pioneer of international finance, Mayer Amschel Rothschild provided the model for the banking powerhouses of recent times, including Goldman Sachs, Morgan Stanley, and Merrill Lynch. For better or worse, he also set in motion the entwinement of international finance and politics. Where today there is widespread unease at the close relationship between the political classes and bankers (particularly given the tendency for financial institutions to blossom in times of political instability), Rothschild set the precedent.

1744

Mayer Amschel Rothschild is born in Frankfurt.

1757

He begins an apprenticeship with the Oppenheimer banking dynasty in Hannover.

1760s

Back in Frankfurt, he expands his trade in rare coins and antiquities to offer credit and other financial services.

1769

He becomes court factor (essentially, a business manager) for Crown Prince Wilhelm of Hesse.

1770

He marries Gutle Shnaper, with whom he has nineteen children, ten of whom survive into adulthood.

1789

The French Revolution provides Rothschild with significant investment opportunities. By the turn of the century, he is among the most important financiers in Europe.

1798

Rothschild sends his son, Nathan, to England. Nathan establishes a lucrative textile trading business.

1809

Nathan Rothschild opens a bank in London.

1811

Jacob Rothschild establishes a bank in Paris.

1812

Mayer Amschel Rothschild dies on September 19 in Frankfurt. His oldest son, Amschel Mayer, takes over his business in Frankfurt. The youngest son, James, sets up a bank in Paris.

1820

Salomon Rothschild bases his financial operations in Vienna.

1821

Carl Rothschild sets up a branch of the family bank in Naples.

so as to spread risk and maximize profit. Coming from a trading background, it was a natural enough step when, in the 1800s, he started to import goods from Britain to the continent in contravention of a blockade imposed by Napoleon. A few years later, he was a key broker in securing finance for the British forces of the duke of Wellington who were going to war with Napoleonic France. As many modern commentators have noted—not least in relation to the twenty-first century conflicts in Afghanistan and Iraq—there is always serious money to be made in war.

Given the close relationship between his financial success and the continent's politics, Rothschild worked hard to develop a communications network second to none. He knew he needed to have all the most important news first if he was to remain at the top of the financial tree. To this end, he employed an army of couriers. It is said that in 1815 his impressive intelligence network provided his London-based son (Rothschild having died three years earlier) with news of Wellington's victory at the Battle of Waterloo even before the British royal family had been notified of the result.

THE FIVE ARROWS

In 1770 Rothschild married and his wife went on to have ten children who survived, five of whom were boys. These were the "five arrows" depicted in the family crest, spearheading the family's advance through Europe. Having worked so hard to make his fortune, Rothschild was determined that it should remain in the family. Furthermore, he saw his sons as vital to expanding the business. As they grew up, he schooled them in the mechanics of banking and imbued them with a fierce loyalty to the family brand.

The oldest son, Amschel, was groomed

to succeed his father in Frankfurt but his brothers would move to other prosperous European cities to establish new branches of the family firm. Salomon, the second oldest, went to Vienna, reaping rich rewards by cultivating a close relationship with the ruling Habsburgs. Nathan, the middle boy, established a bank in London as well as earning a fortune from the old Rothschild game of textile trading. Carl, the fourth son, set up shop in Naples and James, the youngest, established a hugely profitable operation in Paris.

So the Rothschilds established the first truly multinational bank. Furthermore, they continued to diversify their activities, investing in the Industrial Revolution and ploughing money into railways and mining—to say nothing of their roles as political power brokers, patrons of the arts, and philanthropists. When he died in 1812, Rothschild specified in his will that female descendants were to be excluded from direct inheritance, along with their husbands and children. The aim was to ensure that the family wealth was not dissipated by marriages outside the family. It was a move that prompted several cases of inter-family marriage of a type more traditionally associated with the great ruling houses of Europe. And in many ways, that is exactly what Rothschild had created; like the Medicis of Florence (see page 58) Rothschild combined wealth and influence to powerful effect and established a family business that still endures today.

▲ *A depiction of Meyer Amschel Rothschild from 1790. Rothschild established Europe's premier banking dynasty.*

STRATEGY ANALYSIS

STRATEGY TYPE: *Dominance*
KEY STRATEGY: *Provided banking services to governments and kept his business strictly a family affair*
OUTCOME: *The establishment of the world's foremost banking dynasty*
ALSO USED BY: *The Medicis, 1397-1494, and Goldman Sachs, founded in 1869.*

18

PLAY TO YOUR STRENGTHS

GEORGE WASHINGTON LEADS THE NEWLY FORMED CONTINENTAL ARMY TO VICTORY AGAINST BRITAIN

KEY PLAYER: *George Washington (1732–99)*
NATIONALITY: *American*
STRATEGY IMPLEMENTED: *American War of Independence (1775–83)*
CONTEXT: *George Washington led the Continental Army in a quest for independence from the British crown*

Tired of their treatment by the British government in London, the American colonies united in an armed bid for independence in 1775. Where local militia had previously been given defensive duties, a new Continental Army was created under the command of George Washington. Realizing he could not defeat the military strength of the British in pitched battle, he developed a guerrilla-like strategy that ultimately won the day.

America's list of complaints against the British that led to the call for independence was extensive. Between 1754 and 1763 the British had fought what was termed the French and Indian War, against French and Native American forces. It was an arduous struggle and at the end of it London looked to claw back some of the cost from the local population. They imposed highly unpopular taxes on, among other things, sugar, tea, and printed materials. Why should we pay these harsh taxes, the argument went, when we do not even have a right to representation in the British parliament? The British met protests with an iron fist, exemplified by the 1770 Boston Massacre in which five demonstrators were killed.

In 1773 the Boston Tea Party, in which British imports of tea were thrown into the city's docks, signified an irreparable fracturing of relations. Two years later the War of Independence began when British occupying forces in Boston marched to nearby Concord to capture a militia arsenal. Militiamen from nearby Lexington and Concord retaliated, forcing the British to retreat back to Boston with what would be called the "shot heard around the world." Now was the moment for George Washington to enter the fray.

Born into a well-to-do Virginia family, Washington had served the British during the French and Indian War, gaining invaluable experience of battlefield tactics in the process. However, his discontent with rule from London had subsequently grown. At the Second Continental Congress (a meeting of representatives from all 13 colonies) held in 1775, he was put in charge of the newly formed Continental Army. Up until then, each colony operated its own militia—usually a rather ragtag arrangement of part-time, untrained citizen soldiers with little in the way of equipment. There had been an instinctive aversion to a standing army in the colonies but now it was recognized that these unreliable militias had to give way to a properly trained, disciplined, and organized

standing army. Washington's job was to whip them into shape.

MOLDING AN ARMY

Washington had gained a reputation for personal bravery during the French and Indian War. He also learned the rudimentary skills of drilling an army and understood many of the organizational and logistical challenges he now faced. Crucially, he had also become familiar with the strengths and weaknesses of the British. This allowed him to make a realistic appraisal of the resources he had at his disposal.

He recognized, for instance, that he could never hope to match the British for manpower. Even by 1778, he boasted only 20,000 men to the 50,000 of the British. However, Washington possessed significant personal capital. He was already a respected leader who could command support across classes, colonies, and religious affiliation. Furthermore, the British were so untrusting of their loyalist sympathizers in the colonies that Washington was confident he could turn some of them to his side.

DEMOCRATIC IDEALS

Without Washington's skills in marshaling the Continental Army, there would have been no United States and no Constitution. The US Constitution has given impetus to democratic movements around the world. From the French Revolution that began in 1789 through the European revolutions of 1848 to the collapse of the Eastern Bloc at the end of the 1980s and the Arab Spring of 2011, all have referenced the ideals enshrined in that text. As a guiding hand behind it, Washington remains a global icon of democratic liberation. Above Washington accepts the surrender of Lord Cornwallis at Yorktown, Virginia.

TIME LINE

1732
George Washington is born in Virginia on February 22.

1754–63
He serves on the British side in the French and Indian War.

1773
The Boston Tea Party highlights the growing rift between the colonists and the British government.

1775
Outbreak of the War of Independence in April, with the Battles of Lexington and Concord. In June the War's first major battle occurs at Bunker Hill. Washington is appointed chief of the new Continental Army.

1776
Congress proclaims the Declaration of Independence. Following victories in the Battles of Long Island and White Plains, the British take New York. However, American spirits are lifted when they win the Battle of Trenton in December.

1777
Washington wins at the Battle of Princeton. The colonists also triumph at Saratoga.

1778
France allies with the Americans.

1781
After triumphing at the Battle of Camden in August, the British are decisively defeated in October at Yorktown in Virginia.

1783
The Treaty of Paris ends the war. Washington resigns his command.

1787
The US Constitution is enacted.

1789–97
Washington serves as president of the United States.

1799
Washington dies in Virginia on December 14.

He set about building a force that could rely on local support and that had the stomach for the battles ahead. He strove hard to ensure they were properly looked after and provisioned. He was not always successful, since individual colonies were responsible for payment and providing food and equipment, and standards varied greatly. But he did all that he could to create an army that had basic skills, the right equipment, and strong morale.

He knew he held some aces too. The British did not want a long, costly war on territory far from home. Furthermore, such was the geographical expanse of the colonies that to maintain control against a revolutionary force was a tall order. The British desired a quick and decisive battle in which the enemy could be destroyed comprehensively. Washington therefore set about creating a force that would wear down the British without being drawn into major encounters.

HIT AND RETREAT
While few question Washington's credentials as a leader, historians continue to debate his prowess as a military commander. However, his great achievement was that he did not let the bigger British army land a knockout blow. Instead, he encouraged his troops to launch ambushes or engage in low-level local skirmishes that undermined British spirit. He exploited local knowledge of the countryside, using forests for cover and erecting makeshift blockades from which to launch surprise assaults.

Known as Fabian tactics (after the Roman general Fabius), Washington favored the strategy of short, sharp harassment when his forces were at their most vulnerable. All the while, he strived to increase his troops' resilience. For instance, faced with large numbers of desertions at

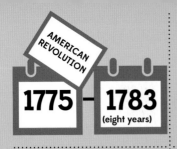

AMERICAN REVOLUTION

1775 – 1783

(eight years)

4,000

British killed in battle

4,435

Americans killed in battle

90k

pounds of tea thrown overboard during the Boston tea party

5

Countries involved: United States, France, Spain, Dutch Republic, and Britain

AMERICAN REVOLUTION IN NUMBERS

Year of Treaty of Paris, which ended the war

1783

Overall American casualties

50,000

---

various times, he extended the enlistment period from one to three years so as to provide stability, increasing punishments for desertion, and offering rewards for staying.

When the circumstances allowed, he dispensed with the hit-and-run tactics to participate in larger assaults. In 1777, for instance, the Continental Army emerged triumphant from the Battle of Saratoga and in 1781 he engineered a victory at Yorktown that all but secured the colonists' ultimate success. The war ended in their favor with the signing of the Treaty of Paris in 1783.

Before the year was out, Washington resigned as commander of the army. Imperfect an institution as it was, he had led it to victory and it would go on to form the basis of the modern US Army. As for Washington, he of course played an instrumental role in drafting the American Constitution and served as the first president of the United States of America. By keeping his army always just beyond the reach of a conclusive British strike, he birthed a nation.

STRATEGY ANALYSIS

STRATEGY TYPE: *Strategy of attack*
KEY STRATEGY: *Avoiding a decisive pitched battle against a stronger enemy*
OUTCOME: *The creation of the United States of America*
ALSO USED BY: *Fabius Maximus against the armies of Hannibal, third century BC; Mao Zedong, 1945-1949.*

19

BACK A WINNER

MATTHEW BOULTON HARNESSED THE POTENTIAL OF JAMES WATT'S STEAM ENGINE

KEY PLAYER: *Matthew Boulton (1728–1809)*
NATIONALITY: *British*
STRATEGY IMPLEMENTED: *1775–1800*
CONTEXT: *A leading figure in the Industrial Revolution, Boulton engineered part-ownership of James Watt's steam engine and made it a force of industrial progress*

Matthew Boulton knew a good thing when he saw it, and when the opportunity arose to secure a financial interest in a new, improved steam engine developed by James Watt, he seized it. Within a few years, the engine was in widespread use in British—and, later, international—industry, accelerating the progress of the Industrial Revolution.

Boulton was an industrialist and entrepreneur with a keen interest in technical innovation despite a lack of formal scientific education. As a young man growing up in the Midlands, England's industrial heartland, he took over his father's business, which produced small metal goods. Within a few years, he had developed it into one of Europe's leading manufacturers, producing everything from buttons to toys to ormolu goods.

He was a man born at just the right time. Britain in the 1800s was the cradle of the Industrial Revolution, which did not just boost the economy but fundamentally changed society. A vast array of technological and scientific developments allied with improvements in transport infrastructure (spearheaded by canal- and railway-building schemes) saw Britain change from a nation of agriculture and cottage industry to one dominated by heavy industry and mass production.

Always keen to improve his business, in the 1760s Boulton worked hard to streamline its industrial processes. To this end he built a complex at Handsworth near Birmingham, which is regularly cited as the first modern, single-site, purpose-built factory. In the same decade, he became a founding member of the Lunar Society, an informal organization that met to ruminate on disparate subjects including science and philosophy. Its membership was varied—including, for instance, Erasmus Darwin (physician), Richard Lovell Edgeworth (politician, writer, and inventor), and Joseph Priestly (theologian)—and together they drove forward many of the developments of the Industrial Age. Historian Jenny Uglow has called them "brilliant representatives of the informal scientific web." Boulton's membership was indicative of his thoughtfulness and openness to progress.

BOULTON AND WATT, 1802
BELL-CRANK ENGINE

STATIONARY ENGINES, CAT. No.82

BELL-CRANK ENGINE, 1800.
(Scale 1 : 8.)
Drawing made in the Museum.

This arrangement of engine was introduced by Messrs. Boulton, Watt & Co. in 1799 to 1806 ; it was designed with the object of obtaining an engine that was self-contained, and more compact than the established beam engine ; one was supplied in 1805 for Robert Fulton's paddle steamer "Clermont"; another was in use at the Soho works until 1896.

The cylinder is vertical and double acting, and by two vertical return connecting rods oscillates the horizontal arm of a bell-crank. From the vertical arm of the bell-crank a horizontal connecting rod extends to a crank on the fly-wheel shaft. A vertical air-pump is provided and is driven from the bell-crank. The engine foundation and the condenser tank are formed by one casting which carries the crank-shaft bearing. The steam is distributed by a long D-slide valve worked by an elliptical cam bolted to the fly-wheel arms.

These engines were made from 4 to 8 h.p.

▲ *A scale drawing of an engine designed by Boulton and Watt. They had started in business together over 25 years earlier.*

BACKING A WINNER

While Bolton was busy building his business, in Scotland an engineer called James Watt was making great strides of his own. Soon their worlds would collide. One of the most important factors in the success of the Industrial Revolution was the harnessing of steam power. In time, it would drive the country's factories and power its transport network. Yet the technology was still in its infancy even as the Lunar Club met for the first time. The very first steam engine had appeared in 1698 and it was not until 1712 that Thomas Newcomen built the first commercially viable example, coming into general usage in the mining industry as a means of pumping water.

In 1764, Watt was given one of these engines to repair and he was struck by its deficiencies. Setting himself the challenge of improving upon it, his great leap forward

TIME LINE

1712
Thomas Newcomen builds the first commercially successful steam engine. It is the first significant power source other than wind or water.

1728
Matthew Boulton is born in Birmingham, England.

1733
Newcomen's patent expires.

1736
James Watt is born in Greenock, Scotland.

1755
The first Newcomen engine is installed in the United States, at a New Jersey mine.

1759
Boulton takes over the family business.

1764
James Hargreaves invents the spinning jenny, revolutionizing the textile industry.

1765
Boulton opens the Soho Manufactory.

1769
Watt receives a patent for his new engine design.

1775
Boulton begins his formal partnership with James Watt.

1782
Watt perfects a rotative engine.

1801
Richard Trevithick builds first steam-powered locomotive.

1809
Boulton dies at his house in Handsworth on August 17.

1814
George Stephenson builds a steam locomotive that ushers in the age of the railway.

1819
Watt dies in Handsworth on August 25.

TEAM-LEADER

Boulton combined an instinctive grasp for technological development with a flair for marketing and entrepreneurship. He was also able to bring out the best in those who worked around him. Among modern-day equivalents, Steve Jobs perhaps offers up the greatest parallels. While he was a computer developer in his own right, he had the knack of surrounding himself with people of greater technical talent, beginning with Steve Wozniak at Apple. However, Jobs's real gift was to inspire his colleagues to reach ever-higher standards and to suggest potential improvements to their work. When he believed he was in possession of a product ready for the consumer, there was no-one who could match his ability to sell it. Boulton and Jobs lived during different commercial revolutions but brought to each many of the same qualities.

was to add a separate condensing chamber that reduced the loss of steam and correspondingly boosted the engine's efficiency. After other, more minor amendments to Newcomen's design, he achieved approximately a four-times greater efficiency, receiving a patent for his design in 1769.

He was backed in this venture by a fellow inventor called John Roebuck. However, in 1773 Roebuck went bankrupt, owing Boulton the then princely sum of £1,200. Ever the wily operator, Boulton saw an opportunity. He would write off the debt in return for Roebuck signing over his interest in Watt's engine. Initially Roebuck refused but Boulton persevered and eventually prevailed in 1774. Boulton could see the vast potential in Watt's creation and also realized that thus far he and his business partners had failed to fully exploit it. Boulton was convinced he was the man to take the enterprise to the next level. However, in order to take full advantage he wanted to go into partnership with Watt. In this way he would be able to guide Watt's engineering genius while he took care of the commercial side of things. Sure enough, in 1775 Watt moved down to Birmingham and the company of Boulton & Watt was born.

DRIVING FORCE

Boulton's Handsworth Manufactory turned out to be the perfect place to build the engines on an industrial scale. As he would come to remark: "I sell here, Sir, what all the world desires to have—Power." Although lacking Watt's technical acumen, he suggested several practical improvements. He saw that the engine had a life that reached far beyond just the mining industry. For instance, he envisaged its application in the booming textile industry. With this in mind, he urged Watt to develop a rotative engine for which they received a patent in 1781.

Boulton's entrepreneurial streak reaped rewards for the partnership from the outset. By 1775, six of the 14 years of available patent had elapsed so he successfully lobbied parliament for a change to the law and had the patent extended to 1800. He also sought innovative revenue streams, such as demanding a third of the savings made by using their engines rather than Newcomen model over 25 years. He was a master of publicity too, making a grand show of using the engines at Albion Mills (his steam-powered flour mill) near London's Blackfriars Bridge in 1786.

Highlighting the engine's use in all sorts of machinery, he made sales to mine-owners, the canal industry, distilleries, and mills producing everything from paper and cotton to flour and iron. In 1783, Richard Arkwright—then perhaps the most important textile factory owner in the world—began using Boulton & Watt's engines in his works. Boulton himself even employed them in the manufacture of coinage after securing a lucrative contract with the Royal Mint.

Boulton & Watt was soon unrivaled as the leading engineering firm of the Industrial Revolution. Between 1775 and 1800 they sold some 400 engines—fewer than the Newcomen version but at a higher price and to the really serious industrialists. Both men were elected to the Royal Society in the 1780s and both earned a fortune from their partnership. Boulton died in 1809, an acknowledged leading light of the Industrial Revolution—an achievement earned by his constant determination to move onward and upward.

STRATEGY ANALYSIS

STRATEGY TYPE: *Innovative*
KEY STRATEGY: *Embraced technical innovation to gain a commercial edge*
OUTCOME: *A surge in industrial efficiency*
ALSO USED BY: *Thomas Edison, inventor and entrepreneur, 1847-1931, and Steve Jobs.*

TACKLE CHANGE HEAD-ON

MAXIMILIEN DE ROBESPIERRE USED BRUTE FORCE IN PURSUIT OF SOCIAL IDEALS

KEY PLAYER: *Maximilien de Robespierre (1758-94)*
NATIONALITY: *French*
STRATEGY IMPLEMENTED: *1793-94*
CONTEXT: *As leader of the Jacobins, Robespierre espoused social equality and anti-monarchism. As a driving force on the Committee of Public Safety, he employed increasingly violent methods to preserve the Revolution*

In his short life, Robespierre emerged as a champion of the poor and oppressed only to die with a reputation as a fanatical despot. In pursuit of undoubtedly noble goals, he was for a time the most important figure of the French Revolution. But as a member of the Committee of Public Safety from July 1793 to July 1794, he consciously utilized terror tactics in a bid to halt counter-revolutionary action.

Born into a comfortable background in Arras, Robespierre trained as a lawyer, as did his father before him. He was interested in social issues and concepts of government from an early age, fostering a fascination with the Roman Empire as a schoolboy and later becoming enormously influenced by the writings of Jean-Jacques Rousseau. Rousseau believed that the truth path to individual happiness rested on a society whose social contract ensured the advancement of the general population's well-being. It was Rousseau's teachings that would underpin Robespierre's later revolutionary fervor.

France, meanwhile, was ripe for revolution. She had recently sided with the Continental Army in the American War of Independence (see page 78), during which radical notions of democracy and freedom had entered mainstream discourse. Domestically, the French economy was struggling. Meanwhile, Louis XVI—who with his wife Marie Antoinette was infamous for a lack of self-restraint in matters of luxury—wanted to increase taxes, despite both the church and nobility being tax-exempt.

In 1789 Louis called the Estates-General in a desperate bid to thrash out a deal. However, neither church nor nobility (the first two Estates) would budge, leaving the Third Estate (i.e. the general public) liable to shoulder the burden. In response the representatives of the Third Estate established a breakaway National Assembly, boasting such weight of numbers that many representatives from the first two Estates joined them. Dedicated to establishing a new constitution that curbed royal powers, the Assembly issued the *Declaration of the Rights of Man and the Citizen*, which owed much to American revolutionary ideals. It was amid this striking climate of change that Robespierre now emerged as a leading figure, having been elected to the Estates General in May 1789.

▲ The storming of the notorious Paris prison, the Bastille, sparked the French revolution.

THE IDEALIST

The Assembly was not immediately intent on doing away with the monarchy altogether but it was soon apparent that there was a schism between the moderate faction (known as the Girondins) and the radicals (Jacobins). As president of the influential Jacobin Club from April 1790, Robespierre became a leading spokesman for the radicals, delivering speeches in which he ferociously attacked the excesses of the royal household and called for the establishment of a republic. Furthermore, he demanded a swathe of liberal reforms, including the ending of the death penalty (somewhat ironically, given later events), the abolition of slavery, an end to government corruption, the vote for all men, and social equality regardless of class or wealth.

A social democrat at heart, Robespierre was tireless in his pursuit of reform. In addition, he led a personal life of noted virtue, living humbly, and earning the name "L'Incorruptible." A champion of the radicalized urban poor (the so-called "sans-culottes"—meaning "without knee-breeches"), by early 1792 his frustration was growing at the lack of progress. Within the Assembly, the Girondins and the Jacobins were engaged in a battle of wills, while in the wider country there were counter-revolutionary moves to restore Louis's absolutist powers.

1758

Maximilien de Robespierre is born in Arras, Artois.

1789

Louis XVI summons the States-General in the hope of agreeing new taxes.

14 July 1789

A mob storms the Bastille, a notorious Paris prison. The following month the National Assembly issues the Declaration of the Rights of Man and of the Citizen.

1790

Louis XVI accepts a new constitution that provides for liberal reforms and reduces his powers.

1791

Louis and his family attempt to flee Paris but are captured. In August, the Holy Roman Empire comes out in support of Louis.

1792

France declares war on Austria. In August, Louis is taken into custody by the National Convention, which abolishes the monarchy the following month. He is put on trial in December.

1793

Louis is executed on January 21. His wife, Marie Antoinette, goes to the guillotine in October. Meanwhile, France declares war on Britain, the Netherlands, and Spain. De facto power increasingly lies with the Committee of Public Safety, which oversees the Terror.

1794

The Terror comes to an end in July, when Robespierre is arrested and executed on July 28 by political opponents.

1795

The Directory assumes de facto power and becomes infamous for its abuses of power.

1799

The Revolutionary period comes to an end when Napoleon establishes a dictatorship.

Furthermore, the Holy Roman Empire backed the king. Against Robespierre's wishes, the Girondins declared war on the empire and France was soon under immense pressure from Austrian and Prussian forces. Then, with popular discontent spiraling, Louis was overthrown in August 1792 after a pitched battle at the Tuileries, his Parisian palace. The National Assembly was replaced by the National Convention, which promptly declared France a republic. By the autumn of 1792 it seemed like Robespierre could rest easy and that the Revolution had won the day. However, instead he was considering setting aside his principles in the short-term to secure the movement's long-term success.

DICTATED LIBERTY

The path from liberator and freedom-fighter to violent autocrat is one that has been trodden with shocking regularity through history. In the twentieth century alone, many of the greatest revolutionary figures calculated that bloodletting and tyranny were justifiable in the interests of their long-term revolutionary goals. One may look toward, for instance, Stalin in Russia and Castro in Cuba. In both cases, historians struggle to reconcile their youthful desire for social equality with their later reliance on state-sponsored terror. Post-colonial Africa, meanwhile, has thrown up many such figures of it own, including Muammar Gaddafi in Libya and Robert Mugabe in Zimbabwe.

ARRESTS AND EXECUTIONS IN THE TERROR

ARRESTS
300,000

CIVIL WAR IN VENDÉE REGION
450,000
DEATHS

POPULATION OF PARIS AT TIME
650,000

EXECUTIONS
16,500

ARRESTS IN PARIS
2,600

THE TERRORIST

After Louis's removal from power, the Paris mob went on the rampage, massacring some 2,000 establishment figures, including priests and nuns. Reforms by the Convention continued to be delayed by internal struggles, heightening the exasperation of the sans-culottes, which threatened to boil over into anarchic street violence. In addition, with the king in custody, there was the ever-present danger that he might be sprung from his incarceration to lead a counter-revolution. Fearful of both this prospect and uncontrolled mob violence, Robespierre began to think that there was no choice but to force the issue.

He came to the conclusion that for the revolution to succeed, the king needed to die, along with those who would bring him back to power. He may have wished another path was available, but he was sure that the ends justified the means—in polar opposition to later social reformers such as Gandhi and Martin Luther King, who both argued that change should be brought about peacefully and that violence could not be justified as a means of forcing social reform (see pages 124 and 192). After a show trial, the king was executed in January 1793. His killing was just the start of the bloodletting; On October 16 he was followed to the guillotine by his wife, Marie Antoinette.

The sans-culottes overthrew the Girondins in June that year, leaving Robespierre as the leading figure in the Convention. Even more significantly, he sat upon the Committee of Public Safety (convened in July), which adopted an official policy of Terror with the approval of the Convention. The constitution and peacetime rights were suspended while violence was authorized in the interests of the revolution's ideals. As his colleague Danton had it: "Let us be terrible in order to stop the people from being so."

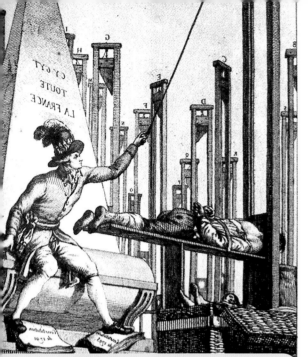

A satirical cartoon of the age shows Robespierre guillotining the executioner after everyone else in France has been put to death.

The Jacobins pursued their opponents ferociously. In its year-long life, the Terror saw over 16,500 people executed and many more murdered or imprisoned without trial (to mention nothing of a barbaric civil war in the Vendée region that claimed as many as 450,000 lives). Among the victims were former allies of Robespierre, including Danton.

So Robespierre transformed from libertarian to state terrorist, from opponent of capital punishment to one of its most prolific exponents. "If the basis of popular government in peacetime is virtue," he would argue, "the basis of popular government during a revolution is both virtue and terror." Perhaps the greatest irony is that his frightened opponents had the last word, arresting him in July 1794 and sending him to the guillotine.

A BLUEPRINT FOR FUTURE DICTATORS

Robespierre adopted terror in the belief that it would preserve the ideals he had fought for, consolidate the authority of his government, and undermine ongoing social unrest. For those who believe in democracy, his experiment was thankfully unsuccessful. Indeed, the Terror was so abhorrent to the nation at large that the Jacobins fell from power far more quickly than if they had adopted a more moderate approach. As for Robespierre, his reputation was forever besmirched in his homeland. Nonetheless, he provided a template for dictators of the future—from Hitler and Stalin to Augusto Pinochet and Idi Amin—whose ideological fervor and desire to retain power induced them to dispense with concern for basic human rights in favour of ruling by fear.

STRATEGY ANALYSIS

STRATEGY TYPE: *Leadership*
KEY STRATEGY: *Employed terror as official government policy*
OUTCOME: *The execution of Louis XVI and a period of despotic rule known as "the Terror"*
ALSO USED BY: *Vladimir Lenin during the Red Terror, 1918–22, and Adolf Hitler, 1933–45.*

DARE TO BE DIFFERENT

HORATIO NELSON EMPLOYS AN INNOVATIVE NAVAL FORMATION TO WIN THE BATTLE OF TRAFALGAR

KEY PLAYER: *Horatio Nelson (1758-1805)*
NATIONALITY: *British*
STRATEGY IMPLEMENTED: *1805*
CONTEXT: *Napoleon planned an invasion of Britain in his bid to secure French hegemony in Europe. However, Lord Nelson, was determined to draw him into a decisive engagement. The battle took place at Trafalgar, off the coast of Spain*

After a brief respite in the Napoleonic Wars, Britain and France resumed their hostilities in 1803. A year later, Spain joined with France, providing Napoleon with the naval muscle to launch an attack on his old enemy. However, as head of the Royal Navy, Nelson knew he had a force strong and skilled enough to defeat the French once and for all. To that end, he dispatched with orthodox naval formation at Trafalgar, instead audaciously attacking in columns that ploughed into the enemy at a 90-degree angle.

Having joined the Navy at twelve years old, Nelson was a captain by the time he was 20, serving variously in Canada, the Caribbean, and the Baltic. But it was when Britain became embroiled in the French Revolutionary Wars in the 1790s that his legend grew. He became renowned for extraordinary personal bravery (he lost an eye at the Siege of Calvi in 1794 and an arm at the Battle of Santa Cruz de Tenerife in 1797), a healthy disregard for his seniors (he famously ignored orders at the Battle of Copenhagen by placing a telescope to his blind eye and pretending not to see them), and for bold strategizing in the heat of battle. That latter quality was never better evidenced than at Trafalgar.

At that time there was a virtually unchallenged orthodoxy in naval battle formation. Ships lined up in long rows so as to be able to signal to each other. It was the only realistic way that a naval commander could ensure his orders were received by all the ships of his fleet. Then, when it came to engaging with the enemy, one ship after another fired broadsides. The problem was that the strategy was so widely employed that battles more often than not ended indecisively. Communication was maintained but so was the status quo. Nelson, though, had such confidence in his Navy that he felt secure enough to dispense with this strategy in order to force a decisive victory over his opponent.

His plan was a simple one. He would split his fleet into two columns, leading one himself while his trusted colleague, Cuthbert Collingwood, led the other. Nelson would use his column of ships to break the French formation and take out its flagship, which was under the command of Pierre-Charles Villeneuve. With the French lines of communication thus broken, Collingwood would force another fracture in the French line. Amid what Nelson

TIME LINE

1758
Horatio Nelson born in Norfolk, England, on September 29.

1770
He joins the Royal Navy and sees action around the world.

1787
He marries Frances Nisbet. However, he will later leave her for a married woman, Emma Hamilton.

1794
He loses an eye while fighting in Corsica.

1797
Nelson is promoted to rear-admiral. Later in the year he loses an arm at the Battle of Santa Cruz.

1798
He crushes Napoleon's fleet in Egypt.

1801
He becomes vice-admiral. In April he defeats the Danes at the Battle of Copenhagen.

1803
Britain declares war on France. Nelson becomes Commander-in-Chief of the Mediterranean Fleet.

1804
France and Spain form an alliance.

1805
Nelson chases the French fleet to the Caribbean and then back across the Atlantic. In September he takes HMS Victory to Cadiz. His finest hour comes a month later in the defeat of the combined French and Spanish forces under Napoleon's command at the Battle of Trafalgar on October 21. However, in the course of fighting Nelson is struck by shot and later dies from his wounds.

anticipated would be a "pell-mell battle," the more highly skilled British sailors would then engage in ship-to-ship combat with their opposite numbers. Boasting more efficient weaponry and superior seamanship, Nelson was confident his fleet would quickly overrun Napoleon's.

NELSON'S COLUMNS

Dreading the prospect of a stalemate using the traditional single-line battle formation that so often resulted in a war of attrition, Nelson wanted to exploit all the natural advantages of his fleet. As his country's leading naval figure for a decade or more, he had ensured that Britain's seamen were the best trained in the world. He also knew that their ships were second to none and their gunnery the fastest available. In short, he knew he had the men and the equipment to best Napoleon.

He was careful in his preparations, identifying the weakest part of the French ships (the sterns, which were constructed from thinner wooden planks) and urging his gunners to focus on them. He also decided to lead his columns into attack at full sail so that each English ship was at its most exposed for the shortest time possible. Furthermore, he looked for historical precedent. While no admiral had led his fleet into battle in quite such an audacious manner, in 1797 Adam Duncan used a "perpendicular assault" strategy against the Dutch at the Battle of Camperdown, as did John Jervis against the Spanish at the Battle of Cape St Vincent the same year. Nelson thus knew that an aggressive "straight at them" approach could work.

In the week leading up to the confrontation, Nelson took every opportunity to school his captains in his radical plan, famously going through the details with them at the table of his

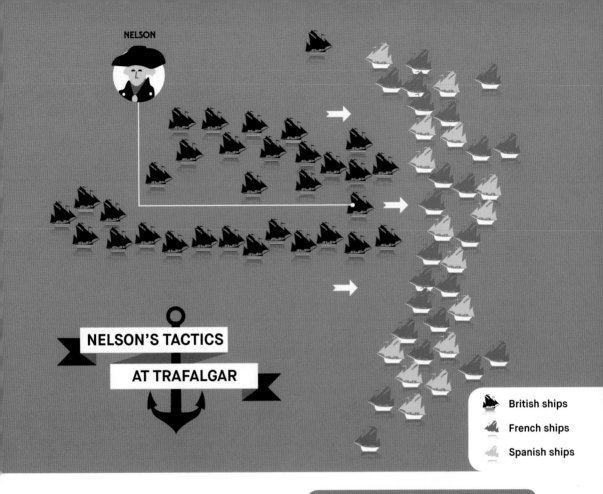

NELSON

NELSON'S TACTICS AT TRAFALGAR

British ships
French ships
Spanish ships

flagship, HMS *Victory*. He also had the ships of his fleet painted in distinctive yellow and black so that they could easily identify each other in the expected melee. Then it was up to the captains to make sure that their individual crews were drilled in what to do. Nelson was taking a calculated gamble but he trusted his men from the lowest to highest ranking to deliver even though he would be unable to directly communicate orders to them during the battle.

ENGLAND EXPECTS

Nelson's other great secret weapon was his personal charisma. Having already led his fleet in numerous notable encounters, his men worshipped him as a leader. As he showed his faith in them, they in turn

RULING THE WAVES

Nelson's victory at Trafalgar was a pivotal moment in Britain's journey to becoming the dominant power of the nineteenth century. By both setting in progress the demise of Napoleon's regime and establishing Britain's position as the world's foremost seagoing force, Britain was set to rule the waves for the next hundred years and more. It was this naval dominance that laid the foundations for the expansion of an empire that, during Queen Victoria's reign, was the largest the world had ever seen.

took inspiration from him. Just prior to the battle, he sent out a signal: "England expects that every man will do his duty." It is a phrase that has gone down in English folklore and spurred his fleet to unmatched acts of valor. As well as being a master strategist, Nelson brilliantly understood the psychology of leadership.

The battle itself occurred shortly after Villeneuve led his Franco-Spanish fleet out of Cadiz. When they met, his force outnumbered Nelson's by some 33 to 27 ships. In fact, the opening and critical phase of battle was won by twelve British ships against 22 Napoleonic ones. Nelson found Villeneuve's vessels aligned in a ragged curve. As Nelson ploughed HMS *Victory* into the enemy line, she took enormous punishment, losing some fifty men (either dead or wounded) before opening fire herself. Victory's gunners finally got into range and became embroiled in a deadly skirmish with Villeneuve's flagship, *Bucentaure*, and at least three other vessels. However, she was able to hold her own and, critically, overwhelmed *Bucentaure*. Villeneuve was left aboard a crippled ship, unable to transmit orders, and master of a fleet that was soon losing its head without clear leadership. The battle gradually played itself out just as Nelson had hoped, with his more skilled men taking apart the enemy a ship at a time. However, at around 1.15 pm, Nelson was hit by a lead ball that would kill him before the afternoon was out; but not before Villeneuve surrendered at 2.15 pm.

A RESOUNDING VICTORY

By the end of the battle, the British had taken 22 enemy vessels for the loss of none. In terms of personnel, the British lost around 1,700 men, against 6,000 enemy casualties and a further 20,000 taken prisoner—a victory astounding in its comprehensiveness. Napoleon's maritime dreams had been shot to pieces and his hopes of ever invading Britain were over for good. As for Nelson, his body was preserved in brandy and sailed back to Britain, where he received a state funeral. England had expected and, through audacious strategy, Nelson had delivered. His innovative—and confident— strategy had successfully seen off the most dangerous threat of invasion that the United Kingdom faced between the Spanish Armada and the Battle of Britain. In establishing Britain's naval dominance, Nelson also set his nation on the path to their "golden age."

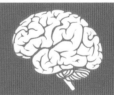

STRATEGY ANALYSIS

STRATEGY TYPE: *Strategic thinking*
KEY STRATEGY: *Attacked the enemy in columns*
OUTCOME: *A century of British naval dominance*
ALSO USED BY: *Admiral Duncan at the Battle of Camperdown, 1797, and Admiral Jervis at the Battle of Cape St Vincent, 1797.*

22 DIVIDE AND CONQUER

NAPOLEON CAREFULLY ORCHESTRATED THE GREATEST MILITARY VICTORY OF HIS CAREER AT AUSTERLITZ

KEY PLAYER: *Napoleon Bonaparte (1769-1821)*
NATIONALITY: *French*
STRATEGY IMPLEMENTED: *December 2 1805*
CONTEXT: *In response to Napoleonic France's aggressive expansionism in Europe, Britain forged an alliance with Austria and Russia in 1803 to form the Third Coalition. The Battle of Austerlitz, fought in what is now the Czech Republic, proved the crucial battle in the conflict*

Napoleon effectively seized power in France in 1799 and set about asserting French military dominance on the continent. Britain resumed war with France in 1803 and persuaded Austria and Russia to join them. So began the War of the Third Coalition, which saw Napoleon's fortunes ebb and flow before Austerlitz. However, at that battle he used all his tactical mastery to split the enemy forces before routing them.

Having suffered defeat at the hands of the British navy at the Battle of Trafalgar in 1805, Napoleon wisely put on hold plans for an invasion of England (see page 95). Instead he decided to confront his chief enemies on mainland Europe, Austria and Russia. Assuming his usual aggressive approach, he mobilized some 200,000 troops to advance deep into the territories of the Holy Roman Empire in double-quick time. In November 1805, his forces topped a succession of victories by taking Vienna, the Austrian capital. However, he now faced the prospect that Prussia—with all its military power—might join the coalition against him. He knew his best chance of success was to bring his Austrian and Russian foes to battle before that occurred. He thus oversaw an elaborate ruse designed to precipitate a battle. His over-riding aim was to seize control of the situation, something he achieved with aplomb.

Napoleon was nothing if not thorough in his preparations. In his own words: "There is no man more pusillanimous than I when I am planning a campaign. I purposely exaggerate all the dangers and all the calamities that the circumstances make possible." Napoleon had spent years reforming the French army so it was the most professional, mobile fighting force in the world. To add to this hard-earned advantage, he now scoped out what he believed would be the most favorable battle location. He hit upon an area close to the town of Austerlitz on the basis that its natural features (including several lakes) would prove disruptive to the enemy, while an adjoining plain would be the perfect ground for his agile cavalry. Before the battle commenced, Napoleon had done all he could to dictate the terms of engagement.

NAPOLEON'S EUROPE, 1810

KINGDOM OF DENMARK AND NORWAY

KINGDOM OF SWEDEN

UNITED KINGDOM

CONFEDERATION OF THE RHINE

GRAND DUCHY OF WARSAW

Paris

AUSTRIAN EMPIRE

FRENCH EMPIRE

✕ Battle of Austerlitz

KINGDOM OF ITALY

Rome

SPAIN

PORTUGAL

BRITISH CONTROL

NAPOLEONIC EMPIRE

DEPENDENT STATES

ALLIES OF NAPOLEON

LAYING THE GROUNDWORK

Now came the job of inducing the enemy into battle. To this end, he gave the impression that fighting was the last thing he wanted. He thinned out the forces of his Grand Armée in order to make them look weaker than they really were. In addition, he sent out word to Russian emissaries that he feared attack and might be open to a peace treaty.

Napoleon guessed that the Allied forces would look to focus on his army's right flank in the hope of breaking the French communication line with Vienna. In the process of launching such an attack, he believed that the Allies would leave their center and own right-hand side exposed. Taking a calculated gamble, he thus made his own right flank appear severely undermanned so as to encourage the Allied advance.

The Allies faced a tough decision: Strike now in the hope of catching Napoleon on the back foot, or bide time and hope for Prussia to join the fray. Austria urged caution but Russia, under the firebrand Tsar Alexander who was eager to supplant Napoleon as Europe's chief power broker, won the day with an argument for quick action. The script was playing out just as Napoleon had written it. As he himself would later observe: "Never interrupt your enemy when he is making a mistake."

By persuading the enemy of his reluctance to fight and, not least, by playing on Alexander's insatiable desire for personal glory, Napoelon had his foe just where he wanted. Now to hammer home his advantage.

SEIZING THE INITIATIVE

The battle commenced around 8 am on December 2. Both armies were remarkably

TIME LINE

1769
Napoleon Bonaparte is born in Corsica.

1789
The French Revolution begins.

1792
King Louis XVI of France is beheaded.

1796–97
Takes command of the French army in Italy. Victories in 1796 at Lodi and Arcole. After victory at the Battle of Rivoli in 1797, he returns to a hero's welcome in Paris.

1798
His campaign in Egypt and Syria is undermined by defeat against the British fleet at the Battle of the Nile.

1799
Napoleon becomes first consul of the French government after a coup d'état.

1803
France goes to war with England, which joins with Austria and Russia to form the Third Alliance.

1804
Napoleon crowns himself as France's emperor.

1805
He additionally becomes king of Italy. In October is defeated at the Battle of Trafalgar. On December 2 he emerges victorious from the Battle of Austerlitz.

1812
Napoleon leads an ill-fated campaign against Russia.

1814
Paris falls to anti-Napoleonic Allied forces. He abdicates and is exiled to Elba.

1815
Briefly resumes his tenure as emperor but abdicates following defeat at the Battle of Waterloo and is exiled to Saint Helena.

1821
Dies on May 5, Saint Helena.

well matched in terms of troop numbers. Sure enough, the Allies sent column after column to attack the French right, but failed to make the inroads they expected. Growing increasingly frustrated, the Allied generals took ever more soldiers from the center, leaving themselves vulnerable to a swift counter-attack. After about an hour of fighting, Napoleon decided the moment had come. "One sharp blow and the war is over," he suggested.

He sent many of his best men to attack the Allies stationed on the high ground of the Pratzen Heights. The combat was fierce and the French certainly did not have it all their own way, but as the clock ticked on Napoleon's highly trained cavalry, backed by artillery support, stole the initiative. Before long, the Allied army had been split asunder. Having gained control of the Heights, Napoleon was able to envelop the enemy in pockets and eventually drive them from the field.

The victory could scarcely have been more comprehensive. France lost around 1,300 men, with a further 7,000 wounded and 500 captured. By contrast, the Allies counted 15,000 men dead or wounded, and 12,000 captured. Austria signed a peace within a couple of days, ceding land and agreeing to pay a huge war indemnity. Furthermore, Napoleon brought down the curtain on the Holy Roman Empire, which had prospered for some thousand years, and established the Confederation of the Rhine to serve as a buffer state between Prussia and France. The Russians, meanwhile, returned home to lick their wounds. The War of the Third Coalition had ended in France's favor with a battle that Napoleon had controlled virtually from start to finish. It served as the springboard for almost a decade of French hegemony in Europe.

This work by Antoine-Jean Gros shows Napoleon offering a hand to Francis II, Holy Roman Emperor, after the battle.

TEXTBOOK STRATEGY

In this age of increasingly mechanized war, it may seem that there is little place for an individual military genius like Napoleon. Yet while the mechanics of war have changed, his example continues to provide apt lessons in the importance of military professionalism, thorough preparation, battlefield psychology, and identifying enemy weaknesses. It is for these reasons that Austerlitz remains a staple of courses in tactics and strategy at military colleges throughout the world.

STRATEGY ANALYSIS

STRATEGY TYPE: *Tactical deception*
KEY STRATEGY: *By cunning manipulation induced the enemy into an ill-considered attack*
OUTCOME: *A resounding defeat for his enemies that left Napoleon as Europe's pre-eminent power*
ALSO USED BY: *The Duke of Wellington at the Battle of Waterloo, 1815, and the Soviets at the Battle of Kursk, 1943..*

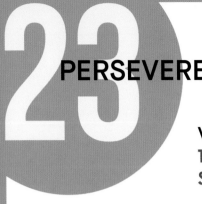

PERSEVERE, PERSEVERE, PERSEVERE

WILLIAM WILBERFORCE INTRODUCED THE LEGISLATION THAT OUTLAWS THE SLAVE TRADE IN BRITISH TERRITORIES

KEY PLAYER: *William Wilberforce (1759-1833)*
NATIONALITY: *English*
STRATEGY IMPLEMENTED: *1807*
CONTEXT: *In the nineteenth century Britain used huge numbers of slaves across its vast empire. Wilberforce was among those who regarded the slave trade as morally unjustifiable*

William Wilberforce entered adulthood as a well-connected Cambridge graduate with a reputation as a wild child. After embracing evangelical Christianity, he emerged as one of the foremost social reformers of his time. As an MP, abolition of the slave trade became the great cause of his life and one that he pursued year-in and year-out, despite parliament repeatedly refusing to back his legislation. In the end, he cunningly hijacked a seemingly unrelated bill in order to achieve his aims.

Born into a wealthy British merchant family, Wilberforce was something of an enfant terrible at university. Nonetheless, he won a seat in parliament in 1780 while still a student. Five years later he underwent a conversion to evangelical Christianity, vowing to devote himself to God's service and becoming a champion of assorted social causes. In 1787 he was introduced to a prominent group of slavery abolitionists including Thomas Clarkson, Granville Sharp, and Sir Charles and Lady Middleton. They were repulsed by the trade that saw British ships swap goods for slaves in Africa, then transport the slaves in inhuman conditions to assorted British territories, principally in the West Indies. It is thought that of some 11 million slaves sent on this route, almost 1.5 million did not even survive the voyage. Wilberforce was a man intent on fighting the good fight and now he had the perfect godly project to pursue.

The abolitionists formally asked Wilberforce to be "their man" in the House of Commons and he agreed, setting about his work with gusto. While anti-slavery committees (often with Quaker origins) had been petitioning parliament to act since the early part of the decade, they had never had a champion so influential as Wilberforce. In particular, he had the ear of Prime Minister Pitt the Younger, with whom he had become close friends at Cambridge. However, the first job was to bring all the disparate abolitionist groups into a closer alliance. In May 1787 the Society for Effecting the Abolition of the Slave Trade met for the first time. Wilberforce kept close ties with them, although he would not join its organizing committee for a further four years. Crucially, they agreed on a general strategy. Wilberforce and the Society would focus first on ending the slave trade specifically. This, they believed, was an achievable and communicable goal that once achieved would ultimately bring an end to slavery in its entirety.

GETTING THE MESSAGE OUT THERE
Wilberforce realized that it was vital to get the public on side and the Society proved adept at spreading the word. The organization set up local groups throughout the country to ensure their cause remained in the public eye. They published pamphlets, held public meetings, lobbied politicians, and boycotted bodies they considered complicit in the trade. They even developed a truly memorable insignia: An evocative image of a slave kneeling above the motto "Am I not a Man and a Brother?" This appeared on widely distributed medals created by no less a figure than potter-to-the-stars, Josiah Wedgwood (see page 70). Wilberforce and his colleagues also organized public petitions that garnered hundreds of thousands of signatures. This was a campaign that stayed on-message in a way that would cause a modern party whip to flush with envy.

It was Wilberforce's intention to introduce a bill for the abolition of the slave trade in the 1789 parliamentary session but ill health thwarted him. Instead, Pitt himself took up the cause on his behalf, ordering a Privy Council report into the matter followed by a parliamentary review. A revitalized Wilberforce returned to the House of Commons later in the year to make his first parliamentary address on the subject. Knowing that many of his fellow MPs had vested colonial interests that meant they were resistant to see the end of slavery altogether, he concentrated his attack on the slave trade itself. Using

THE ABOLITION OF SLAVERY AROUND THE WORLD

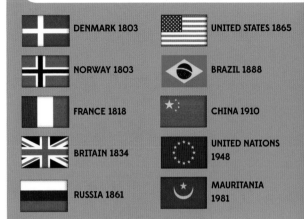

DENMARK 1803

UNITED STATES 1865

NORWAY 1803

BRAZIL 1888

FRANCE 1818

CHINA 1910

BRITAIN 1834

UNITED NATIONS 1948

RUSSIA 1861

MAURITANIA 1981

35,800,000
live in modern slavery globally today

A GLOBAL MOVEMENT

Although illegal throughout the world, slavery remains a modern-day blight. The 2013 Global Slavery Index, for instance, suggested some 30 million people were living as slaves, predominantly in Asia and Africa. Nonetheless, Wilberforce was instrumental in ridding slavery of any claim to social acceptability. He not only set the precedent by which the United States outlawed the system in 1865 but laid the foundations for Article 4 of the Universal Declaration of Human Rights: "No one shall be held in slavery or servitude; slavery and the slave trade shall be prohibited in all their forms."

1759

William Wilberforce is born on August 24 in Kingston upon Hull, United Kingdom.

1780

He becomes a member of parliament.

1787

The Society for Effecting the Abolition of the Slave Trade is formed. Although not a founding member (joining formally in 1891), Wilberforce agrees to be the parliamentary figurehead of the abolitionist movement.

1789

He makes his first attempt to guide through parliament a bill to abolish the slave trade, making arguably his most famous anti-slavery address in the process to the House of Commons.

1805

Wilberforce sees his eleventh anti-slave trade bill fail.

1806

Parliament passes the Foreign Slave Trade Abolition Act, outlawing British trade in slaves to foreign countries.

1807

The Slave Trade Act is passed, killing off the trade in the British Empire.

1823

He co-founds the Society for the Mitigation and Gradual Abolition of Slavery, which campaigns to end slavery throughout Britain's dominions.

1825

Wilberforce resigns from parliament because of failing health.

1833

An active campaigner until the end, he dies on July 29 in London. Shortly afterward, parliament passes the Slavery Abolition Act, ending slavery in all its forms.

documentary evidence, he painted a startling picture of the conditions slaves faced as they were transported. He then introduced a dozen resolutions condemning the trade. However, to allay the fears of the vested interests, he hinted that the existing slave population could be replenished by natural reproduction. Wilberforce realized that in order to push through such radical legislation, he must keep his opponents as close as possible.

DUE PROCESS

Despite his best efforts, the bill was waylaid by delaying tactics as Wilberforce's opponents pushed for parliament to hold its own hearings into the subject, which inevitably overran the parliamentary session. It was not until April 1791 that the bill went to the vote. Wilberforce gave an impassioned speech, elucidating an argument that remains powerful to this day: "Never, never will we desist till we have wiped away this scandal from the Christian name ... and extinguished every trace of this bloody traffic, of which our posterity, looking back at the history of these enlightened times, will scarce believe that it has been suffered to exist so long a disgrace and dishonour to this country."

Nonetheless, the bill was easily defeated. It was, in part, a victim of circumstance: The revolutionary fervor sweeping Europe (and especially France since 1789) had seen the British ruling classes adopt a new conservatism. Slave revolts in the French West Indies further hardened certain hearts against the legislation. Nonetheless, Wilberforce did not let the setback knock him off course.

He continued to propose legislation on an almost annual basis, to be met by repeated delaying tactics and other obstructions (11 bills were defeated in the 15 years to 1805). However, by the turn of the nineteenth century there was a growing public appetite for abolition. In 1806 Lord Grenville became prime minister and put his weight behind the campaign. Meanwhile, Wilberforce hit on a new tactic. The government had proposed a Foreign Slave Trade Abolition bill, prohibiting British subjects from importing slaves into territories of foreign powers. Wilberforce hardly commented on the bill, which was easily voted through as an apparently essential war measure against the French. By keeping his counsel, his enemies did not realize the bill's full implications until it was too late.

The reality of the trade was that most British participants were sailing under foreign flags and supplying French colonies. Now these traders lost a vital source of revenue (which they had used in part to lobby support) as well as focusing public opinion against the industry as a whole. The following year the Slave Trade Act was waved through both Houses of Parliament with prime ministerial backing. Wilberforce had won the day through intelligent manipulation of the parliamentary system.

Wilberforce continued his fight against slavery for the rest of his life but poor health saw him retire from front-line politics in 1825. He made his final public anti-slavery address in April 1833, shortly before an attack of influenza took its toll. He died at the end of July, with the Bill for the Abolition of Slavery poised to be passed into law. His life had been a triumph of idealism tempered by astute pragmatism.

▲ *A portrait of William Wilberforce, "The Abolitionist." Wilberforce was steadfast in his determination to have slavery abolished in law.*

STRATEGY ANALYSIS

STRATEGY TYPE: *Perseverance*
KEY STRATEGY: *Unstinting perseverance and the wily use of the legislative process*
OUTCOME: *Wilberforce paved the way for the ending of slavery in the British Empire*
ALSO USED BY: *Abraham Lincoln and the Emancipation Proclamation, 1863, and Florence Nightingale, 1850s–1910.*

THINK BIG

VISIONARY ENGINEER **ISAMBARD KINGDOM BRUNEL** CREATED "GOD'S WONDERFUL RAILWAY"

KEY PLAYER: *Isambard Kingdom Brunel (1806-59)*
NATIONALITY: *English*
STRATEGY IMPLEMENTED: *1835-59*
CONTEXT: *Appointed chief engineer for the Great Western Railway, which was to provide a direct link between London and Bristol, Brunel faced a succession of engineering and administrative obstacles*

Brunel was the greatest civil and mechanical engineer of his day, overseeing landmark projects that included bridges and tunnels, railways, and steamships. His work on the Great Western Railway (GWR) helped produce arguably the finest railway anywhere in the world up to that point and required Brunel to marry his brilliant engineering vision to utter pragmatism in order to see the scheme through to a successful conclusion.

In the early 1830s, the merchants of Bristol were keen for the city to maintain its position as the leading English port for trade with America, but faced stiff competition from Liverpool. So a number of Bristol's leading citizens came up with a radical new idea—a double-tracked rail connection linking the port directly with London. They decided to appoint Brunel as their chief engineer since, despite being only 27, he was already making considerable waves in the engineering world.

The son of a French-born engineer, Marc Isambard Brunel, Isambard grew up immersed in complex engineering conundrums. Aged just 21, he was appointed resident engineer on the Thames Tunnel, a pioneering project to build a tunnel beneath London's great river spearheaded by his father. Although beset with problems, it was a revolutionary scheme and the first time a tunnel was laid beneath a navigable river. So, from the outset of his career, Brunel was involved in projects that demanded he think far and wide around a problem. Then in 1831 he won a competition to design the Clifton Suspension Bridge across the River Avon near Bristol. With its ground-breaking design and record-breaking span of 702 feet (214 m) (making it the longest bridge in the world when it finally opened), the project vastly raised Brunel's public profile, making him a natural choice for the London-to-Bristol rail link.

THE COURAGE OF HIS CONVICTIONS

It was 1835 before an act of parliament gave the formal go-ahead for the project, which was to be called the Great Western Railway (or, according to its fans, God's Wonderful Railway). By then, Brunel had tirelessly and meticulously surveyed the land between the two cities, even obliging his lawyer to row him along a stretch of river at one point. While

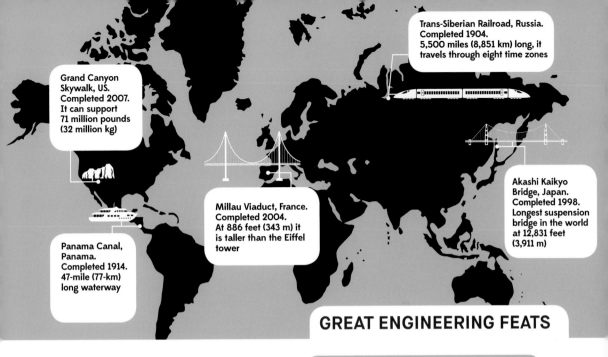

Grand Canyon Skywalk, US. Completed 2007. It can support 71 million pounds (32 million kg)

Trans-Siberian Railroad, Russia. Completed 1904. 5,500 miles (8,851 km) long, it travels through eight time zones

Millau Viaduct, France. Completed 2004. At 886 feet (343 m) it is taller than the Eiffel tower

Akashi Kaikyo Bridge, Japan. Completed 1998. Longest suspension bridge in the world at 12,831 feet (3,911 m)

Panama Canal, Panama. Completed 1914. 47-mile (77-km) long waterway

GREAT ENGINEERING FEATS

he entertained great hopes for the railway, Brunel knew that the key to success was attention to detail. He therefore hit upon a route that, as far as possible, avoided going through major population hubs in a bid to head-off potentially costly and time-consuming local opposition. He also steered clear of steep gradients and obstacles that would require excessive re-routing of the tracks.

The railway was always going to be a costly project and to secure financing he needed his plans to be watertight. Only then could he navigate his way around the countless powerful committees he had to face. His experience with the Clifton Suspension Bridge commission had confirmed for him the importance of communicating often highly complex ideas in a clear and appealing manner. On that occasion, he had told his brother-in-law: "… of all the wonderful feats I have performed… I think yesterday I performed the most wonderful. I produced unanimity among 15 men who were all quarrelling about that most ticklish subject—taste."

So he devoted inordinate hours to preparing his scheme for the GWR. Once he had established his preferred route, he drew up plans for many of the notable features to be constructed along its length. These included termini at Paddington in London and

INSPIRING EXAMPLE

Brunel has inspired countless engineers to dream big. Without him, it is possible we may never have had other grand schemes born in the nineteenth century such as Egypt's Suez Canal (opened in 1869) or the Panama Canal in Central America (opened in 1914). Equally, Brunel's spirit is evident in such modern mega-infrastructure projects as the Øresund Bridge (which carries rail and road traffic between Sweden and Denmark and opened in 2000) and the Channel Tunnel, which links the United Kingdom to mainland Europe.

1806
Isambard Kingdom Brunel is born on April 9 in Portsmouth, England.

1827
Brunel becomes resident engineer on the Thames Tunnel.

1831
Wins the commission to build the Clifton Suspension Bridge.

1833
Brunel is signed up as chief engineer of the Great Western Railway.

1835
Government grants permission for construction of the GWR. Brunel lays out plans for a transatlantic steamship service.

1836
Work begins on the SS Great Western. Brunel marries Mary Horsley.

1838
SS Great Western has her maiden voyage to New York.

1841
The GWR route from London to Bristol starts operating.

1843
The Thames Tunnel opens. Brunel is appointed engineer of the South Devon Railway.

1845
The SS Great Britain has her maiden voyage.

1854
Paddington station opens in London.

1858
The SS Great Eastern launches after multiple problems.

1859
Brunel dies on September 15 in London.

1864
The Clifton Suspension Bridge is finally opened.

Temple Meads in Bristol, along with a locomotive works at Swindon, the Maidenhead Railway Bridge (the longest brick arch bridge ever envisaged at that point) and the Box Tunnel between Chippenham and Bath (then the world's longest railway tunnel).

Sure enough, Brunel proved a master, not only of having vision but of selling it to others. For instance, when he was called to address the House of Lords, a witness described him as "rapid in thought, clear in language" and complemented him for not saying too much and for keeping his presence of mind throughout. The engineering genius had done enough to persuade the greatest powers in the land that he could deliver a railway of a grandeur never before seen.

DREAMING BIG

Almost before the ink had dried on the act of parliament that sanctioned the GWR, Brunel was imagining something even more formidable. His ambition, he said, was to build a network that allowed an individual to buy a ticket in London and travel all the way through to New York. While even he drew the line at extending his railway across the Atlantic Ocean, instead he envisaged the passenger changing from train to steamship at Bristol. Sure enough, he established the Great Western Steam Company and in 1838 the SS *Great Western* became the first steamship to offer a transatlantic service, completing its maiden voyage in a mere fifteen days. Brunel simply refused to put a cap on his ambition.

Of course, his appetite for innovation and his rejection of the merely conventional brought with it risks. Brunel was by no means unfamiliar with failure. The Thames Tunnel, for instance, was abandoned for several years because

▲ *Work on the Clifton Suspension Bridge in Bristol—one of the engineering marvels of the Victorian age—extended from 1836 until 1864.*

of construction difficulties while his plans for an "atmospheric railway" (run using atmospheric pressure) in South Devon also came to nothing. In the latter case, Brunel took personal responsibility for its downfall and refused his fee. That was characteristic of the man, with private investors and he himself always taking the financial risk, rather than the public. And of course, Brunel learned as much from his failures as his successes.

His one great error on the GWR was to use a non-standard broad gauge, which he believed would guarantee a more efficient and smoother ride. While the theory was sound, it caused severe problems wherever the GWR met up with the wider rail network and in 1846 the government legislated that all railways should run on standard gauge track. Nonetheless, this setback was absorbed and the necessary adjustments made. Having begun operating its full route from London to Bristol in 1841, the GWR went from strength to strength until it was subsumed into the nationalized British Railways in 1948. It serves to this day as testament to Brunel's ability to blend vision, ambition, cutting-edge technology, and pragmatism.

STRATEGY ANALYSIS

STRATEGY TYPE: *Innovative*
KEY STRATEGY: *Found the practical means to implement visionary engineering solutions*
OUTCOME: *Completion of the foremost railway of the age*
ALSO USED BY: *Jorgen Nissen, Klaus Falbe Hansen, Niels Gimsing, and Georg Rotne, designers of the Øresund Bridge (2000).*

25 MOBILIZE THE MASSES

MARX AND ENGELS PUBLISH A CALL TO ARMS IN THE MOST INFLUENTIAL POLITICAL MANIFESTO IN HISTORY

KEY PLAYERS: *Karl Marx (1818–83) and Friedrich Engels (1820–95)*
NATIONALITY: *German*
STRATEGY IMPLEMENTED: *1848*
CONTEXT: *In the mid-nineteenth century, Europe was in a tumult of revolution amid growing dissatisfaction with the old order. In their Communist Manifesto, Marx and Engels elucidated a theory of world history that encouraged the proletariat (wage-laborers) to overthrow their capitalist masters*

Karl Marx and Friedrich Engels were two German-born social and political scientists who met in Paris in 1844. In 1847 they were both resident in London and members of a radical workers' organization called the Communist League. The League asked them to write a manifesto, which was published the following year. It urged workers across the globe to rise up against the existing capitalist system. Marxist theory subsequently underpinned communist regimes around the world.

When Marx and Engels met, the former was working as an editor of a radical left-wing newspaper aimed at bringing together French and German socialists, while the latter had just finished his influential book, *The Condition of the Working Class in England*. Both were influenced by the philosophical writings of Hegel and believed that the capitalist system that dominated Europe was detrimental to the good of the masses, and that the desire for material wellbeing caused the alienation of individuals from each other and themselves. Engels would report after their first meeting that he and Marx were nearly in "complete agreement in all theoretical fields" and the pair decided to

INTERNATIONAL EDITIONS OF THE COMMUNIST MANIFESTO PUBLISHED BEFORE 1880

work together, so combining Marx's brilliant political theorizing with Engels knack for communicating complex messages to a wide audience.

Both believed that political theory was of little value if it did not promote action. As Marx would comment, too many philosophers "only interpreted the world in various ways; the point is, to change it." No wonder they were both drawn to the Communist League, with its aims of overthrowing the bourgeoisie (the class consisting of employers and owners of the means of production) in favor of rule by the proletariat in a society without class divisions or private property. When they were asked to compose the League's *Communist Manifesto*, they realized it was a prime opportunity to spread the communist word to a mass audience open to the idea of a radical social overhaul. After all 1848—the year of the *Manifesto's* publication—would see revolution across the continent. Marx and Engels felt the hunger for change and seized the moment with both hands.

THE MARCH OF HISTORY
Weighing in at some 12,000 words, the *Manifesto* offered a concise introduction to the aims of communism and its theoretical basis. Marx used a draft work by Engels called *The Principles of Communism* as its basis but expanded on its ideas and added new ones of his own so that in 1883 Engels would write in a preface to a German edition that the *Manifesto* was essentially Marx's work. It begins with a sentence that became one of the key tenets of Marxism: "The history of all hitherto existing society is the history of class struggles." It was a radical interpretation of history, which was traditionally seen as a collection of stories about notable individuals. Marx instead argued that all human development was based on the exploitation of one class by another until such relationships became incompatible with changing means of production. Then a revolution installs a new dominant class. The "march of history," he contended, was thus driven by economics rather than "great men."

The Manifesto declared that nineteenth-century European industrial society in which the bourgeoisie oppressed the proletariat was ripe for overthrow. Marx and Engels argued this could only be achieved by a revolution of the workers that would see an end to private property and traditional class divides, leaving a society of

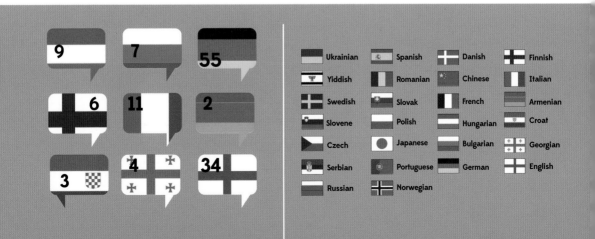

1818
Karl Marx is born in Prussia on May 5.

1820
Friedrich Engels is born in Prussia on November 28.

1844
The two meet while working in Paris.

1845
Engels publishes The Condition of the Working Class in England.

1848
Now based in London, Marx and Engels collaborate on The Communist Manifesto. *Meanwhile, a wave of revolutions overtakes continental Europe before fading out.*

1867
The first volume of Marx's Das Kapital *appears in 1867. Further completed volumes appear in 1885 and 1894.*

1883
Marx dies in London on March 14.

1895
Engels dies in London on August 5.

1917
Russia becomes the first world's first communist state.

1949
A communist government wins power in China.

1991
The collapse of the Soviet Union marks the end of the Cold War.

2007
The start of the global economic crisis prompts a re-examination of capitalism.

FOR THE MODERN AGE

With the collapse of the Soviet Union and the economic liberalization of China at the end of the twentieth century, it appeared that the Marxist experiment had run its course. People spoke of the "end of history" as liberal capitalism seemed to have won the day. However, the global financial crisis that rippled across the planet from 2007 caused us to re-evaluate the strengths and weaknesses of capitalism. Marxism suddenly found new advocates, not least in prominent protest movements such as Occupy. Marxism may never hold political sway as it did in the last century, but it doubtless maintains a modern relevance in its questioning of the prevailing economic ideology of our age.

equals. Having outlined the historical justification for communism, Marx wrote a stirring call to arms: "Let the ruling classes tremble at a Communistic revolution. The proletarians have nothing to lose but their chains. They have a world to win. Working men of all countries, unite!" Marx and Engels thus fulfilled their ambition of expounding theory in the hope of making a real-world impact.

IDEAS THAT SHAPED THE WORLD

As the revolutions of 1848 faltered one by one, it seemed possible that communism's moment had been and gone. Nevertheless, both men kept up their work, with Engels using his personal wealth to prop up the efforts of the poverty-stricken Marx. In 1867 Marx published the first volume of his masterpiece, *Das Kapital*, a historical analysis of capitalism that with the Manifesto constituted the founding documents of twentieth-century socialism. While many political philosophers believed change could be effected by appealing to the utopian dreams of the individual, Marx and Engels sought nothing less than to mobilize a whole class of people at once. This, they believed, was the most efficient way to engineer progress.

Both men were dead before the century was out so missed seeing the full extent of their impact, which reached its zenith over the next hundred years. Marxism provided the theoretical framework upon which the Soviet Union was based, with Lenin, who led the communist revolution in Russia in 1917, commenting: "In their scientific works, Marx and Engels were the first to explain that socialism is not the invention of dreamers, but the final aim and necessary result of the development of the productive forces in modern society." Without Marx and Engels, there would have been no USSR, communist Eastern Bloc, Maoist China, or Castro's Cuba.

Yet the excesses of these regimes did much to discredit Marxism as a workable political theory. Communist regimes became synonymous with shortages, corruption, oppression, and the Cold War. In the USSR alone, it is conservatively estimated that Stalin was responsible for the deaths of at least 20 million of his comrades. Meanwhile, the world's leading extant communist regime, in China, bears little resemblance to the classless, private-property-less ideal that Marx and Engels described. However, it is unfair to blame the credo's principal theoreticians for the faults of those who implemented it after their deaths. With *The Communist Manifesto*, Marx and Engels set out to define a philosophy that changed the world. For better or worse, they achieved that goal.

▲ *This statue of Marx (left) and Engels resides in Berlin. Their political philosophy had a profound impact on global politics in the twentieth century.*

STRATEGY ANALYSIS

STRATEGY TYPE: *Communication*
KEY STRATEGY: *Refining a new political philosophy designed to effect social change*
OUTCOME: *The birth of communism, an ideology that came to mold world history*
ALSO USED BY: *Thomas More, author of* Utopia, *1516, and Mao Zedong's* Little Red Book, *1964.*

26 FOLLOW YOUR GUT

FLORENCE NIGHTINGALE, "THE LADY WITH THE LAMP," USHERED IN THE MODERN AGE OF NURSING

KEY PLAYER: *Florence Nightingale (1820–1910)*
NATIONALITY: *English*
Strategy implemented: *1850s–1910*
CONTEXT: *At a time when nursing was little-respected and often conducted in a haphazard manner, Nightingale turned it into a respectable and far more effective profession underpinned by proper training*

When she was sixteen, Nightingale felt a "calling" to do important work. Over time, she realized her passion was for nursing, even though it was a poorly-paid profession regarded as suitable only for those of low social standing. Nightingale, however, wished to turn it into a respectable career choice. She tirelessly campaigned for proper training so that nurses could make a real contribution to alleviating suffering and improving public health.

Born into a wealthy family in 1820, Nightingale's early interest in the nursing profession was opposed by her mother and father. They considered it an unsuitable job for a woman of her background and wished her to make a advantageous marriage instead. But in 1851, after years of arm twisting, she persuaded her parents to give her their blessing to train as a nurse. She had overcome their resistance through sheer determination—a quality that would become a hallmark of her long career.

After completing her training at Kaiserswerth in Germany, she returned to London and became the lady superintendent of a hospital for invalid women. In 1854 the Crimean War began, with Britain sending an army to Turkey to fight the Russians. The newspapers were soon full of reports about the hellish conditions troops faced. Within a few weeks, some 8,000 men had gone down with either malaria or cholera. Despite official reluctance to allow women into the crucible of battle, Nightingale volunteered her nursing services and was eventually granted permission to take a further 38 nurses with her to the front. For her, it would prove a horrifying but formative experience. Stationed at the military hospital at Scutari, she found circumstances every bit as awful as had been suggested. Unwashed men lay in their dirty battle clothes in packed rooms without such basics as blankets or decent food. Typhus, cholera, and dysentery were all rife. This was, Nightingale soon became convinced, no way to carry on. She determined to do everything in her power to change things.

BIRTH OF AN ICON

In the 1850s, medical understanding of hygiene was still very basic and germ theory was hardly out of its infancy. Indeed, Nightingale herself was unconvinced by the idea of

NIGHTINGALE'S CHART: THE CAUSES OF MORTALITY IN THE ARMY IN THE EAST

APRIL 1854 TO MARCH 1855

Measured from the centre of the diagram the area of the blue wedges represent deaths from preventable diseases

Measured from the centre of the diagram the area of the black wedges represent deaths from all other causes

Measured from the centre of the diagram the area of the orange wedges represent deaths from battle wounds

Note: The black line in November 1854 marks the boundary of deaths from all other causes during the month. In October 1854 the black area coincides with the orange.

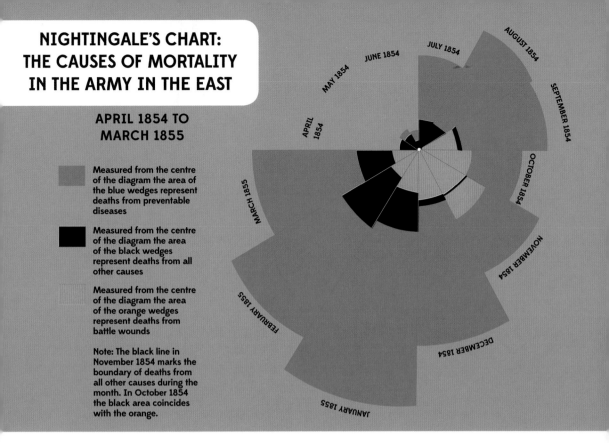

MAY 1854 · JUNE 1854 · JULY 1854 · AUGUST 1854 · SEPTEMBER 1854 · APRIL 1854 · OCTOBER 1854 · MARCH 1855 · NOVEMBER 1854 · FEBRUARY 1855 · DECEMBER 1854 · JANUARY 1855

disease spreading via germs. However, she instinctively believed that good sanitation was key to health. So she began to press for improvements in the running of military hospitals, arguing that greater cleanliness would see far fewer men succumb to their wounds or, more commonly, to diseases they picked up in the hospitals themselves. She also championed compassion as a key aspect of nursing care.

Her suggestions for reform met with immediate resistance from the male-dominated medical profession and military hierarchy, who had scant regard for the opinions of an upstart nurse. When word reached England of the "ministering angel" who glided around the hospital making life more comfortable for her charges, the legend of the merciful "Lady with the Lamp" (she carried a small lamp when it was dark) was born. Although Nightingale never felt comfortable with this popular perception, she understood that her fame granted her power and influence she would not otherwise have had. Sure enough, public support ensured she was given the job of reforming the hospital at Scutari. She oversaw an immediate improvement in conditions and medical outcomes.

She returned to Britain at the end of the war in 1856 as a national heroine and had the opportunity to personally brief Queen Victoria and Prince Albert on her plans to improve military hospitals. Now she set out to improve nursing provision in wider society too.

AN ENDURING LEGACY

Nightingale perfected a multifaceted approach to reform. She consulted experts in health and medical provision, consulting the latest studies and creating her own where they

TIME LINE

1820
Florence Nightingale is born in Florence, Italy, on May 12.

1837
Nightingale has her first thoughts of going into nursing but her parents oppose the idea.

1851
She travels to Kaiserwerth in Germany to train.

1853
She becomes superintendent of a hospital for gentlewomen in Harley Street. Meanwhile, the Crimean War breaks out between an alliance of Britain, France, the Ottoman Empire and Sardinia on one side and Russia on the other.

1854
Nightingale leads a team of nurses at the barrack hospital at Scutari. During her time there, she vastly improves conditions for patients.

1855
Nightingale meets Mary Seacole, a fellow nursing trailblazer.

1856
Nightingale returns to the UK and begins work on a Royal Commission to explore the health of the British Army.

1859
She publishes the landmark Notes on Nursing.

1860
She establishes the Nightingale Training School at Saint Thomas' Hospital, London, and becomes the first woman to be elected a fellow of the Statistical Society.

1883
She is awarded the Royal Red Cross by Queen Victoria.

1907
She becomes the first woman to receive the Order of Merit.

1910
Nightingale dies in London on August 13.

were needed. She was a great documenter of data (she helped develop a distinctive type of pie chart, see page 113) and backed up her arguments with as much credible evidence as she could muster. Meanwhile, she garnered public support for her ideas via publications such as 1859's *Notes on Nursing* and by regularly contributing to public debate in arenas such as *The Times* letters page.

She also became a tremendous lobbyist, writing countless letters and using her enviable social contacts to wield influence. She was widely credited with getting Earl de Grey installed as minister of war in 1863 because she knew he was sympathetic to her cause. She was also a crack money-raiser, securing sufficient funds to open the first nursing school at Saint Thomas' Hospital in London in 1869. Nursing was now a respectable career for women of all classes. In order to achieve her grand goals, she had become an expert at playing the game with the rich and powerful.

If the army had much to be grateful to her for, so did the poor, for it was Nightingale who saw the law changed so that trained nurses were employed in workhouses. Previously the role had normally fallen to untrained nurses who were themselves resident in the workhouse and often more intent on purloining their patient's few meager possessions rather than helping them. In demanding a health safety net for the poorest in society, Nightingale helped establish the principles that birthed the National Health Service in the middle of the twentieth century. Indeed, many of the fundamentals she championed continue to underpin the nursing profession throughout the world. By following her instinct and then acting with great determination Nightingale succeeded in transforming the nursing profession.

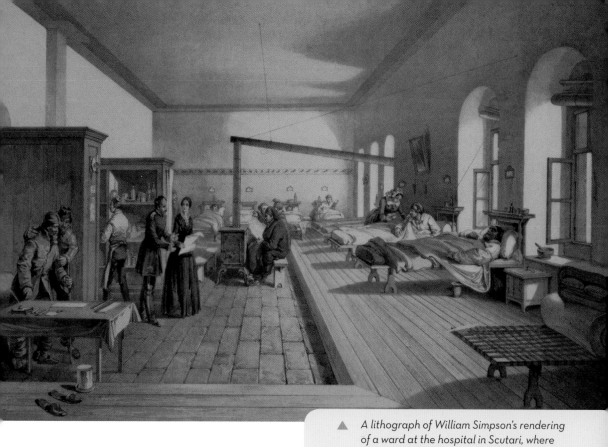

▲ A lithograph of William Simpson's rendering of a ward at the hospital in Scutari, where Nightingale made vast improvements.

LASTING LEGACY

For evidence of Nightingale's enduring impact, look no further than the Nightingale Initiative for Global Health—an organization created in 1999 by international scholars. With a mission "to inform and empower nurses and other healthcare workers and educators to become "twenty-first century Nightingales," it aims to build a grassroots movement among nurses, healthcare workers, and educators toward the adoption of health as the universal priority of the United Nations and its member states. A remarkable legacy indeed.

STRATEGY ANALYSIS

STRATEGY TYPE: Leadership
KEY STRATEGY: Lobbying for reform using determination and a strong evidential basis
OUTCOME: The foundations of modern nursing and the welfare state
ALSO USED: Mother Teresa, social campaigner, 1910-97, and Margaret Sanger, US birth control pioneer, 1879-1966.

"COMPETITION IS A SIN"

JOHN D. ROCKEFELLER BUILT AN OIL EMPIRE, SUCCESSFULLY DOMINATING THE MARKET

KEY PLAYER: *John D. Rockefeller (1839-1937)*
NATIONALITY: *American*
Strategy implemented:
1870-1911
CONTEXT: *John D. Rockefeller got into oil just as the industry boomed and in 1870 he established the Standard Oil Company. Using aggressive tactics, he bought up rival firms to ensure a virtual monopoly*

John D. Rockefeller opened his first oil refinery in 1863 and by the time he died 74 years later, his personal wealth was equivalent to about 1.5 percent of the United States's entire GDP. He achieved this remarkable feat by fine-tuning his oil operations so that he had a hand in all stages from production to distribution. But perhaps even more importantly, he was ruthless in his pursuit of market domination.

Rockefeller was born into a poor and dysfunctional family and this no doubt drove his determination to work hard to secure complete economic security. Even as a child, he would purchase sweets in bulk at discount so that he could sell them in individual portions to his siblings at profit. He got his first job at sixteen, working as a bookkeeper for a small firm, and training himself in the importance of keeping a close eye on all incomings and outgoings. In 1859 he went into business in his own right, setting up a wholesale foods operation with a partner, Maurice B. Clark.

Around this time, there were significant oil discoveries being made in various corners of the United States. Furthermore, the Civil War had raised demand for kerosene while whale oil, which had traditionally been used to fuel lamps, was in short supply. So when the opportunity arose to get into the oil business in 1863, Rockefeller leapt at it. Along with Clark and two of Clark's brothers plus a chemist called Samuel Andrews, Rockefeller set up Andrews, Clark & Company. They built an oil refinery in an area of Cleveland called The Flats, which at the time was enjoying an industrial boom. The company was immediately successful and within two years Rockefeller had accumulated enough capital to buy out the Clark brothers: An early indicator that Rockefeller liked to maintain as much personal control of business as he could.

He dedicated himself to running the company as best he might. Rather than enjoying the high life, he favored reinvestment, not only using the firm's healthy profits but also borrowing heavily against them. In 1866 he entered into partnership with his brother, who had opened a new refinery in the state. Rockefeller ran a network of staff to provide him with intelligence about developments in the market and was quick to respond to altering circumstances. He also kept a close eye on costs, looking to maximize economies of

▲ *John D. Rockefeller was ruthless in his commercial dealings, buying out or scaring off his rivals at every opportunity.*

scale and seeking out commercial opportunities involving waste products from the refining process.

AN EYE FOR THE MAIN CHANCE

By 1868 Rockefeller had interests in two refineries in Cleveland and a marketing operation in New York. Realizing that transporting his oil was one of his chief expenses, he decided to flex his commercial muscle with the railroad companies. He hammered out a deal with the Erie Railroad whereby he was given a significant rebate in exchange for guaranteeing a certain volume of shipments. Where the Erie Railroad had gone, many of its competitors felt compelled to follow. It set a trend for Rockefeller's sometimes ruthless treatment of suppliers, of a sort many modern-day superstores are accused of exercising.

In 1870 he invested one million US dollars to set up Standard Oil of Ohio, which was then America's largest corporation, accounting for 10 percent of national oil refining. The railroads were hungry for its business and several joined together in secret to form the South Improvement Company, a cartel that agreed mutually beneficial terms with

TIME LINE

1839
John Davison Rockefeller is born on July 8 in Richmond, New York.

1855
He gets his first job with a produce-shipping firm.

1863
Rockefeller co-founds Andrew, Clark & Company, opening an oil refinery in Cleveland.

1864
He marries his first love, Laura Celestia ("Cettie") Spelman.

1865
He buys out the Clark brothers to form Rockefeller & Andrews.

1870
Rockefeller founds Standard Oil of Ohio.

1872
He takes control of all but four of Cleveland's 26 refineries.

1877
He controls 90 percent of America's oil refining business.

1897
Rockefeller formally retires from day-to-day management of Standard Oil.

1911
Standard Oil is forced to dismantle after the US Supreme Court rules it is running a monopoly.

1913
The Rockefeller Foundation is established to promote "the well-being of mankind."

1937
Rockefeller dies on May 23 in Florida.

SELF-MADE MEN

Late nineteenth-century America saw the emergence of several self-made men who, like Rockefeller, came to wield significant influence—among them Andrew Carnegie and Cornelius Vanderbilt. The technological revolution of the last forty years has seen the rise of a new generation of such figures. The story of Microsoft-founder Bill Gates, in particular, has obvious parallels with Rockefeller's life. Both entered their industries just as they were about to explode and negotiated commercial deals that guaranteed unprecedented market share (indeed, both faced long-running anti-trust cases). Furthermore, just as Rockefeller ran a double life as part-business supremo and part-philanthropist, so too has Gates reinvested much of his wealth back into the society that made him rich in the first place.

Standard Oil. Rockefeller persuaded them that not only should he have a 50 percent rebate on his oil shipments, but that he should receive additional rebates when his rival's oil was shipped. In practice, this meant rival firms faced a sudden price hike for transportation. There was inevitable uproar from the oil companies and railroads who were not in on the deal, and for a while it was put on hold. However, Rockefeller was not to be deterred by the disapproval of the public, and even less so by that of his rivals.

In what became known as the "Cleveland Massacre," he spent much of 1872 approaching his competitors with offers to buy them out. If they resisted, he gave them a simple choice: Reconsider or prepare to be driven out of the market place. Standard Oil was already big enough that it could keep costs down, offering differential pricing so as to maximize profits where competitors were few and selling at cost (or even beneath it) in order to destroy his rivals. By the end of the year, he owned 22 of the 26 refineries in Cleveland. It wasn't pretty, but he had created a state-wide monopoly. Rockefeller, though, did not see that as a bad thing. For him, a monopoly brought order in place of the chaos of unhindered competition.

When the stock market crashed the following year, he swept in to pick off yet more rivals, buying at rock-bottom prices and extending his reach in New York, Pittsburgh, and Philadelphia. In 1877, he engineered a stand-off with the Pennsylvania Railroad Company, who feared Rockefeller was going to build a network of pipe lines. The result was a railroad war that ended in Rockefeller's favor, with further cuts to shipping costs. By 1878 Rockefeller was in control of 90 percent of all the oil refined in the United States. He officially retired in 1897.

GIVE AND TAKE

While he ascended the list of world's wealthiest people, Rockefeller never ceased to give away a share of his wealth. A devout Northern Baptist, he believed that as money came to him, so he should give a proportion of it away. From his days as a teenage bookkeeper, he gave 10 percent of his salary to good causes. By the end of his life, he had donated upward of US$500 million, benefiting the needy and financing prominent educational, scientific, and cultural institutions. The ruthless monopolist was imbued with significant humanity after all.

Because of legal complications, Rockefeller's empire was run on a state by state basis but in 1882 he established the Standard Oil Trust that consolidated some 41 different companies. Soon it was in control of 90 percent of refined oil, not merely in America but globally. However, on his relentless march to greatness, Rockefeller had made many enemies and he faced legal case after legal case testing the legitimacy of his undeniable monopoly. Finally, in 1911 the US Supreme Court ruled that he was operating just such a thing and that the Trust was to be broken up into 34 companies, inevitably breaking Standard Oil's stranglehold on the industry. Yet Rockefeller, resilient as ever, did not himself suffer greatly. In the process of splitting up and selling off the Trust, the resulting companies' net worth increased by some 500 percent and Rockefeller saw his own bank account swell to some US$900 million. On his death, the *New York Times* estimated he had earned US$1.5 billion over his lifetime. In terms of personal wealth-to-US GDP, he was perhaps three times more wealthy than Bill Gates is today. Yet while he had taken much, he had given a lot back too.

STRATEGY ANALYSIS

STRATEGY TYPE: *Dominance*
KEY STRATEGY: *Bought up the opposition to ensure market domination*
OUTCOME: *A 90 percent share of the global oil refinery business*
ALSO USED BY: *De Beers, diamond merchants, in the nineteenth and early twentieth centuries, and Bill Gates, 1980–..*

28 KNOW YOUR CUSTOMER

THE **WOOLWORTH BROTHERS** FOUNDED A RETAIL EMPIRE THAT OFFERED BOTH BARGAINS AND CUSTOMER SERVICE

KEY PLAYERS: *Frank Woolworth (1852-1919) and Charles Sumner ("Sum") Woolworth (1856-1947)*
NATIONALITY: *American*
Strategy implemented: *1879-1997*
CONTEXT: *Frank Woolworth realized that there was money to be made by selling fixed-price lines and treating all his customers, whatever their spending potential, as equals*

Even as physical shops give way to cyber-commerce, we continue to make purchases according to a model that owes much to the Woolworth brothers. Before them, "browsing" was a rarity—instead, shoppers presented a list of desired merchandise that staff then assembled. It was also a general rule that the richer you were, the better you were treated. The Woolworths, however, realized a dime is a dime whoever spends it.

The Woolworth brothers, Frank and Sum, were born into a farming family in Jefferson County, New York. Times were hard as the country recovered from the horrors of the Civil War. Frank left school to work full-time on the farm when he was 16 but already harbored plans to take a different direction in life. When he was 21 he took a six-month sabbatical to go and work for Augsbury and Moore, a much-loved hardware store in nearby Watertown. So began a retail odyssey that reconfigured the way the world shopped.

By then Frank already had strong ideas about how to treat customers, rooted in an experience he had as a teenager in search of a present for his mother's birthday. He and Sum pooled their worldly wealth so that they could buy a gift to a value of 50¢. In the end, they opted for a scarf but when they presented the shop assistant with their collection of shrapnel in payment, they noticed all the staff had gathered round and were laughing at them. One even made a wisecrack that perhaps they could get the matching gloves for their mum's next birthday. The two boys thus had their act of generosity hijacked and they left feeling humiliated. From that moment, Tom vowed that someday you would be able to buy ten decent items for 50¢, and get treated with respect into the bargain.

LEARNING THE MARKET

At Augsbury and Moore, Frank set about accumulating the knowledge to achieve his goal. He spent hours in the stockroom, preparing the merchandise and gradually learning how to spot a winning product line and what to avoid. He was also given responsibility for product displays, developing the vivid red color-scheme that would become a hallmark of the Woolworth company.

Crucially, he also learned of a tactic employed by an erstwhile rival store in Watertown to dispose of slow-moving goods. The store, Bushnells, used to load up a table with the problem merchandise beneath a sign proudly proclaiming: "Nothing on this table over 5¢." A proverbial light bulb pinged on in Frank's brain. If such a tactic was successful in clearing excess stock, might it not work on a more permanent basis? Could you get rich from a fixed-price table selling a range of lines, each offering some margin for profit?

He persuaded his boss, William Moore, to give it a go. After an initial rush of sales, interest dwindled and Moore suspected the fixed-priced table worked best as an occasional offering only. He also feared its permanent presence might detract from the store's upmarket ethos. Frank, though, was convinced he could make a go of things. He turned to Moore for advice on the practicalities of setting up an entire 5¢ store and was told it would cost in the region of $300 to rent an appropriate site, pay for fixtures and fittings, and buy suitable goods to sell.

Frank turned to his friends and relations for start-up capital. He found a site in Utica, New York, that was off the town's main commercial drag but was affordable. He kept costs as low as possible, employing staff on temporary contracts and using upturned packing crates as counters. He draped them in signature red cloths and created a red and gold sign to hang outside. "The Great Five Cent Store" opened on February 22 1879.

After an initial boom, sales soon fell off and in May he decided to cut his losses and close the operation. Frank had identified his niche and was determined to realize its potential, but knew better than to flog a dead horse.

TWEAKING THE FORMULA

He was convinced that the Utica store had failed because of its poor location. Now he decided to open a new shop in a prime location in Lancaster, Pennsylvania. He also decided to add a 10¢ line. This was to be the first true "five-and-dime." With a large local Amish community, he was confident he was accessing a market who would appreciate the bargains he had on offer. He stocked everything from cups and handkerchiefs to police whistles and toy dustpans, each bought in bulk at prices that allowed for at least a little profit despite the low prices. (He would later be a pioneer of loss-leading lines—selling products at a loss in order to get customers through the doors to buy other products that would turn a profit—but this was not the time for such largesse.)

WOOLWORTHS IN NUMBERS

Woolworth building cost US $13.5m

At its peak operated over

3,000

retail stores around the world.

Territories: Barbados, Canada, Germany, Ireland, Jamaica, Mexico, Spain, Trinidad and Tobago, the UK, the USA and Zimbabwe

1909
first branch opens outside of North America.

WOOLWORTH BUILDING OPENED 1913

TIME LINE

1852
Frank Winfield Woolworth is born on April 13.

1856
Charles Sumner ("Sum") Woolworth is born on August 1.

1873
Frank takes first job in retail, working for the Augsbury & Moore Dry Goods Store in March.

1879
Frank opens his first 5¢ store, in Utica (New York) on February 22 but it closes after a few weeks. In June, he opens a second store in Lancaster, Pennsylvania. It is an immediate hit. A month later, Sum opens a store in Harrisburg, Pennsylvania.

1890
Frank Woolworth visits Europe for the first time, reaching purchasing deals direct with manufacturers.

1891–94
The brothers ally themselves with other relations and hand-picked associates to establish a syndicate

1913
Work finishes on the company's new headquarters, the Woolworth Building in New York. It is the world's tallest skyscraper, a record it holds until 1930.

1919
Frank dies on April 8.

1932
Woolworth's introduces a 20¢ line for the first time.

1935
The company does away with selling price limits.

1947
Sum dies on January 7.

1997
The last of Woolworth's US shops closes, although other shops bearing the name continue to operate around the world.

Again, initial sales were brisk. But this time they kept up their momentum. The good people of Lancaster could not resist Frank's heady combination of value products and his staff's courteous, attentive treatment of their customers. Within a month, his brother Sum was installed as manager of a store in nearby Harrisburg, working to the same formula. Sum eventually bought out Frank to own the flagship branch of Woolworth's in Scranton, Pennsylvania, so creating the Woolworth's syndicate model.

As the retail empire grew, each new store was established in the same way. Trusted partners were brought in to set up new branches, putting up the stake money for a share of the profits. This kept partners motivated and minimized the risk of contagion from any single failing store. Each store was thus effectively independent and they were far enough apart that they did not directly compete with each other. So it was that a chain of "friendly rivals" was born, with syndicate members meeting regularly to share ideas and maximize their buying power.

Frank remained the driving force of innovation. For instance, he sourced supplies directly from Europe so as to cut out expensive middlemen. In 1912 almost 600 syndicate stores incorporated to become the F. W. Woolworth Co., prospering until hard times hit in the 1990s, long after the Woolworth brothers had departed the scene. By successfully identifying a new market and then serving their needs by providing desirable products at a low price and making customers feel valued, two farming boys from New York State laid the foundations of the modern chain store that was unrivaled in its commercial dominance until the internet came knocking.

▲ *Shoppers thronged to the new Woolworth's stores—such as this one in Washington, D.C.— reveling in an innovative retail experience.*

RETAIL THERAPY

Today, the customer is always right but it was only in the aftermath of the Woolworth brothers that the consumer became king. The two men helped turn shopping from a necessary part of life into an experience to be enjoyed. Frank also realized the power of a "bargain" to attract custom. His influence can be traced through, for instance, the "Pile 'em high and sell 'em cheap" philosophy of Tesco founder, Jack Cohen, through to the low price and easy shopping experience that has fueled the exponential growth of Amazon in the twenty-first century.

STRATEGY ANALYSIS

STRATEGY TYPE: *Innovation*
KEY STRATEGY: *Identified a new market and created a retail model to meet their needs*
OUTCOME: *A retail brand that earned the brothers a fortune and prospered for decades after their deaths*
ALSO USED BY: *Jack Cohen, founder of the Tesco, 1929, and Jeff Bezos, Amazon, 1994–.*

THE POWER OF NONVIOLENCE

GANDHI PREACHED A DOCTRINE OF NONVIOLENT PROTEST TO SECURE INDIA'S INDEPENDENCE FROM BRITAIN

KEY PLAYER: *Mohandas Gandhi (1869–1948)*
NATIONALITY: *Indian*
STRATEGY IMPLEMENTED: *c.1893–1947*
CONTEXT: *After becoming involved in securing rights for Indian citizens in South Africa, Gandhi returned to India and led demands for independence from the British Raj, pioneering the use of nonviolence in a mass movement*

Mohandas (also known by the honorary name Mahatma, meaning great soul) Gandhi led India's nationalist movement against the British Raj. Turning his back on traditional forms of violent protest, he taught a creed of nonviolence and proved its efficacy for a real-life mass protest movement. Britain granted India independence in 1947.

Born into a relatively affluent family, Gandhi trained as a barrister in London and in 1893 took a job as a legal representative in Durban, South Africa. It was here that he underwent a political awakening, becoming active in the movement to secure basic rights for the country's immigrant Indian population, many of whom endured appalling treatment.

In some twenty years spent there, he served several prison sentences for his protest activities and developed his philosophy of *satyagraha* ("devotion to truth") that espoused spiritual purity above all else. It was an ethos that was influenced not only by his own Hindu beliefs but also by elements of Jainism and Christian teachings. He was also profoundly touched by Henry David Thoreau's *On Civil Disobedience* and Tolstoy's 1894 work, *The Kingdom of God is Within You* (Gandhi and Tolstoy corresponded for a while before Tolstoy's death in 1910). Eventually, the South African government agreed to compromise and met a number of Gandhi's demands in 1914. He had proven that change could be engineered without recourse to brutality.

Shortly afterward, he returned to India and began organizing protests against unfair taxes and crude discrimination employed by the occupying British forces. In 1919 the British passed the Rowlatt Acts that paved the way for the large-scale internment of suspected seditionists. In response, Gandhi launched a new satyagraha.

NONVIOLENCE, NOT PASSIVITY

In 1920 the British responded to protestors in Amritsar by opening fire, killing somewhere between 300 and a thousand people. The massacre brought the satyagraha sharply into the public eye and turned Gandhi into a major political figure. In the wake of this incident he became the leading force within the Indian National Congress. Under him, Congress adopted a formal policy of nonviolence and peaceful non-cooperation.

▲ *Gandhi, sporting a traditional home-spun dhoti, arrives in Delhi for talks on Indian independence with the British authorities.*

His first major task was to convince skeptics within his own ranks that nonviolence stood any chance of success. On the face of it, it seemed a fairly blunt weapon against the might of a British Empire reluctant to loosen its grip on power. The ability to turn the other cheek might be an admirable trait in an individual, but there was precious little evidence that it worked as a tool for social change. Gandhi responded by arguing that nonviolence was not the same as passivity. Rather than accepting the oppression heaped upon his people, he called instead for widespread, active protest. The only condition was that it should not inflict violence on another. This was not simply a political strategy, as far as he was concerned, but a profound moral philosophy and, ultimately, a way of life. While others saw protest as a means to an end, Gandhi believed in a much closer relationship between the two, with the latter not justifying the former. As he put it, "the means may be likened to the seed, the end to a tree."

If his critics felt that it all sounded rather nice but ineffectual, Gandhi was quick to show that nonviolence and action were not mutually exclusive. As well as initiating peaceful protests and speaking eloquently against the excesses of Raj rule, he also called for boycotts of British goods and institutions. He urged Indians to withdraw from the British court system and take their children out of British schools, while Indian-born civil servants were encouraged to resign their positions. Meanwhile, he adopted the

1869
Mohandas Gandhi is born on October 2 in Gujarat.

1891
He qualifies as a barrister in England.

1893
He moves to South Africa to work as a lawyer.

1894
He founds the Natal Indian Congress, campaigning for Indian rights and serving a number of prison terms in the process.

1915
Gandhi returns to India.

1919
The Rowlatt Acts and Amritsar Massacre fire anti-British sentiment.

1920
Gandhi advocates non-cooperation with the British.

1922
He receives a six-year sentence for sedition.

1930
Congress declares Indian independence.

1931
Gandhi leads his March to the Sea. He also travels to London for a Round Table Conference with the British. However, he spends much of the next decade in and out of prison.

1942
The UK offers India dominion status, which Gandhi rejects. Opposing Indian involvement in the war, he is imprisoned.

1947
London grants Indian independence, while also partitioning the new state of Pakistan.

1948
Gandhi is assassinated on January 30 in New Delhi.

traditional home-spun dhoti (an item of male apparel) and shawl as an explicit rejection of British clothing and urged his fellow citizens to set aside time each day to spin yarn so they need not buy imported clothes. By such means he showed how pressure could be exerted on the oppressor without causing physical harm.

MORAL AUTHORITY

By the early 1920s, Gandhi had moved beyond merely demanding greater rights from the British to campaigning for outright independence. His willingness to accept the punishment dealt out to him while maintaining his nonviolent stance only increased his moral authority. In 1922 he was one of thousands of protestors

INSPIRATION

Gandhi's successful use of nonviolent protest has provided an inspiration for countless subsequent protest movements. His influence may be found in the American civil rights movement of the 1960s, in the teachings of James Bevel and, most notably, Martin Luther King (see page 192). George Orwell was among those who commended Gandhi while arguing that his tactics would only work against a relatively benevolent opponent such as the British. In South Africa, Nelson Mandela seemed to illustrate this as he was eventually forced to surrender his nonviolent approach against the intransigent apartheid regime. However, the likes of Aung San Suu Kyi in Burma and Vaclav Havel in Czechoslovakia showed that nonviolence does have a place even against hardline opponents.

arrested that year, receiving a six-year prison sentence for his peaceful protests. Released after two years, he re-entered the political fray with renewed vigor in 1928, addressing mass rallies, organizing petitions, and giving orations that permitted nonviolent forms of disobedience, non-cooperation, and direct action. Fasting was another tactic that he used, going without food and risking his own life in a way designed to humble the authorities. Such actions also played well with his supporters, who could see that his nonviolent approach was in no way rooted in a desire to avoid physical peril. Indeed, he taught that nonviolence required a level of courage that not everyone could be assumed to have.

All the while, he kept channels of communication open with the British. Not only was this politically pragmatic, but it reflected his belief that no individual had the monopoly on *satya* (truth) and that dialog was essential to understand others' motivations and gain a grasp of the full picture. Furthermore, he believed that to be heard, one must also listen.

In 1930 Congress unilaterally declared Indian independence, a move unrecognized by the British. The following year he championed a campaign against a newly imposed tax on salt, leading thousands on a 250 miles (400-km) walk that became known as the March to the Sea. The British hit back in heavy-handed fashion, rounding up some 60,000 people in the aftermath. As Gandhi had always hoped it would, his nonviolent approach was beginning to heap shame upon his opponents.

LEADING THE WAY

In 1942, amid anger that India had been dragged into World War II as part of the British Empire, he called for the British to "Quit India" and rejected an offer of dominion status. He spent most of the rest of the war in prison, often fasting—a fact the British did all they could to conceal. However, by the end of the war, the British were ready to open serious negotiations. Two years later, an act of parliament granted India independence. Gandhi had achieved his goals without ever resorting to violence—the first time such a major political and social movement had attained success in this way.

Nonetheless, Gandhi did not rest. He had not wanted partition (which saw the creation of Muslim Pakistan, while India remained predominantly Hindu) and worked hard to improve relations between the religions. On January 30 1948 he paid the ultimate price when a Hindu fanatic murdered him. In 1936, Gandhi had said: "I do not claim to have originated any new principle or doctrine. I have simply tried in my own way to apply the eternal truth to our daily life and problems." Einstein, another great humanitarian of the age, saw it differently: "He has invented a completely new and humane means for the liberation war of an oppressed country ..."

STRATEGY ANALYSIS

STRATEGY TYPE: *Strategy of attack*
KEY STRATEGY: *Nonviolence as a form of protest*
OUTCOME: *Indian independence in 1947*
ALSO USED BY: *Martin Luther King, 1955-68, and Aung San Suu Kyi in Burma.*

PRACTICAL SOLUTIONS

EBENEZER HOWARD LEADS THE GARDEN CITY MOVEMENT

KEY PLAYER: *Sir Ebenezer Howard (1850–1928)*
NATIONALITY: *British*
STRATEGY IMPLEMENTED: *1899*
CONTEXT: *At the end of the nineteenth century, Britain's cities were blighted by overcrowding and pollution. Against this backdrop, Howard introduced his vision of small, self-supporting cities combining elements of the town and country*

Ebenezer Howard was not by profession either an architect or an urban planner, yet his ideas on urban design have influenced planners and architects around the world through the present day. Deeply concerned with social reform, he believed the industrial cities of the nineteenth century had failed to provide working people with a decent place to work and live. His idea was to start again from scratch, creating towns that offered the benefits of both urban and rural living.

Born in London in 1850, Howard grew up in a city that magnificently served the rich but left the poor to struggle. Building projects were undertaken by individuals and corporations almost exclusively concerned with their own profits. This was not, Howard came to believe, how things ought to be. Instead, development should be undertaken for the good of society as a whole. It was an idealistic outlook that he developed after moving to the United States in 1871.

Having arrived in New York, he made his way to Nebraska and began farming. However, it was a short-lived enterprise and Howard soon got himself a job as a courtroom stenographer in Chicago. The city had suffered a devastating fire in 1871 and was in the process of extensive regeneration when Howard arrived, including the creation of new suburbs and large public parks. He also became aware of an experimental development in Illinois called Riverside, the brainchild of one Frederick Law Olmsted, a famous landscape architect. Olmsted's aim was to create a town that took elements of town and country living, blending them into the perfect mix. Howard was profoundly influenced by these projects, which were in such sharp contrast to the directionless urban sprawl that he had witnessed in London. Taking inspiration from Olmsted, he evolved many of their shared ideals into an entire philosophy of urban planning.

When he returned to London in 1876 to work as an official parliamentary reporter, he was increasingly interested in social reform. In 1889 he read a novel by Edward Bellamy called *Looking Backward*, which told the story of a Bostonian who wakes from a coma in the year 2000 to discover a new, idealized society fueled by technological advancement and new social structures. Around the same time, he also read *Fields, Factories, and*

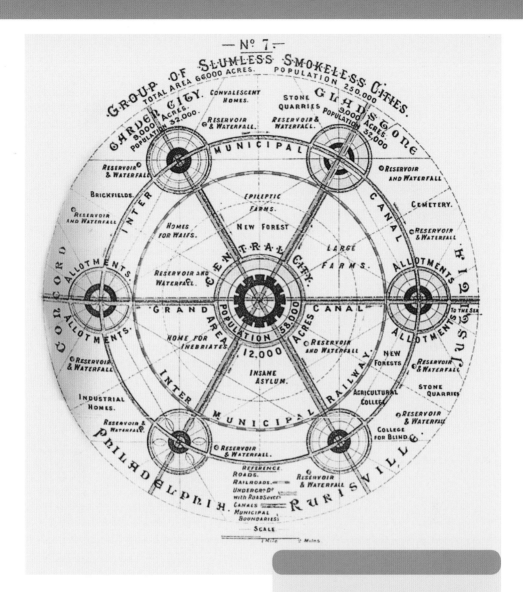

Workshops by the Russian author Peter Kropotkin and *Progress and Poverty* by the American author Henry George. These envisaged new communities, with George proposing nationalization of land. Under their influence, Howard distilled his own thoughts into a book published in 1898 as *To-morrow: A Peaceful Path to Real Reform*, which was reissued four years later as *Garden Cities of To-morrow*. This book became the founding gospel of the Garden City movement.

GARDEN CITY MODEL

Howard drew up a detailed plan for a network of garden cities. Each of the six garden cities would have 32,000 citizens and be 9,000 acres. The central "social city" meanwhile would cater for 58,000 people and cover 12,000 acres. The total population of the development would be 250,000 with a total area of 66,000 acres.

TIME LINE

MODEL TOWNS

Howard started out from the premise that existing cities suffered from overcrowding, offering the working classes unacceptable living conditions and leaving them vulnerable to ill health. Meanwhile, the countryside was suffering from a mass exodus to the cities that had caused an agricultural depression. His answer was to create a new type of town that provided decent residential living, space for industrialization, and plentiful green spaces, all surrounded by a permanent greenbelt. Such cities were to be as self-contained as possible, so that people did not have to commute far to and from work. In addition, the land was to be taken out of private ownership and held in trust, with residents paying a regular, reasonable rent. In his own words, he was intent on "helping to bring a new civilization into being."

His guidelines for these new utopias were very specific, although he would argue he was happy for them to be adapted on a case-by-case basis. He envisaged a cluster of six Garden Cities of 32,000 citizens each, centered on a larger development of 58,000 people, which together formed a "Social City." Each part would be linked to the others via rapid transport links and Howard called for electricity to be the chief source of energy so as to reduce pollution. The basic city would take up around 6,000 acres of land and was to be built in a concentric pattern, with a handful of wide boulevards emanating from the center. At the center would be a large public garden surrounded by the main civic buildings and amenities, including a concert hall and a hospital. It was a radically new vision that his critics derided as self-indulgent utopianism.

Deciding to put his money where his mouth was, Howard established the Garden City Association in 1899 and three years later set up the Garden City Pioneer Company to put his theory into action. In 1903 he decided on a site, Letchworth, in Hertfordshire a little over 30 miles from London. Building work began in 1904 under the guidance of architects Barry Parker and Paul Unwin, who were selected by public competition. Although they tweaked many of the finer details of Howard's master plan, they remained faithful to his underlying principles. It took a while for the population to grow (there were 10,000 residents by 1917) but Howard had proved his vision could be realized.

During World War I, Prime Minister David Lloyd George promised "homes fit for heroes" for returning troops. But to Howard's disappointment, the 1919 Housing Act made no provision to replicate his Letchworth model. Fired into action once more, he decided to build a second town, this time at Welwyn in Hertfordshire. Again, he saw the project through fruition, and it was not long before Welwyn Garden City was supporting a population of several thousand. By the time Howard died there in 1928, he had shown that Letchworth was no fluke and that his planning principles could be practically applied.

AN INTERNATIONAL TEMPLATE

Howard never gained much financially from his new towns but he did establish a template that, after his death, began to gain significant momentum—not only at home but abroad too. It turned out that his had been a vision just a little too ahead of its time. By the mid-twentieth century his philosophy had won an international audience. Garden cities that exhibited clear signs of his influence appeared throughout the United States, Canada, South America, Australia, and South Africa. There were also echoes in the redevelopments of post-colonial super-cities, including New Delhi. That a layman could have such a profound influence on urban development across the globe is little short of astonishing. Yet Howard communicated his vision with such clarity and passion, backing up his words with deeds, that it is perhaps not so surprising after all. In 1964 a memorial plaque erected in his honor at Welwyn stated: "His vision and practical idealism profoundly affected town planning throughout the world." He could not have hoped for more.

MODERN HOMES

The Sunnyside neighbourhood in Queens, New York, is testament to Howard's enduring impact. As the Big Apple struggled to find suitable housing for its booming population in the early twentieth century, three leading architects—Marjorie Sewell Cautley, Clarence Stein, and Henry Wright—laid out plans for the development, which provided high-quality garden homes for families along with ample public green spaces. The 77-acre area underwent its facelift between 1924 and 1928. It was the first such "garden city" development in the country and its importance was recognized in 1984 when Sunnyside was listed on the National Register of Historic Places. Today, it continues to support a population of almost 30,000.

STRATEGY ANALYSIS

STRATEGY TYPE: *Innovative*
KEY STRATEGY: *Developing and implementing a pioneering practical solution to answer the social problems he saw*
OUTCOME: *A new approach to urban planning.*
ALSO USED BY: *Architect Walter Burley Griffin in Canberra, 1910s-20s, and Cautley, Stein, and Wright in New York, 1924-28.*

31

FIGHT FOR YOUR RIGHTS

EMMELINE PANKHURST DECIDED IT WAS TIME TO STOP PLAYING NICE IN THE STRUGGLE FOR EQUAL RIGHTS

KEY PLAYER: *Emmeline Pankhurst (1858-1928)*
NATIONALITY: *British*
STRATEGY IMPLEMENTED: *1903-28*
CONTEXT: *At a time when women were expected to do everything—even protest—with grace and decorum, Pankhurst realized such tactics were ineffective in furthering women's rights. Instead, she promoted militancy*

It was the crusade to secure all adult women the right to vote that dominated Pankhurst's life. Having tried to campaign peacefully through traditional political channels, she grew increasingly frustrated with her lack of progress. So in 1903 she established the Women's Social and Political Union (WSPU), whose motto was "Deeds, not words." Pankhurst championed a new, aggressive form of protest that included breaking the law.

Pankhurst was born in 1858 to progressive parents who were active social campaigners. However, she soon noticed that there were vastly differing expectations for herself and her brother. She struggled to reconcile her parents' apparently liberal attitudes with their expectation that she should become a good, middle-class homemaker. When she was fourteen she attended a life-changing talk by Lydia Becker, a leading women's campaigner of the day. At the time, serious campaigning for votes for women was barely a decade old but Emmeline was soon wedded to the cause. As she would later write: "Women had always fought for men, and for their children. Now they are ready to fight for their own human rights."

Emmeline nonetheless make a good marriage: To a lawyer who was one of the people responsible for drafting the first women's enfranchisement bill to go to a parliamentary vote. It was a marriage that combined domestic contentment with shared political ideals. Emmeline, with the support of her husband, actively campaigned for the female vote. She forged ties with the Independent Labour Party (ILP), the political organization that seemed best placed to move forward the cause of women. However, when she was refused membership of a branch of the ILP on the grounds of her gender, she decided enough was enough. Sensing that she could never achieve her ends by working within a political system naturally skewed against women, she determined to adopt a more direct approach.

Pankhurst viewed arrest as a means of publicizing her cause. Here she is being led away in 1914 after trying to accost King George V.

1858

Emmeline Pankhurst is born in Manchester, England.

1866

MP John Stuart Mills unsuccessfully attempts to have the Reform Act amended to give the vote to both genders.

1872

Pankhurst attends a meeting at which prominent women's activist, Lydia Becker, leaves a lasting impression.

1903

The Women's Social and Political Union is established.

1905

The Women's Enfranchisement Bill does not make it through Parliament. Pankhurst decides to pursue a more militant course. She is arrested and serves the first of many stints in prison.

1908

The WSPU's window-smashing campaign begins.

1910

After clashing with police in Parliament Square, Pankhurst in one of several WSPU members arrested.

1913

The government passes the "Cat and Mouse Act." In June, Suffragette Emily Davison dies when she jumps in front of King George V's horse during the Epsom Derby race. There is a general upsurge in suffragette militancy.

1914

The onset of World War I sees Pankhurst draw back from militancy.

1918

The Representation of the People Act extends the vote to women over 30.

1928

Pankhurst dies on June 14. A few weeks later the Equal Franchise Act grants women the vote on the same basis as men.

HITTING WHERE IT HURTS

In 1903 Pankhurst established the WSPU—and made sure that membership was exclusively for women. Despite the membership requirements, she was quick to emphasize that this was not an organization fighting against men, but one fighting for women. Pankhurst ensured that the WSPU maintained ties with the ILP in the hope that the two organizations could mutually benefit each other.

To begin with, the WSPU focused on peaceful protests. Members spread the word of their campaign in public forums, wrote letters to the press, and petitioned MPs for change. However, the 1905 campaign by some MPs to call time on a women's enfranchisement bill through filibustering incensed Pankhurst and spurred her on to a radical new approach. Deciding that playing by the book was getting her organization nowhere, she decided the time had come to follow a more militant agenda.

The first great act of defiance came shortly afterward when Pankhurst's daughter, Christabel, and another WSPU colleague were arrested after disrupting a meeting of the Liberal Party, demanding of the candidate whether his Party would extend the franchise and refusing to leave when asked. The two women both served short prison sentences. The WSPU had made a bold statement: It would break the law in pursuit of its aims.

A RADICAL NEW DIRECTION

Christabel proved a great influence on her mother in making the WSPU more radical. It continued with its program of civil disobedience, but adopted increasingly aggressive tactics to complement this approach. In 1908 the Suffragettes of the WSPU began to break windows as a sign of protest, with Pankhurst describing "the broken window pane" as the "most valuable argument in modern politics." As she put it: "There is something that government cares for more than human life, and that is the security of property, and so it is through property that we shall strike the enemy." In addition, WSPU members took to systematically disrupting public meetings and even to chaining themselves to the Ladies Gallery at the Houses of Parliament. Another campaign focused on using small incendiary devices to destroy letter boxes and their contents. There was inevitably some "collateral damage," with innocent individuals occasionally receiving minor injuries as a result of these gestures. But the emphasis was always on violence against property and not against people. The WSPU always practiced civil disobedience rather than terrorism. The real aim was to commit crimes (and to be arrested for doing such) in order to bring publicity to the cause of women's suffrage.

▲ Pankhurst's doctrine soon spread. Pictured here are suffragettes being accompanied by police from New York's City Hall.

It was to Pankhurst's great chagrin that arrested suffragettes were treated as common criminals and not the political prisoners she believed them to be. She therefore came to champion the hunger strike as another weapon in the WSPU arsenal and a highly effective means of maintaining publicity even when behind bars. It was grueling on the women who put themselves through the ordeal but it ultimately won them much respect. When the government responded in 1913 with the heavy-handed "Cat and Mouse Act" (which allowed fasting prisoners to be freed until they had regained sufficient strength to be re-imprisoned for the remainder of their sentence), the Suffragettes had a public relations triumph.

ADAPTING TO CHANGING CIRCUMSTANCES

1913 saw an upsurge in WSPU militancy after a new suffrage bill was dropped from the parliamentary session. Members continued their window-breaking program but also cut telegraph lines and perpetrated bomb and arson attacks. Meanwhile, in June that year, Emily Davison achieved notoriety by throwing herself in front of the King's horse at the Epsom

HUNGRY FOR CHANGE

Pankhurst originated a blend of civil disobedience, militancy, and self-sacrifice that has been replicated by civil rights activists around the world. Particularly impactful was her adoption of the hunger strike as a political weapon. It is an act of civil disobedience that leaves the authorities with a conundrum—either to leave the striker to their fate or to force-feed them. Either action places them in the position of brutalizer, so reducing their moral authority. It is a strategy that subsequent political protestors have embraced, from Irish republicans to Cuban dissidents and Gandhi in India.

Derby, dying in the process. Yet just as Suffragette militancy was reaching a crescendo, World War I arrived and Pankhurst called on her members to cease violent tactics in order to put all their energies into the war effort.

Here she showed remarkable foresight. The war created myriad new roles for women and few could ignore their contribution to ultimate victory. In 1918 the government at last granted women the vote (to those over 30 at least). A year later, Nancy Astor became the first female MP and in 1928 women were given the same voting rights as men. Just a few weeks before that legislation was passed, Pankhurst died, perhaps content her life's work was done. It had not always been pretty, but she had refused the demand to be lady-like, instead adopting militant tactics in pursuit of her rights as a woman.

FAR-REACHING IMPACT

It was an approach that had international ramifications too. In particular, Pankhurst was a profound influence on the suffrage movement in the United States. Not only did she lecture on several occasions there, but several of its leading lights also spent time campaigning with her in Britain. Perhaps most important of these were Alice Paul (1885–1997) and Lucy Burns (1879–1966). In 1910 Paul and Burns, disillusioned with the direction being taken by the National American Woman Suffrage Association, set up the rival National Woman's Party (NWP), adopting many of the militant strategies developed by Pankhurst. In 1917 the NWP became the first organisation to picket the White House, when the "Silent Sentinels," as the protestors became known, were arrested on charges of obstructing traffic. It was an action that brought renewed national attention to their cause. In October that year, Paul, Burns, and a number of fellow protestors received lengthy sentences to be served at the Occoquan Workhouse in Virginia. There the women were exposed to harsh conditions, including beatings. Appalled at the treatment the women had received, public opinion decisively turned in their favor. After being blocked by the Senate in 1918 and 1919, the Nineteenth Amendment to the Constitution was passed in 1920, granting women the vote.

It was a momentous change in no small part thanks to Pankhurst, who had refused to play by the rules that her oppressors had tried to impose. Her adoption of militant action was truly shocking for a society still governed by the polite social mores of the Victorian age. As well as garnering support by her willingness to put herself in danger, perhaps her greatest achievement was to jolt the patriarchal powers-that-be out of their complacency, forcing them not merely to take the suffrage movement seriously but to recognize that they were fighting a losing battle.

STRATEGY ANALYSIS

STRATEGY TYPE: *Strategy of attack*
KEY STRATEGY: *Employing direct action and civil disobedience in pursuit of female suffrage*
OUTCOME: *Votes for Women*
ALSO USED BY: *Rosa Parks, on a bus in Montgomery, 1955, and Malala Yousafzai, 2012-.*

32 BREAK IT DOWN

HENRY FORD CREATED A CAR FOR THE MASSES AND A REVOLUTIONARY NEW WAY TO PRODUCE IT

KEY PLAYER: *Henry Ford (1863-1947)*
NATIONALITY: *American*
STRATEGY IMPLEMENTED: *1913*
CONTEXT: *Having vowed to create a car cheap enough for mass ownership, Ford and his team spent five years perfecting the moving assembly line*

When the age of the motorcar began in the late-nineteenth century, it was exclusively a rich man's game. However, in America Henry Ford was determined to make the automobile an object to which ordinary people could aspire. To this end he created the landmark Model T car, which dominated the market for decades. But in order to keep the price down, Ford required a new method of manufacturing.

Ford entered the motor industry in 1899 but his company went bankrupt within a year. It was only at the third attempt (under the guise of the Ford Motor Company) that he started to have success. Introducing the Model A in 1903, it was soon one of the best-selling cars in the country. Nonetheless, it was still relatively expensive, with a team of skilled craftsmen taking upward of twelve hours to produce a single vehicle. Ford hungered for a car that the ordinary man in the street could afford—in his own words, "motor cars for the multitude."

He knew that the secret was to come up with a model that did without some of the style and luxuriousness demanded by the current market. He decided to concentrate instead on a car that was simple but reliable. The time had come to change the automobile from a status symbol into something eminently practical and, dare it be said, rather humble. So he surrounded himself with the best engineers he could find and in 1904 began work on what would become the Model T.

MOTORING FOR THE MASSES

In the meantime, the Ford Motor Company unleashed on the world the Model N. It did well and Ford's good name continued to grow. However, no-one would be quite ready for the ground-breaking Model T. After four arduous years of development, Ford and his team introduced it to the market in 1908. It came with a price tag of US$825—still a significant outlay for the time but less than its rivals. Sales were brisk from the outset.

Simplification was key to the lower price, although that did not mean unduly compromising on the mechanics. However cheap a car was, nobody would want it if it didn't work very well. Instead, design features were kept basic and the finish was

TIME LINE

1863
Henry Ford is born in Michigan on July 30.

1891
He starts working for the Edison Illuminating Company.

1899
He founds the Detroit Automobile Company.

1900
It goes bankrupt.

1901
He re-enters the market with the Henry Ford Company.

1903
After leaving following a fall-out with shareholders, he founds the Ford Motor Company. The Model A is its first car.

1908
Production begins of the Model T.

1910
The Highland Park factory opens in Michigan.

1913
Model T is produced on a moving assembly line for the first time at Ford's custom-designed Highland Park plant.

1917
Work begins on Ford's River Rouge Plant, which becomes the world's biggest industrial complex.

1921
Ford produces over one million cars in a year for the first time.

1927
Model T production stops after over 15 million models have been sold.

1942
Ford's Willow Run plant begins producing the B-24 Liberator Bomber, the first mass-production aeroplane.

1947
Henry Ford dies on April 7 at Fair Lane, Dearborn, Michigan.

rudimentary when compared to, say, the flamboyance of a Rolls-Royce. Ford was after those purchasers who wanted to get from A to B by a means other than foot, train, or horse and cart. Such people were largely unconcerned with the finer details of, for instance, the upholstery they were sat upon.

His attitude in this respect is perhaps best illustrated by his oft-quoted observation: "Any customer can have a car painted any color that he wants so long as it's black." In fact, the early Model Ts were available in a choice of colors but black paint was quicker drying and cheaper than the alternatives, so to streamline operations he insisted on a reduced color palette. Such tweaks saw the price of the Model T tumble. By 1912 it was about a third cheaper than when it was introduced and by 1922 you could buy a model for under US$300. By 1914, Ford cars accounted for more than half of all the US market. As he had hoped, he had brought motoring to the mass market.

THE MOVING ASSEMBLY LINE
Indubitably, the crucial factor in making the Model T affordable was the introduction of the moving assembly line. Ford cannot claim credit as its inventor but he was the man who introduced it to mainstream industry, so changing the face of manufacturing forever. It is a production method that was taken up around the world for virtually every consumer good you can think of.

Until Ford adopted it for his own purposes, the assembly line had been used in industries based on fairly simple production processes. For instance, mills, breweries, and bakeries all utilized the method. But no-one had ever dared try something as complicated as building a car in this manner. However, Ford could

FAMOUS FORD CARS

Top speed
30 mph
(48 km/h)

$750

**Model A,
1903-1905**

Top speed
42 mph
(68 km/h)

$825

**Model T,
1908-1927**

Top speed
120 mph
(193 km/h)

$2,695

**Thunderbird model,
1955-1977**

Top speed
94 mph
(151 km/h)

$2,368

**Mustang,
1964**

Top speed
106 mph
(171 km/h)

$13,995

**Ford Focus,
1998-2001**

see no reason why not. Again, he employed a talented set of underlings to work with him on honing a system and allowed himself the time to get it right. In the event, it took more than five years.

Where teams of skilled laborers had hitherto worked upon a single car, Ford wanted a system where the car moved logically from one individual to another, each trained in just one aspect of the manufacture. Construction would start with the components of the engine and end with the body of the car being attached to the chassis. In the end, the Ford team identified 84 distinct production processes. Ford then employed motion-study experts to refine each process, making it as quick and simple to execute as possible. In addition, he developed machinery that could speedily produce components.

Initially, the car was moved from one process to the next by a system of ropes and pulleys operated at specific lengths and time delays to ensure each stage went smoothly. In time Ford built a plant at Highland Park especially designed to accommodate the production line system, including a power-driven assembly line that moved at six feet per minute. His innovation reduced the time taken to produce a car from over 12 hours to nearer two-and-a-half.

There were downsides for employees, though. Such automated work was repetitive, boring, and arduous. This was reflected in a rapid turnover of staff (at one stage, Ford employed 53,000 people a year to fill 14,000 posts). His response was to double wages (to US$5 per day in the first instance), introducing a model of mass production and high wages that came to be known as Fordism.

MOTOR GIANTS

Ford introduced the moving assembly line on December 1 1913 and it fueled the ongoing phenomenal success of the Model T. By the time it ceased production in 1927, over 15 million vehicles had been produced and sold. Even more importantly, industry had been changed forever.

Ford's production model also proved invaluable to the United States in World War II. Though Ford himself was a dedicated pacifist, following the attack on Pearl Harbor in 1941 Ford Motor Company became one of the key US military contractors. The company supplied airplanes, engines, jeeps, and tanks. To produce the B-24 Liberator bombers Ford had a mile-long assembly line built at the Willow Run plant, Dearborn, Michigan. The assembly line was able to produce bombers at the rate of one plane per hour and, by the end of the war, the company had built 86,865 complete aircraft.

The ground-breaking assembly line at Ford's Highland Park works, Michigan, that paved the way for a new industrial age.

Henry Ford, left, with Major Henry Cunningham leaving the White House. Ford was instrumental to aviation in World War II.

In the motoring industry, Ford's initiative was the driving force behind the emergence of the United States as the world's leading car manufacturer, a crown it retained until Japan overtook it in the 1980s. Today, America remains the second-largest automobile manufacturer, with some eight–ten million models rolling off its production lines annually. In 1970, at the industry's peak, that figure had been close to 15 million. Ford, Chrysler, and General Motors were the largest of the homegrown producers and, as of 2012, Ford still provided jobs for some 80,000 Americans.

CHANGING INDUSTRY

It is difficult to overestimate the impact Ford's innovations had on society in the twentieth century and through to the present day. His influence extends far beyond simply bringing motoring to the masses. His development of the assembly line came to be adopted in virtually every manufacturing process, from refrigerators and clothing to fast food. Indeed, there is a chance that World War II may have played out differently if the United States had not been able to supply its allies with plentiful materials, produced according to Ford's assembly line method. Furthermore, the creation of high-wage, low-skilled factory jobs spurred the movement of large numbers of people from the countryside into cities, promoted social mobility, and even fueled patterns of international migration. Ford changed the very face of the world we live in.

STRATEGY ANALYSIS

STRATEGY TYPE: *Innovative*
KEY STRATEGY: *Ford introduces the moving assembly line*
OUTCOME: *A manufacturing revolution*
ALSO USED BY: *International armaments factories during the Second World War, and General Motors, who introduced the robotic arm to the assembly line in 1961.*

KEEP AHEAD OF THE CURVE

BY DESIGNING FOR THE MODERN WOMAN **COCO CHANEL** TURNED THE FASHION WORLD ON ITS HEAD

KEY PLAYER: *Coco Chanel (1883-1971)*
NATIONALITY: *French*
STRATEGY IMPLEMENTED: *1913-71*
CONTEXT: *Chanel turns her back on the fussy and uncomfortable clothes in the Victorian and Edwardian age, designing clothes to suit the needs of the modern woman*

When *Time* magazine named its hundred most influential people of the twentieth century, there was only one name from the world of fashion: Coco Chanel. The diminutive French designer is a legendary figure, whose designs, which focused on simplicity and wearability, continue to inform couture to the present day. She is an object lesson in adapting to the evolving needs of the market.

Coco Chanel's start in life was not promising, but her visionary skills as a designer of women's fashion would bring her wealth, fame, and legendary status. She spent a lifetime creating clothes that women actually wanted to wear, rather than ones into which they were forced to cram themselves in the interests of achieving a male-imposed image of femininity. Her tough beginnings doubtless contributed to giving her the fierce determination she needed to challenge the fashion status quo. The world and the role of women within it was changing, she saw, and she was intent on being the one to meet its demands.

Gabrielle Bonheur Chanel was born in 1883, the daughter of a laundrywoman and street hawker. When she was twelve her mother died and she spent much of the next few years in a convent, where she learned to sew. From there she found work as a seamstress, altering clothes so that women could achieve the unearthly silhouette that had been demanded of them for so long. This was very much still the age of corsets and bustles.

But where women once quietly accepted their lot, Chanel could sense change in the air. Women were beginning to have a life outside the home. Many had careers of their own, and vastly more would join their ranks during and after World War I. They wanted clothes that were at once esthetically pleasing, comfortable, and practical. Yet no-one in the fashion world was reflecting this fundamental change in women's lives. So Chanel set out to do it herself and became a trailblazer for every designer since.

The impeccably stylish Coco Chanel, seen here with Duke Laurino of Rome. Despite her humble birth, Chanel was at ease among the rich and powerful. ▶

TIME LINE

1883
Gabrielle Bonheur "Coco" Chanel is born on August 19.

1895
Her mother dies. She subsequently lives in a convent where she learns to sew.

1910
Chanel opens her first shop, exclusively selling hats, in Paris.

1913
She opens the first of her own general fashion shops, in Deauville.

1915
Her second shop opens for business, this time in Biarritz.

1921
The legendary Chanel No. 5 perfume is launched.

1923
She debuts the "Chanel suit" to journalists.

1924
A Chanel range makes costume jewelry truly fashionable for the first time.

1925
She debuts the cardigan jacket.

1926
Her famous "little black dress" hits the catwalks.

1939
Chanel closes her shops, claiming that war offers "no time for fashion." She spends most of the war based at the Ritz Hotel in Paris.

1945–53
She lives in effective exile in Lausanne.

1954
Chanel relaunches her career after a 15-year hiatus. Soon re-establishing herself as a giant of the industry.

1971
Chanel dies in Paris on January 10.

MONEY TALKS

While Chanel did not lack for vision and drive, she was short of cash to start a business. But her difficult childhood had instilled in her both fight and pragmatism. Even as she dreamed of changing the world of fashion, she knew she could not do it without money in the bank. Chanel knew she had the power to captivate men from all ranks. Among them was Étienne Balsan, a textiles heir who took her as his lover. In 1910 she was happy to let him bankroll her first serious fashion venture, a milliners outfit named Chanel Modes. The foundations of her future empire had been set in place.

By then she was also engaged in an affair with Balsan's friend, a rich Englishman called Arthur Capel, who in 1913 financed her first general fashion shop, in the coastal town of Deauville. A second branch, in Biarritz, opened two years later. Against the odds Chanel

TREND FORECAST

If Chanel changed fashion forever, her ability to sense a changing market is an example to entrepreneurs in all sectors. Take, for instance, one of the great innovators of the modern technological age, Steve Jobs. Just as Coco saw that women needed a new style of clothing at a time when design had largely stagnated, Jobs also had an unerring eye for the changing landscape of technology. The products he introduced to the market stand as both design classics and commercial smashes—Steve Jobs: The Chanel of the Gizmo Age.

had established a fashion chain and leveraged her social contacts to build a roster of well-connected clients. Always alert to a marketing opportunity, she even recruited a couple of youthful, glamorous relatives to parade about Deauville in her garments. So spectacular were her creations that the Chanel boutique was soon in profit. In fact, within a couple of years she was able to return Capel's "seed money." She may have needed a helping hand to get started, but she was determined to make the business work on her own terms.

DARLING OF PARIS

By 1918, Chanel was able to fund a move to rue Cambon in Paris's fashion heartland. Within a decade, she owned a large stretch of the street. Among the many changes wrought by World War I, the role of women in society had been utterly changed. It was now quite normal for women to have jobs and to pursue careers. Chanel was at the forefront of dressing them for their new lifestyles. She offered elegant but practical cardigan jackets and trenchcoats, loose-fitting jumpers, and pleated skirts, utilizing revolutionary new materials like jersey fabric, previously only used for underwear. In an age of emerging female liberation, she provided clothes that physically liberated women.

Chanel was also a genius at using her exotic and wealthy social circle to create priceless publicity. She mixed with artists, entertainers, socialites, and royalty. At one stage, she was rumored to be about to marry the fabulously wealthy Duke of Westminster, only to later explain her refusal thus: "There have been several duchesses of Westminster. There is only one Chanel." All the while, she was able to make sure that her clothes were seen on all the best people at all the best places. Having become the fashion queen of Europe, she even took her skills to Hollywood, designing wardrobes for several movies. So Chanel developed into one of the great self-publicists of her age.

It would be remiss to ignore the fact that Chanel's single-mindedness had its dark side too. She could be tough on her workforce and her reputation took a serious knock when she took a Nazi officer as her lover during Germany's occupation of France. Nonetheless, today many of her creations are familiar to those even with only the most passing interest in couture. The Chanel suit, the "little black dress," and the Chanel bag are all highly treasured and much imitated—famous for their simple and utilitarian yet chic design. Coupling creative vision with drive and business acumen, she changed the way women dressed to meet the challenges of the modern world. All those who have followed in her footsteps, from Mary Quant to Stella McCartney and Karl Lagerfeld, owe Coco an enormous debt of gratitude for her trailblazing.

STRATEGY ANALYSIS

STRATEGY TYPE: *Innovative*
KEY STRATEGY: *Satisfying the demands of a new age*
OUTCOME: *Creation of the most famous fashion house in history*
ALSO USED BY: *Allen Lane, Penguin Books, 1934, and Steve Jobs, 1974–2011.*

34 THE WOLF IN SHEEP'S CLOTHING

ARMED SHIPS DISGUISED AS MERCHANT VESSELS WERE DEPLOYED TO COUNTER THE U-BOAT THREAT IN WORLD WAR I

KEY PLAYER: *The Royal Navy*
NATIONALITY: *British*
STRATEGY IMPLEMENTED:
1915-18
CONTEXT: *All the combatants in World War I knew that victory would be secured by the side that best marshaled its resources. When Germany unleashed its U-boats (armed submarines) against Allied merchant shipping, the Allies desperately searched for ways to protect its sea routes*

Q-ships were vessels disguised specifically to trap German U-boats. Sometimes also known as Special Service Ships or Mystery Ships, they were heavily disguised to appear easy prey, they sailed in the hope of inducing U-boats to the surface to launch an attack. Behind their apparently vulnerable exteriors, the Q-boat were equipped with weaponry that then pounded their unsuspecting assailants.

Germany wished nothing less than to starve Britain out of the war and by 1915 its efforts at cutting off Atlantic supply routes were proving highly effective. The Germans' most potent weapon was the U-boat, which could stalk its target unseen before launching a devastating torpedo attack. In one month alone, almost 900,000 tonnes of Allied shipping was sent to the bottom of the ocean. The British adopted all sorts of tactics to counter the threat, including the highly effective convoy system in which merchant ships traveled together for mutual protection, usually with some form of armed guard. But even more innovative was the Q-ship initiative, which updated the Trojan horse strategy (see page 10) for a modern warfare context.

The basic idea was elegantly simple. Take the most innocuous-looking merchant ships you can find (from trawlers and cargo ships to schooners and steamers) and heavily arm them. Guns were hidden behind lifeboats and in fake funnels, or were painted to camouflage them. It was hoped that the ship would appear so harmless that U-boat captains hungry to up their strike-rates would be unable to resist launching an attack. Furthermore, because their prey appeared defenseless and often far from robust, German commanders would opt not to waste their valuable torpedoes but would instead come to the surface to attack. Crucially, a U-boat was at its most vulnerable when on the surface, where it could be downed by gunfire or even rammed. A widely-adopted strategy the Q-boats became a potent weapon in the Allied armory against the U-boat threat.

THE ELEMENT OF SURPRISE

The crews of the Q-boats were well trained and kept up their ruse until the last moment. Often they would make as if they were abandoning ship to ensure the foe was kept off-

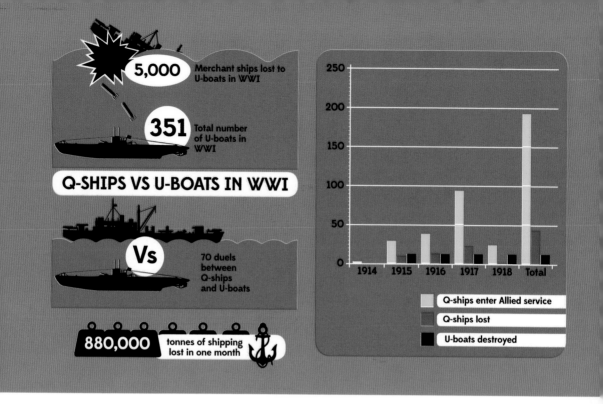

5,000 Merchant ships lost to U-boats in WWI

351 Total number of U-boats in WWI

Q-SHIPS VS U-BOATS IN WWI

Vs 70 duels between Q-ships and U-boats

880,000 tonnes of shipping lost in one month

Q-ships enter Allied service

Q-ships lost

U-boats destroyed

guard. Furthermore, their vessels routinely carried cargoes such as balsa wood or cork so that even if they received a direct hit, they had a reasonable chance of staying afloat long enough to inflict damage. Once a U-boat had surrendered the protection offered by complete submergence, the Q-boat teams swung into action, stripping away whatever casings were hiding their armaments before unleashing a shock attack on the U-boat.

In such a way, the Allies hit upon a method that allowed a tiny, old fishing trawler to sink a state-of-the-art German sub. It was a case of David and Goliath revisited (see page 14). Alternatively, if a Q-ship itself could not down the enemy, it might buy time and opportunity for Allied naval vessels to come in and make the kill. Such was the case with the first successful Q-boat encounter, which occurred off the Scottish coast in June 1915 when a British submarine worked in tandem with a Q-ship to sink a U-boat. The following month came the first successful strike by an unassisted Q-boat. What started as an audacious attempt at misdirection undertaken in hope rather than expectation was shown to be a genuinely effective military strategy.

By the end of 1915, 29 Q-boats had entered service, destroying two U-boats that year for the cost of nine decoy boats. But their job only got harder when the Germans introduced a policy of unrestricted submarine warfare, which effectively meant merchant shipping was fair game and that their crews did not have to be given time to abandon ship before an attack was launched. Furthermore, U-boat commanders naturally became more wary of apparently tame merchant vessels after news of the first few Q-boat attacks spread. Q-boat operations were officially secret but it is thought that by the end of the war, the British had used over 350 such vessels, losing around 60 in the process of destroying 15 German submarines. The plucky little decoy boats accounted for around 10 percent of all U-boat sinkings, an undeniably important contribution to the war effort.

TIME LINE

IN DISGUISE

The art of disguise in warfare, begun by the Trojan horse and perpetuated by Q-ships, continues in the modern era. Take, for instance, the British stage magician Jasper Maskelyne who, according to his memoirs, volunteered his service as an illusionist during World War II, becoming head of a unit made up of assorted tricksters, con-men, and technical experts that became known as the Magic Gang. They specialized in creating epic deceptions to confuse the enemy, from making maps disguised as playing cards to persuading German intelligence that a double-agent had blown up a British military installation (he hadn't) to, allegedly, creating a dummy army that fooled Germany's Erwin Rommel. Devoted to making things appear other than they really were, Maskelyne would no doubt have approved of the Q-ships.

GETTING INSIDE THE ENEMY'S HEAD

Given the nature of the strategy, the Q-boats were most effective when they could exploit the element of surprise. As the war went on and the Germans got wise to the tactic, the Q-boats struggled to make the same impact and by the end of 1917 were reaching the end of their usefulness. However, even more important than the number of U-boats they took out of action was their role in turning the tide against the U-boats at a moment when they seemed almost unstoppable. Where German captains had previously enjoyed their status of silent, unseen ocean killers, the Q-boats made them nervous. No longer could they launch strikes with virtually no fear of reprisal. The rules of engagement had been changed in the favor of the Allies.

TURNING THE TABLES: THE "PRIZE" HOISTING THE WHITE ENSIGN AND OPENING FIRE ON THE U-BOAT AT SHORT RANGE.

▲ *On April 30 1917, British Q-ship, HMS Prize, feigned panic before unleashing a deadly counter-attack against German U-boat 93.*

When Allied shipping faced similar threats in World War II, the navies of the United Kingdom and the United States both introduced new fleets of Q-ships. However, time had moved on and just as their effectiveness waned as World War I progressed, this time round they struggled to make any inroads. Nonetheless, their reintroduction goes to show that those who had seen at first hand their operations from 1915 until 1918 did not forget the vital contribution these little boats had made to countering what had seemed an overwhelming threat. Indeed, in more recent years it has even been suggested that the Q-ship tactic might be adapted to counter the thoroughly modern threat of piracy that has spread such fear and wreaked economic havoc in the waters around Somalia and adjoining countries.

STRATEGY ANALYSIS

STRATEGY TYPE: *Tactical deception*
KEY STRATEGY: *Apparently easy target shipping was used to induce U-boat attacks, only for the submarines to face a surprise armed onslaught*
OUTCOME: *Helped stem the U-boat peril*
ALSO USED BY: *Trojan horse, between the eleventh and fourteenth centuries, and the Allied forces, Operation Bodyguard, 1944.*

35 STRONG LEADERSHIP

COMMITTED TO BEING ONLY THE BEST BARON VON RICHTHOFEN LED WORLD WAR I'S MOST FEARED FLYING UNIT

KEY PLAYER: *Manfred von Richthofen (1892-1918)*
NATIONALITY: *German*
STRATEGY IMPLEMENTED: *1917-18*
CONTEXT: *Von Richthofen proved himself a master fighter pilot in World War I and in 1917 took command of a crack squadron that he molded in his own image*

World War I was the first conflict in which aerial power played a serious role and, to a large extent, pilots and their commanders made up the rules as they went along. The German Manfred von Richthofen was not only blessed with a natural aptitude for flying but displayed great personal bravery and a cold-blooded desire to down his opponents. It made him the most feared pilot in the war, while the squadron he commanded set the benchmark for all others as a rapid-response special operations unit.

THE HUNTER AND THE HUNTED

In August 1916 Oswald Boelcke signed up von Richthofen to his new fighter squadron, Jagdstaffel 2 (known as Jasta 2). His first dogfight came over Cambrai in France on September 17 and he absorbed all the lessons he could from the skilled Boelcke. When Boelcke died in combat at the end of October 1916 in front of von Richthofen, it must have been a truly sobering experience but he made sure to remember the key tenets his commander had told him. Principal among these was the idea that a good fighter pilot was not the one who could do the most spectacular tricks. While he had the ability to throw his plane around the sky with the best of them, von Richthofen developed into a reasonably conservative flyer, avoiding unnecessary risk wherever possible.

Instead, he took a sanguine, tactical approach. He liked to attack from above and strove to keep the sun behind him at the crucial moment. He also sought protection from his fellow pilots, urging them to cover his tail and flanks as he launched an assault. Similarly, he would provide the cover for them when they needed it. As a young boy, he had loved hunting, tracking game in the forests of his native Silesia and displaying his hunting trophies with pride. He used similar tactics now, tracking his prey with patience, waiting for the perfect opportunity to strike. For each plane he bested in a dogfight, he had a small silver cup commissioned and inscribed with the details of the battle—each a symbol of the pride he took in his work.

By early November 1916 he had reached the milestone 10 "scores." Later that month he downed arguably the most prestigious opponent of his career, Lanoe George Hawker (known as "the British Boelcke"). It was around this time that he started to paint his

plane red, an audacious gesture that earned him the moniker of the "Red Baron." In January 1917 he was given command of his own squadron, Jasta 11. The hotshot pilot now became a true leader of men.

CIRCUS RINGLEADER

The Red Baron instilled in his men the same discipline he himself demonstrated. Each member was expected to read up on the latest tactics and to approach each dogfight like a scientist, considering the best angles of attack, optimum flying speed, and precise weapons requirement. He also demanded utter ruthlessness. If fighting a single-seater aircraft, aim for the man and be sure to hit him. If it was a double-seater, focus on the observer first (who, as he well knew, had the best chance of firing his weapon at you) and then the pilot. Where viable, no-one should be allowed to emerge from the wreckage.

Von Richthofen was not known for his warmth by his men. He was cold and aloof yet this distance seems to have helped ensure their respect. They knew he practiced exactly what he preached as they carried out their grim work and so they were prepared to follow him to the ends of the earth. In April 1917 ("Bloody April" as it became known), Jasta 11 shot down no fewer than 89 aircraft. In June 1917 Jasta 11 joined with three other squadrons to form Jagdgeschwader 1 (JG1), under the Red Baron's command.

TIME LINE

1892
Manfred von Richthofen is born near Breslau in Germany on May 2.

1911
Von Richthofen enrols as a cavalry officer.

1914
World War I breaks out in August. Von Richthofen is variously posted on the Western Front and in Russia in its early months.

1915
He transfers to the Fliegertruppe (Air Service), working as an observer before beginning training as a pilot.

1916
In September he gets his first "score" of the war when he shoots down an Allied plane.

January 1917
Given command of his own squadron. In the same month he shoots down his eighteenth plane and receives "the Blue Max," Prussia's highest military honor.

June–July 1917
Von Richthofen forms the so-called Flying Circus. In July he is shot down and seriously wounded but returns to action within a few weeks.

November 1917
The Flying Circus is scrambled from Ypres to counter British offensive maneuvers at Cambrai.

April 1918
Von Richthofen's plane is shot down in France and he dies in the crash. He is buried with full military honors. Under Hauptmann Wilhelm Reinhard, the Flying Circus goes on to win its 300th victory in May and its 500th victory follows in July.

November 1918
The Circus retires as the war ends. It has destroyed almost 650 Allied aircraft, losing 52 pilots in the process, with a further 67 wounded.

SPECIAL FORCES

Von Richthofen could look to many forebears who like him led by example, from Julius Caesar and Joan of Arc to Lord Nelson and Napoleon (see pages 38, 62, 91, and 96). However, perhaps his greatest long-term achievement was to establish the Flying Circus as the modern model for special operations units. He brought together the very best fighter pilots available to create a force that was skilled, reliable, and clinical. Always on-call and prepared to step into front-line action at short notice wherever it was most needed, the Flying Circus created a template that such revered organizations as the British SAS and the American Navy SEALs would follow later in the century.

Before long, it was known as the Flying Circus, reflecting not only the bold colors of its aircraft and the acrobatic skills of its pilots, but also its ability to travel quickly to wherever its services were demanded. The unit became renowned for its ability to pitch a makeshift camp on a spare patch of airfield in record time. Furthermore, by rapidly countering Allied offensives at disparate locations, time and again it brought the German forces extra time and room for maneuver. In November, for instance, the Flying Circus sped from Ypres to Cambrai on the Western Front, bringing some stability just as it seemed British forces were about to cut loose. Boasting many of Germany's elite pilots, the Flying Circus came to epitomize its leader's values and wreaked havoc against its enemies.

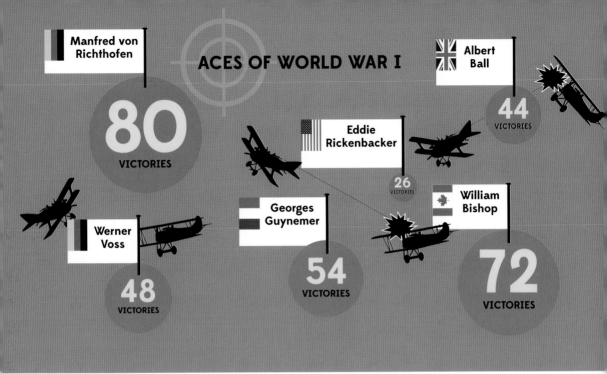

ACES OF WORLD WAR I

Manfred von Richthofen

80
VICTORIES

Albert Ball

44
VICTORIES

Eddie Rickenbacker

26
VICTORIES

William Bishop

72
VICTORIES

Werner Voss

48
VICTORIES

Georges Guynemer

54
VICTORIES

LEGEND OF THE SKIES

The Red Baron was himself shot down in July 1917 and suffered a serious head injury but he quickly returned to active service. However, on April 21 1918, he was felled again over the skies of France and this time did not survive. He was just 25 but was already a legend, his enemies even granting him full military honors. At the time of his death, he was credited with 80 scores, the highest total of anyone in World War I. His was a gory business, but combining skill, bravery, and desire for victory he became a true leader of men and even won the grudging respect of those he sought to kill. Meanwhile, his Flying Circus carried on to the end of the war, claiming hundreds of vital "scores" and bolstering the front line wherever it was needed.

STRATEGY ANALYSIS

STRATEGY TYPE: *Leadership*
KEY STRATEGY: *Developing a rapid-response squadron made up of the finest pilots and characterized by a ruthless will to win*
OUTCOME: *The most efficient aerial killing-machine of the age*
ALSO USED BY: *Shayetet 13, the Israeli Navy's special forces; British SAS; and US Navy SEALs..*

CONTROL THE MESSAGE

VLADIMIR LENIN USES PROPAGANDA TO SECURE BOLSHEVIK SUCCESS IN THE RUSSIAN REVOLUTION

KEY PLAYER: *Vladimir Lenin (1870-1924)*
NATIONALITY: *Russian*
STRATEGY IMPLEMENTED: *1917*
CONTEXT: *Keen to replace the discredited rule of the Russian tsars with a new society based on Marxist principles, Lenin realized the need to spread the Marxist philosophy among the working class*

Although Karl Marx was convinced that it was the European state least likely to be the first to espouse communism, Russia became the world's original communist state in 1917. The brainchild behind the revolution that overthrew the previous, widely loathed tsarist regime was Vladimir Ilyich Lenin, an astute political operator who better understood the power of propaganda (information slanted to promote a particular cause) than anyone else of his time.

Born into a relatively well-to-do family, Lenin was drawn to Marxist doctrine (see entry on page 108) from a young age and became increasingly radical in his outlook after his brother's execution in 1887 for plotting to murder Tsar Alexander III. In 1893 Lenin was a prominent figure in the Russian Social Democratic Labor Party (RSDLP) and by the mid-1890s, he was in Moscow, orchestrating the Union for the Struggle for the Liberation of the Working Class. Having come to the attention of the authorities, he was imprisoned for a year and exiled to Siberia for a further three. On his release, he moved to Western Europe, where he felt he could more freely practice his activism.

Assuming the name Lenin in this period (having been born Vladimir Ilyich Ulyanov), by 1903 he was in London, where he set up the Russian Social-Democratic Workers' Party. Already, he was proving himself extremely adept as a propagandist, having published a pamphlet the previous year entitled *What Is To Be Done?* In it he argued that the working classes could not be expected to spontaneously revolt against their capitalist oppressors, but that instead a "vanguard" of committed revolutionaries needed to organize themselves to spread the Marxist message to the workers. To take popular power, he already understood, the Marxists needed to capture the hearts and minds of the masses.

PEACE, BREAD, LAND

What Is To Be Done? contributed to the schism within the RSDLP between Lenin's Bolsheviks (who advocated an organized and disciplined seizure of power) and the Menshevik faction who believed in a more democratic progression toward the socialist idyll. In 1905, revolution in Russia forced Tsar Nicholas II to agree to limited reforms and Lenin took the opportunity to return home. However, the tsar soon resumed his old, authoritarian ways and Lenin was again exiled in 1907. Returning to Western Europe, he became ever more convinced that the existing regime must be overthrown. By 1912, the Bolsheviks and Mensheviks had split into separate entities, with Lenin intent on fomenting revolution in his homeland. He spent the following years tirelessly campaigning, speaking, and writing to spread the Marxist doctrine (the newspaper *Pravda* was adopted as the party's official organ of mass media), and awaiting the ideal circumstances to challenge the status quo.

He was quick to grasp that World War I offered him his opportunity, opposing it as an imperialist folly in which capitalist overlords sent proletarian troops to their slaughter. By 1917 the war had indeed wrought havoc on the Russian population, causing unprecedented numbers of casualties

▲ *A 1920s Soviet propaganda poster proclaims: "All power to the Soviets! Peace to the people! Land to the peasants! Factories and mills to the workers!"*

and utterly destabilizing the economy. That year saw the February Revolution, in which popular protests in Petrograd (now St Petersburg) forced Nicholas II's abdication.

Lenin knew the time had come to strike. With assistance from Germany—which was hopeful that he would undermine the Russian war effort—Lenin secretly returned to Russia. On his journey from Switzerland he composed the April Theses, in which he described how the February Revolution was merely a first stage that saw the bourgeoisie supplant the discredited ruling class. Now, he argued, the Bolsheviks were to lead a true socialist revolution of the proletariat (workers and peasants). To this end, he argued that the Bolsheviks should remove the Provisional Government and place power with the soviets (local workers' councils). His rallying cry of "All power to the soviets!" was radical in the extreme but by espousing a slogan of "Peace, bread, land," Lenin began to win over doubters. Having secured Bolshevik control of Petrograd, he launched the October Revolution that saw the Provisional Government deposed and the Bolsheviks swept to power. Vast crowds chanted Lenin's memorable slogans. He had done what Marx had believed impossible by garnering mass support through extraordinary propaganda skills.

KING OF AGITPROP

Once in power, Lenin knew he must keep momentum up. After narrowly escaping an assassination attempt in August 1918, he was in no doubt that the revolution's future

1870

Vladimir Ilyich Ulyanov is born in Simbirsk, Russia.

1897

His political activities earn him three years in Siberian exile.

1903

Having traveled to Western Europe he establishes the Russian Social-Democratic Workers' Party in London.

1905

He returns to Russia after the 1905 Revolution.

1907

Renewed exile sees Lenin return to Western Europe.

1912

Lenin's Bolsheviks formalize their split with the more moderate Mensheviks.

1914

Outbreak of World War I, in which the Russian populace endures significant hardships.

1917

The February Revolution sees Nicholas II abdicate. The Provisional Government is formed and Lenin comes back to Russia in April. An attempted Bolshevik coup fails in July but they seize power during the October Revolution. Civil war between the Bolsheviks and White Russians ensues.

1918

Russia exits World War I in March. Nicholas II and his family are murdered in July. Lenin orders the Red Terror, a period of political oppression and bloodletting.

1921

The civil war ends, with the White Russians crushed.

1922

The Soviet Union is established. Lenin suffers two strokes during the year.

1924

He dies in Gorki on January 21.

remained precarious. By that time the Bolsheviks had already dispensed with any notion of democracy, instead declaring themselves representatives of a "dictatorship of the proletariat." As Lenin sought to nationalize industry and redistribute wealth, he was on the one hand ruthless in suppressing opposition (epitomized by the violence of the Red Terror, a campaign of torture, imprisonment, and execution), while on the other hand he remained intent on harnessing popular opinion in his favor.

So, for instance, a train filled with writers, artists, and actors toured the country, putting on shows and printing posters and pamphlets (there was a printing press on board). While *Pravda* carried on elucidating Lenin's philosophy, other less flattering newspapers were censored. In addition, the Communist

RULING MINDS

While Lenin was an undoubted master of manipulating the mass media, the modern age has seen plenty of other macabre exceptional exponents. His successor, Joseph Stalin, arguably took an even tighter control of the organs of mass communication, allowing him to ride out catastrophic policy decisions that cost millions of Soviet lives. Meanwhile, the Nazi minister of propaganda, Joseph Goebbels, was instrumental in Hitler's ascent to power and also the spread of anti-semitic sentiment in the Third Reich. In today's world, we need look no further that Kim Jong-Un's North Korea for an example of how propaganda can support a political regime.

A mass demonstration in St Petersburg, 1917, of mostly women and children, in favor of Lenin and his Bolshevik forces.

Party trained up professional "agitators," who traveled into the heart of Russia via train and ship to spread the Marxist credo to the peasantry. Even a People's Commissariat of Enlightenment was established to increase literacy, using specially written textbooks to further indoctrinate the population.

As such, Lenin won for himself a reputation as the founding father of "agitprop" (he would set up a government department for agitation and propaganda), a strategy in which propagandists (using primarily printed materials) and agitators (relying on speech) highlighted social deficiencies and urged the populace to support change. He set in place the foundations for seventy years of Soviet state control of the media, in which notions of propaganda and brainwashing became synonymous.

STRATEGY ANALYSIS

STRATEGY TYPE: *Communication*
KEY STRATEGY: *Using propaganda to spread the message of revolution*
OUTCOME: *The overthrow of the tsar and the establishment of a communist state*
ALSO USED BY: *Marx and Engels, 1848, and Mao Zedong in China, 1949–76.*

37 EXPAND YOUR MARKET

GERARD SWOPE BROUGHT CONSUMER CREDIT TO THE MASSES

KEY PLAYER: *Gerard Swope (1872–1957)*

NATIONALITY: *American*

STRATEGY IMPLEMENTED: *1922–44*

CONTEXT: *When Swope is appointed president of the General Electric Company in 1922, the company is principally involved in industrial electrics and engineering systems. Swope decides to expand into the mass market*

General Electric, founded by Thomas Edison in 1890, was already a giant in the electrical industry when Swope became its head. Swope believed that meeting the booming demand for household electrical appliances offered not only a new revenue stream but would bolster the industry as a whole. Having taken the company in its radical new direction, he made the even more seismic decision to offer credit on purchases.

Born in St Louis, Missouri, in 1872, Swope studied electrical engineering at the Massachusetts Institute of Technology, during which time he had his first interaction with General Electric. As was often to be retold in the future, he served as a helper at the company's repair store at the 1893 Chicago World's Fair for the princely sum of a dollar a day. What could have been a brief, youthful dalliance turned into a marriage in later life as Swope and General Electric evolved into soulmates. However, Swope actually started his post-MIT career with a commercial rival, the Western Electric Company. He learned about the business from top to bottom as, variously, a repairman, an accountant, and a designer. After he oversaw a large order to his hometown, St Louis, he was brought into the commercial department and it was here that he discovered that he was a better salesman than an engineer. In 1908 he became general sales manager for what was by then the largest electrical manufacturing company in the country, in which role he established a subsidiary in China. Swope knew not only how electrical machinery worked, but how the business did too. His experience broadened still further when, during World War I, he was drafted into the War Department as a director of procurement. By the time peace returned, Swope had a reputation as a first-class manager and industrial coordinator.

THE WHITE GOODS REVOLUTION

In 1919, General Electric's chairman, Charles Coffin, invited Swope to head up a new division, the International General Electric Company. He substantially expanded General Electric's business abroad, especially in Europe and the Far East. In fact, so successful was he that in 1922 the board of directors appointed him company president. Owen D.

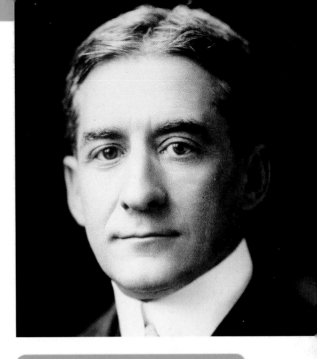

Young was named chairman of the board at the same time and the two formed a remarkable commercial partnership that saw the company go from strength to strength. Key to this was expansion into the consumer electrical goods market.

Swope's initial motivation was that by selling consumer goods, electricity consumption would increase, growing demand for the generators and other industrial equipment that had always been the core of General Electric's business. Before long, however, Swope realized that demand for consumer goods was booming and so he increasingly diverted his employees' attention to satisfying it.

He oversaw a huge upturn in the sale of items for home use, including vacuum cleaners, washing machines, and—most successfully of all—refrigerators. These modern inventions offered households the possibility of more leisure time than ever before and they were willing to pay a premium for it. To fully capitalize, Swope demanded a rebranding that meant General Electric maintained a single trademark for all its goods. In addition, he funded a huge surge in advertising, increasing the relevant budget six-fold between 1922 and 1930. Sure enough, by 1930, consumer products accounted for fully half of the company's business.

CREDIT TO THE NATION

The only problem was the natural limit to how many products the company could sell. For all its economies of scale, General Electric could not manufacture white goods (large electrical goods used domestically) for sale at prices every household could afford. Fridges and washing machines demanded large financial outlays to the extent that they were seen by many as a status symbol more than a domestic staple.

BAD CREDIT

Swope had a pivotal role in the introduction of easy credit in first the United States and then the wider world. Economists continue to debate its impact. On the one hand, credit has fueled spectacular growth in the developed world for the last century or so. However, where credit goes, debt follows. In 1920, US household indebtedness equated to 15 percent of GDP. By 1929 it had risen to 32 percent. In 1930 the economist Charles Pearson argued: "... The existing depression [the Great Depression] was due essentially to the great wave of credit expansion in the past decade." The international financial crisis that began with the US credit crunch in 2007 has similarly been laid at the door of too much easy credit and irresponsible lending. Swope's legacy is thus a complex one.

TIME LINE

1872
Gerard Swope is born in St Louis, Missouri, on December 1.

1895
He graduates in engineering from the Massachusetts Institute of Technology and takes a job with the Western Electric Company.

1919
Swope joins General Electric as head of a new international division.

1922
He becomes company president and begins diversifying its activities into consumer goods.

1931
Proposes the influential "Swope Plan" to bring about economic recovery in the US after the Great Depression.

1932
He oversees the setting up of the GE Credit Corporation.

1939
Swope retires as GE's president.

1942
He resumes his former role for a further two years.

1957
Swope dies on November 20 in New York.

In 1932 Swope managed the establishment of the GE Credit Corporation (later to become GE Consumer Finance). Instantaneously, he had made a mass market still more massive. The company reaped immediate rewards and secured a publicity coup into the bargain. American householders who had previously only dreamed of filling their homes with white goods rushed out to snap up General Electric's stock. When Swope became the company president in 1922, General Electric had annual sales of US$200 million but when he retired in 1944, the figure had rocketed to US$1.35 billion. In a little over two decades, Swope pioneered a revolution in American commercial culture, making previously inaccessible technological innovations accessible to everyday folk. It was a revolution that quickly spread across the globe and continues to the present day in a world where it is considered a virtual human right to have access to a flat-screen TV and a smart phone.

Swope's answer was quite revolutionary: He would offer approved consumers a credit line so that they could pay for their purchases in monthly instalments. While General Electric was not the first company to offer consumer credit (for instance, hire purchase agreements allowing customers to spread payments were in use in the United Kingdom back in the nineteenth century), never had such a prominent company offered the provision to so many people.

STRATEGY ANALYSIS

STRATEGY TYPE: *Innovative*
KEY STRATEGY: *Opening up the market for electrical goods by providing consumers with credit to pay for them*
OUTCOME: *A consumer revolution*
ALSO USED BY: *General Motors, from 1927, and Frank McNamara, founder of the Diner's Club charge card in 1950.*

38

MARKET CREATIVELY

WALT DISNEY'S CARTOON CREATIONS CONQUERED THE WORLD

KEY PLAYER: *Walt Disney (1901-66)*

NATIONALITY: *American*

STRATEGY IMPLEMENTED: *1929-66*

CONTEXT: *Walt Disney started his career as a promising cartoonist. With a keen eye for commercial opportunities and a talent for creating memorable animated characters, his empire soon grew*

Walt Disney was a creative powerhouse who combined artistic innovation with an unrelenting business strategy of expansion and diversification. He built Walt Disney Productions into the first media conglomerate, operating across multiple commercial sectors. Never missing a chance to promote the Disney brand, he established Disneyland as the original themed entertainment park in 1955.

Walt Disney's earliest ambition was to be a newspaper cartoonist but by 1919 he found himself working in animated film after meeting a talented young artist named Ub Iwerks. Before long Disney had built a catalog of well received works including animated advertising movies, short sketches called "Laugh-O-Grams," and *Alice in Cartoonland*, the first of a projected series of seven-minute fairy-tale adaptations that mixed animation with live action. There was no doubt he was making a cultural splash. However, his first business ventures proved less successful. His Laugh-O-Grams Studio closed within months of opening in 1922, crippled when a deal with a New York distributor collapsed. Walt was learning the harsh lessons of the business side of movie making.

Undeterred, the following year he ventured to Hollywood with his brother Roy, where they set up the Disney Brothers Cartoon Studio. Roy was a banker with an eye for the bottom line and just the man Walt wanted in his corner as his business manager. Knowing the finances were in good hands, Walt was able to explore his artistic vision. Soon he invited Iwerks to join them, ensuring the burgeoning studio was a hotbed of creativity. But Walt would never forget that creativity was worthless in the absence of money to realize it.

It was not long before the studio was earning a reputation for its strong output. In particular, one Mickey Mouse proved an instant hit after hitting the screens for the first time in 1928. In fact, he took the world quite by storm. After a cameo in a silent short film (*Plane Crazy*), he hit the big time with *Steamboat Willie*, the first cartoon with a synchronized soundtrack. Walt put much of himself into his creation, voicing Mickey until 1947 and reputedly even making Mickey's gestures as he recorded the mouse's words. It was natural then that Mickey should become the poster boy (or poster mouse) of the Disney empire. Today he is among the most recognizable figures in the world.

AUDIENCE APPEAL

Having won a mass audience, Disney was quick to hammer home his advantage with a string of follow-up successes. First came the Silly Symphonies series before the creation of a slew of animated immortals including Donald Duck, Pluto, and Goofy. In 1932, Disney received an Oscar in recognition of creating Mickey Mouse, as well as one for the company's first color offering, *Flowers and Trees*. In 1933 Depression-era audiences were cheered by *The Three Little Pigs*, confirming Disney's Midas touch when it came to connecting with the American public.

Disney himself was keen to make hay while the sun shone. America might be in the midst of a crushing economic downturn but he made sure his company cashed-in on its popularity. Having incorporated their business as Walt Disney Productions in 1929, Walt and Roy devised a strategy that involved granting franchising rights to sell dolls, shirts, watches, and other tie-in items for Mickey Mouse and Donald Duck. Disney had launched the era of film merchandising.

While Roy continued to look after the books, Walt realized that ongoing success relied on meeting new technical and artistic challenges. In 1937 Disney released its first full-length animated feature, *Snow White and the Seven Dwarfs*. Ahead of its premiere, many commentators believed it was an artistic goal too far but it proved an immediate critical and commercial triumph. More features followed, including the masterpieces *Fantasia* and *Pinocchio* (both 1940), *Dumbo* (1941), and *Bambi* (1942). They were not cheap to produce but Roy kept things ticking over until the box-office tills began to ring.

As for Walt, he never let standards slip and continued to innovate. For instance, in the 1940s he was a pioneer in mixing animation and live action in film such as *Song of the South* (1946). Ollie Johnstone and Frank Thomas, members of his original team

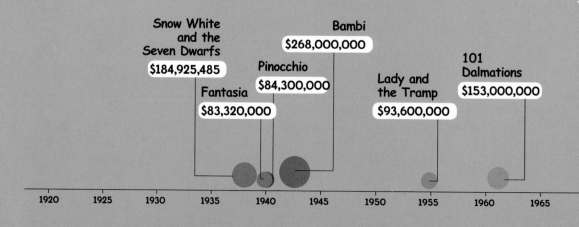

DISNEY'S BOX OFFICE HITS

Snow White and the Seven Dwarfs
$184,925,485

Fantasia
$83,320,000

Pinocchio
$84,300,000

Bambi
$268,000,000

Lady and the Tramp
$93,600,000

101 Dalmations
$153,000,000

1920   1925   1930   1935   1940   1945   1950   1955   1960   1965   19

of animators, recalled that "there were actually three different Walts: The dreamer, the realist, and the spoiler." Committed to creating groundbreaking works of art, he was also realistic about the demands of animation and about what would work. He maintained a stern critical eye and if the audience would not love it, he would not issue it.

DIVERSIFICATION

Walt was constantly alive to opportunities—not only artistic but also commercial. After succeeding in those early merchandising experiments, he eagerly continued to expand and diversify Disney's operations. He quickly grasped the potential of television as a medium for the kind of family entertainment for which his company was known. A series of films and programs for television followed. The first, made in cooperation with the Coca Cola Company, was *One Hour in Wonderland,* broadcast on the NBC network on Christmas Day, 1950. In 1954, the ABC network aired Disney's first regular television output, the anthology

IT'S A DISNEY WORLD

Almost half a century after his death, the Walt Disney Company (as it is now called) continues to thrive, with divisions involved in publishing, music, radio, merchandising, and online media, in addition to moviemaking and theme parks. Incredibly, it continues to produce a stable of animated films as critically lauded and money-spinning as any that Walt himself created. In 2013, Disney released Frozen, *inspired by Hans Christian Andersen's tale* The Snow Queen. *Raking in some US$1.3 billion in box-office receipts within a year, it became the world's highest-grossing animated film of all time, and the fifth highest-grossing film of any genre ever. Meanwhile, it picked up two Oscars along the way and the industry in* Frozen *spin-off merchandise continues to boom. Walt's impressive empire shows no signs of waning anytime soon.*

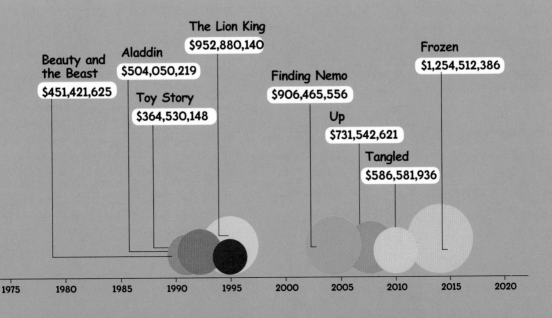

Beauty and the Beast
$451,421,625

Aladdin
$504,050,219

Toy Story
$364,530,148

The Lion King
$952,880,140

Finding Nemo
$906,465,556

Up
$731,542,621

Tangled
$586,581,936

Frozen
$1,254,512,386

1975   1980   1985   1990   1995   2000   2005   2010   2015   2020

TIME LINE

1901
Walter Elias Disney is born in Chicago, Illinois.

1919
Disney begins working as a commercial artist.

1922
He establishes the Laugh-O-Gram studio.

1923
He moves to Hollywood and sets up the Disney Brothers Cartoon Studio with his brother, Roy.

1926
The company is renamed Walt Disney Studios.

1928
Steamboat Mickey, *which marks the full debut of Mickey Mouse, is the first cartoon to feature a full soundtrack*

1929
Walt Disney Productions is founded.

1930
The company begins producing Mickey Mouse-themed merchandise and inaugurates The Mickey Mouse Club, *which soon boasts over a million members.*

1937
Disney's first full-length feature, Snow White and the Seven Dwarves, *is released.*

1947
The Walt Disney Music Company is founded.

1953
The Buena Vista Film Distribution Company begins operations.

1955
Disneyland opens in California.

1956
Disneyland Records is established.

1966
Walt Disney dies on December 15 in Burbank, California.

series *Disneyland*, while the *Davy Crockett* and *Zorro* mini-series were also big hits. From 1955–59, the company had its own daily TV show, *The Mickey Mouse Club*, on ABC. All the while, Walt kept up the cinematic output, both live-action (e.g. *Treasure Island* in 1950) and animated (e.g. *Lady and the Tramp*, 1955, and *One Hundred and One Dalmatians*, 1961).

Renowned for its musical output, the company established a music publishing division in 1949 and a record production and distribution company, Disneyland Records, in 1956. This was partly to capitalize on the success of "The Ballad of Davy Crockett" from their mini-series. In addition, they established their own distribution arm, the Buena Vista Film Distribution Company, in 1953. If there was money to be made from their creative output, Walt and Roy were determined to keep it in-house.

IT'S A SMALL WORLD

Perhaps Walt's most visionary commercial idea came in the 1940s, when he began to draw up plans for a new breed of family-focused entertainment park. There had been amusement parks before, such as that at Coney Island in Brooklyn, New York, but these focused on promenades and fun rides. Walt's idea was for a themed park, hidden from the surrounding area and accessed via a single entrance, with rides that prioritized storytelling over thrills and spills—all focused on Disney characters and the Disney brand.

His original idea was for an entertainment complex, "Mickey Mouse World," for fans—many of whom had been writing to him asking to visit Walt Disney Studios in Burbank, California. Eventually he purchased a vast 160-acre (65-hectare) site in Anaheim, California. Costs quickly soared so Roy and Walt went

DISNEY RULES THE WORLD

18.6 million people visit the Magic Kingdom every year

When it opened in 1955 adult admission cost **$3.50**, today it costs **$85**

11.2 million visit EPCOT

There are more than **25** Disney Resort hotel locations

10,000 people attended the soft opening in 1971

Mickey Mouse has more than **290** outfits and Minnie Mouse has over **200**

Tree of Life in the Animal Kingdom is **145 ft (45 m)** tall and its trunk is **50 ft (15 m)** wide

10.2 million visit the Animal Kingdom

Cinderella's Castle is **189 ft (58 m)** tall

10.1 million visit Hollywood studios

into partnership with Western Publishing and ABC to build the park. Constructed between 1953 and 1955, its final cost was US$17 million.

Disneyland opened to the public at 10 am on July 18 1955. Some people had queued eight hours to secure entrance. Anticipation was sky high, as evidenced by a 90-minute live show, *Dateline Disneyland*, on the ABC TV network that was watched by 90 million people. This was perhaps the pivotal moment in Walt Disney Production's journey to becoming a media conglomerate and the world's leading purveyor of family entertainment. It was an empire Walt had built on foundations of artistic skill, cultural sensitivity, and business acumen.

STRATEGY ANALYSIS

STRATEGY TYPE: *Marketing*
KEY STRATEGY: *Building a global brand out of cultural innovation*
OUTCOME: *The world's first media conglomerate*
ALSO USED BY: *George Lucas for the Star Wars franchise, 1977, and J. K. Rowling, creator of the Harry Potter franchise, 1997–.*

LIGHTNING WAR

HITLER ADOPTED THE SCHLIEFFEN PLAN'S STRATEGY OF BLITZKRIEG TO DEVASTATING EFFECT IN WORLD WAR II

KEY PLAYER: *The Wehrmacht (German Armed Forces)*
NATIONALITY: *German*
STRATEGY IMPLEMENTED: *1939-41*
CONTEXT: *At the start of World War II, Hitler was persuaded to use a combination of aerial attacks, light tank divisions, and fast-moving artillery and infantry to speedily conquer Nazi Germany's enemies*

World War I had been characterized by static armies caught in debilitating and futile face-offs. Hitler himself had seen the ineffectiveness of trench warfare first-hand, so come World War II he was determined to implement a strategy in which agile forces moved quickly to overwhelm the enemy. The result was Blitzkrieg, in which foreign powers were overrun by highly disciplined troops supported by the latest in technological innovation.

Blitzkrieg (a term coined by the Allied press) described the battle strategy employed by Germany in the early phases of World War II. It relied on a formidable blend of speed, surprise, and coordination, with the result that it sowed panic within the enemy ranks. As a *Time* magazine editorial observed in 1939: "The battlefront disappeared, and with it the illusion that there had ever been a battlefront. For this was no war of occupation, but a war of quick penetration and obliteration."

In fact, the Blitzkrieg strategy had its roots even before World War I. In 1905 General Count Alfred von Schlieffen finished work on the famous Schlieffen Plan, which envisaged a pan-European war in which Germany fought on two fronts: Against the French to the west and Russia to the east. Aware that Germany would stand little chance if drawn into a long war against combatants superior in numbers and resources, he argued instead for quick and decisive strikes to cripple the enemy.

In World War I Germany had been wholly unable to execute his plan, instead getting dragged into precisely the exhausting arm-wrestle Schlieffen had feared. By the time Hitler came to power in 1933, he was intent that there would be no repeat of this. Furthermore, technological advances meant Schlieffen's plan was now much more achievable. In particular, a German officer called Heinz Guderian looked at how dive bombers and tanks might be employed to effect rapid, crushing advances against the enemy. He wrote a pamphlet called *Achtung Panzer!* (Panzers being German tanks) that fell into Hitler's hands. The Führer was impressed and when Guderian subsequently advised him that German forces could reach the French coast within a matter of weeks, Hitler believed him even as many of his military colleagues doubted the claim.

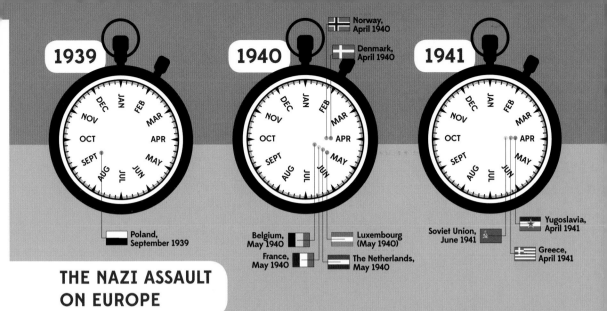

1939

1940

Norway,
April 1940

Denmark,
April 1940

1941

Poland,
September 1939

Belgium,
May 1940

France,
May 1940

Luxembourg
(May 1940)

The Netherlands,
May 1940

Soviet Union,
June 1941

Yugoslavia,
April 1941

Greece,
April 1941

THE NAZI ASSAULT ON EUROPE

THE ELEMENT OF SURPRISE

While it is debated whether Blitzkrieg was ever formally adopted by the German authorities, it was nonetheless the Nazis's de facto military strategy come the outbreak of World War II. Its implementation was relatively straightforward. First, weaknesses in the enemy lines were identified. Once a target had been selected, dive bombers were sent in to knock out transport and communications infrastructure and to cause general panic. In the meantime, tank divisions made their way to the target location, the air force only retreating on their arrival. Reinforcements followed, often in armored vehicles with tracks so that they could move quickly cross-country without having to rely on a road network.

Communications between units was maintained by radio, keeping everybody well informed of developments. The defenders themselves enjoyed no such luxuries, instead finding themselves on the back foot and often in disarray. Their job was regularly made even harder as they were confronted by frantic civilian retreat. Amid the confusion, the German land forces encircled the enemy in pockets and cleared out any remaining resistance. Blitzkrieg thus reaped a whirlwind. Poland was the first to fall to the strategy, succumbing in just over a month in September–October 1939. Then it was France's turn, beginning on May 10 1940. It came as an almighty shock when their forces collapsed before the end of June 1940. As the French Prime Minister Paul Reynauld put it:

> The truth is that our classic conception of the conduct of war has come up against a new conception. At the basis of this…there is not only the massive use of heavy armored divisions or cooperation between them and airplanes, but the creation of disorder in the enemy's rear by means of parachute raids.

Blitzkrieg was so effective in that it handed virtually complete control to the German attacking forces. Because of its heavy reliance on the element of surprise, Blitzkrieg was always likely to become less effective the more it was utilized. Yet it reaped almost

TIME LINE

1905
Alfred von Schlieffen completes his Schlieffen Plan.

1914–18
During World War I, the Schlieffen Plan fails to be implemented.

1933
Hitler comes to power in Germany.

1937
Heinz Guderian publishes Achtung Panzer!

March 1939
Germany invades Czechoslovakia.

September 1939
Germany invades Poland. Britain and France declare war on Germany.

April–May 1940
Germany invades Denmark and Norway in April. The following month Luxembourg, the Netherlands, Belgium, and France are invaded.

June 1940
Mass evacuation of British forces from France at Dunkirk. Later that month German troops enter Paris.

September
The Battle of Britain comes to an end, with Hitler postponing his planned invasion of the United Kingdom.

1941
Berlin launches Operation Barbarossa against the Soviet Union. After initial successes, German progress slows. The United States enters the war.

1943
The Siege of Leningrad ends with Germany's forces retreating across Russia. Its ally, Italy, surrenders.

1944
The Germans lose their foothold in the USSR while the momentum also swings against them in North Africa and on the Western Front.

1945
Germany surrenders.

unimaginable rewards for the Berlin authorities in the early stages of the war. Hitler had hit upon a strategy for modern warfare that made the best use of the latest technical developments, while his enemies were too often still married to tactics that were archaic even by the end of World War I.

THE TIDE TURNS

As late as 1941 Blitzkrieg seemed to have put Hitler in the ascendency, especially when Operation Barbarossa got off to such an impressive start. Surprise attacks on Russian airfields all but neutralized the Russian air capability, while vast quick-moving panzer divisions tore into the unprepared Soviet forces on the ground. However, where Polish and French defences had collapsed under the strain, the Russians held on. Having failed to

SHOCK AND AWE

The modern US strategy of "shock and awe," as outlined by its authors Harlan K. Ullman and James P. Wade in the mid-1990s, shares many of the same principles as Blitzkrieg. It aims for rapid dominance, which paralyzes the enemy's will to carry on and renders them incapable of executing strategic resistance. This strategy saw real-world use during the 2003 invasion of Iraq. While Saddam Hussein's forces were indeed soon overwhelmed, the experience led many commentators to question the strategy's suitability to the modern theater of war given its tendency to cause unpalatable "collateral damage" and to alienate the local population.

German Panzer tanks approaching the city of Bydgoszcz, Poland. Such vehicles were instrumental to the execution of Blitzkrieg.

overrun the country by the end of 1941, Hitler found himself in an unwelcome situation: Embroiled in a struggle that would last for years and caught up once again in a dreaded war on two fronts.

Although Blitzkrieg had given Germany a foothold in Russia, it had failed to secure Moscow's surrender. For the strategy to work, it was essential to take down the enemy quickly and immediately move on to the next target. Instead, the Eastern Front would become the scene of a painfully drawn-out stand-off. The result was millions dead on both sides before Germany was chased out of the USSR after a series of crucial military reverses in 1944. The Soviet Union had drawn the sting out of the Nazi tail. Meanwhile, to the west the other Allies were adopting Blitzkrieg-style tactics of their own, launching rapid and flexible attacks combining land and air forces to seize back the initiative in North Africa and Western Europe. Hitler had, it might be said, been hoisted by his own petard.

STRATEGY ANALYSIS

STRATEGY TYPE: *Strategy of attack*
KEY STRATEGY: *Lightning war—a short, shocking military assault from the ground and air designed to secure rapid victory*
OUTCOME: *Early military successes, including the subjugation of Poland and France*
ALSO USED BY: *Israeli forces in Syria and Egypt, 1967, and the US-led forces in Iraq, 1993.*

THE FINAL SOLUTION

NAZI GENERAL **REINHARD HEYDRICH** BROUGHT INDUSTRIAL EFFICIENCY TO MASS MURDER

KEY PLAYER: *The Nazi regime (1933-1945)*

NATIONALITY: *German*

STRATEGY IMPLEMENTED: *c.1941-45*

CONTEXT: *Hitler had brought the Nazis to power on a wave of anti-semitic feeling. During World War II, he and his fellow regime leaders devised a plan to slaughter European Jewry on an industrial scale*

Widely regarded as the darkest episode in human history, the Holocaust saw the mass extermination of European Jews by Germany's Nazi government. Hitler made little secret of his loathing for Jews and authorized swathes of anti-Jewish legislation before the war's start. However, from 1941 his regime developed a complex, industrial system to facilitate mass executions that shocked even his greatest enemies when evidence of the crime came to light.

In the six years after he came to power as chancellor of Germany, Hitler enacted some 400 anti-Jewish decrees, regulations, and articles of legislation. Virtually no aspect of public or private life was left untouched. Business practises were restricted and boycotts of Jewish businesses encouraged. Basic civil rights were denied, including the rights to vote and hold citizenship. Jews were also prohibited from entering certain professions, banned from designated public areas, and forced to carry identification at all times. The list of encroachments on basic liberties went on and on.

Nor could anyone argue that Hitler's ardent anti-semitism was a surprise. In his autobiographical work of the mid-1920s, *Mein Kampf (My Struggle)*, he detailed his fear of the "Jewish peril" centered around a groundless conspiracy theory that Jews were intent on a global takeover of power. He held the Jewish population responsible for virtually all of Germany's woes, which at the time included grave economic hardships resulting from the strict terms of the post-World War I Treaty of Versailles.

Indeed, he regarded that war as their responsibility too and would argue that were they, in his opinion, to cause another such conflict, he would seek nothing less than the wholesale destruction of European Jewry. Alas, many of his opponents and critics regarded his rantings as simply that—the runaway ideas of a fanatic anti-semite that would never be realized within the civilized cradle of twentieth-century Europe. As history would show, it was a devastating miscalculation.

MURDEROUS INTENT

Regardless of the disjointed nature of his politics, Hitler was an accomplished organizer and, to his supporters, an irresistibly charismatic figure. It was these skills that saw him

THE TERRIBLE SCALE OF THE FINAL SOLUTION

% OF PRE-WAR JEWISH POPULATION KILLED IN EACH OF THE EUROPEAN COUNTRIES

6,000,000

Jews were killed during the Holocaust (two-thirds of the Jews living in Europe before WWII).

5,000,000

non-Jewish undesirables were also killed in the death camps.

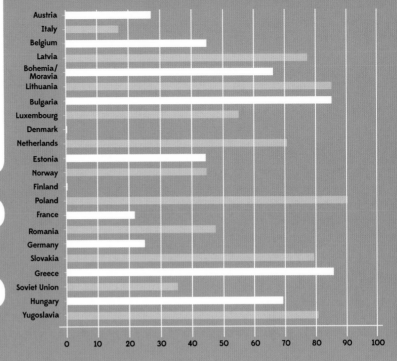

build up his party and become the leading power in the nation. In office, these talents enabled him to persuade not only his followers but also large sections of the general populace that the state bureaucracy should be turned over to a campaign of persecution.

Of course, the Jews were not the only subjects of Hitler's vitriol. In his pursuit of a "pure" fatherland, he came out against several other groups of "social undesirables" including communists, gypsies, and homosexuals. However, the Final Solution, as it was developed, related specifically to Jews and identified them as its prime target. Yet there is little evidence to suggest that Hitler and his regime entered the war with a clear plan to systematically destroy the continent's Jewry. Certainly, Jewish lives were considered dispensable and their deaths were celebrated rather than mourned by the administration. However, the Final Solution seems to have evolved as a strategy over a period of time, the natural development of a vaguer plan to first move Jews to the edges of European society and then away altogether.

The first stage of the war, from 1939–41, saw a more haphazard approach to what the Nazis termed "the Jewish question." In Germany and its occupied countries, holding areas were established, either in the form of camps or ghettoes within existing population hubs. Jews were rounded up and housed in often inhuman conditions, with hunger and disease causing significant "natural wastage" as a result. Many more died in labor camps, where they were treated as slave labor, working until they literally dropped. Others perished from disease, cold, and exhaustion on the journeys to these camps, undertaken in overcrowded, sealed cattle trucks without water, sanitation, or room to sit.

There were sporadic massacres too, though nothing on the scale of what was to follow. Meanwhile, in 1940 the Jewish Department of the Foreign Affairs Ministry proposed the Madagascar Plan, which envisaged relocating Europe's Jewish population to the island

TIME LINE

1933
Hitler becomes German chancellor and introduces swathes of anti-semitic legislation. The SS establish the Dachau concentration camp, this serves as a model for the concentration camp system implemented to effect the Final Solution.

1939
Adolf Eichmann heads up a branch of the Gestapo devoted to "Jewish affairs and evacuations."

1940
The Madagascar Plan suggests relocating Europe's Jews to the island off the east coast of Africa.

1941
Gas vans and murder squads hunt down Jews on the Eastern Front. Mass deportations begin from German-held territories. Chelmno in Poland commences operation as an extermination camp in December.

1942
Austwitz-Birkenau begins operating in January. Over a million Jews will be killed there. The Wannsee Conference meets to coordinate the Final Solution.

1943
The number of Jews killed passes the million mark.

1944
Auschwitz-Birkenau ceases gassings in October.

1945
Russian troops liberate Auschwitz-Birkenau in January. As Allied forces liberate other camps, the full horror begins to emerge. Hitler commits suicide on April 30.

1945–46
The Nuremberg Trials assigns some personal responsibility for the Holocaust though many of its chief architects avoid justice.

A BLOODY LEGACY

Genocide, the deliberate mass killing of a particular social group, is considered a crime against humanity yet we are burdened with too many recent examples. Among the most notorious was that perpetrated in Rwanda in 1994, when over a hundred-day period between half a million and a million ethnic Tutsi were massacred by members of the Hutu majority. In less than three months, some 70 percent of the resident Tutsi population was killed in an outpouring of violence carried out by government-backed murder squads. Almost contemporaneously, in the wars that marked the break-up of Yugoslavia, genocide found its way back to Europe when some 8,000 Bosniak ("Bosnian Muslim") boys and men were killed by Republika Srpska troops in the town of Srebrenica.

of Madagascar in the Indian Ocean. Some take this as evidence that the Nazis were still some way off formulating the Final Solution at this time, although others have suggested it served as a convenient smokescreen for Berlin's real intentions.

THE INDUSTRIALIZATION OF DEATH
There can be no doubt that the climate had changed by 1941. In that year, Germany invaded Russia and utilized death squads to hunt down and kill "undesirables," including Jews. They also employed gas vans in which prisoners were rounded up and gassed using carbon monoxide. Nonetheless, the regime seems to have judged that this approach was somewhat inefficient. At the end of July 1941 Hermann Goering, Hitler's right-hand man, gave SS General Reinhard Heydrich responsibility for preparing a "complete solution of the Jewish question." His answer would be death camps.

Although there is no record of Hitler having personally given the go-ahead for the Final Solution, few serious historians give credence to the argument that he was somehow kept out of the loop. Under Heydrich and colleagues including Adolf Eichmann and Heinrich Himmler, the Final Solution quickly gained momentum and became one of the Nazi regimes most terrible strategies of attack. By the autumn, the first camps built solely for the purpose of killing were established, all of them in Poland. Furthermore, Zyklon B was being tested as a more efficient gassing agent

▲ *Reinhard Heydrich, pictured here in 1934, was one of the Holocaust's chief architects. He died after being attacked by assassins in Prague in 1942.*

than carbon monoxide. The first systematic gassings of Jewish prisoners took place in the death camp at Chelmno, near Łódź in Poland, on December 8 1941.

With the system already up-and-running, the Nazis convened the Wannsee Conference on January 20 1942 under Heydrich's chairmanship. Representatives from all relevant government departments attended so that details of Final Solution coordination could be hammered out. As Himmler would confirm as the Posen Conference in October 1943, "the extermination of the Jewish people" was official state policy.

Trains to the death camps from throughout German-held territories brought prisoners. Once there, they were shorn of their hair, disinfected, and stripped in acts designed to dehumanize. Their valuables were taken—even down to their gold teeth—and they were then told they were to be showered, only for the showerheads to release poisonous gas. The bodies were later burned in industrial ovens.

UNIMAGINABLE SCALE

The statistics of the Holocaust remain mind-boggling. Auschwitz-Birkenau, the most infamous of the death camps, operated like a commercial abattoir. At its peak of activity, some 9,000 Jews were murdered there every day (in fact, it had provision to kill 12,000). There were nine million Jews in Europe in 1933. By 1945, two-thirds were dead—about half of them killed in the death camps imagined by the Final Solution. The industrialization of murder also saw the Nazis kill an estimated five million other "undesirables" in the course of World War II. There is no greater stain on European history.

STRATEGY ANALYSIS

STRATEGY TYPE: *Strategy of attack*
KEY STRATEGY: *Bringing industrial efficiency to mass murder and dehumanizing an act of genocide*
OUTCOME: *The deaths of some six million Jews*
ALSO USED BY: *Hutu militia against Rwanda's Tutsi minority, 1994, and Republika Srpska troops, Yugoslavia, 1992-95.*

41 STRIKE WHERE IT HURTS

VÕ NGUYÊN GIÁP REDEFINED HOW GUERRILLA WARFARE COULD SERVE THE MODERN REVOLUTIONARY

KEY PLAYER: *Võ Nguyên Giáp (1911-2013)*

NATIONALITY: *Vietnamese*

STRATEGY IMPLEMENTED: *1942-75*

CONTEXT: *Võ Nguyên Giáp was the military leader of the Vietnam Independence League (Vietminh). Developing a theory of a "people's war," he updated guerrilla tactics to defeat the Japanese, French, and Americans*

Guerrilla warfare traditionally utilizes small, mobile military units who unleash frequent, damaging, but small-scale attacks before retreating. Thus avoiding major confrontations, guerrilla fighters can wear down a seemingly stronger opponent. While such tactics have been practiced since ancient times, Giáp overhauled them for use in a modern context.

A schoolteacher by profession, Giáp immersed himself in communism and nationalism from a young age. In the early 1940s he found himself thrust into the military limelight when he was put in charge of the Vietminh's armed wing. He set about educating himself in the ways of the master military strategists including Napoleon (see page 96) and the great Prussian general Carl von Clausewitz, who famously proclaimed: "The political object is the goal, war is the means of reaching it, and the means can never be considered in isolation from their purposes."

Giáp's first struggle was against the Japanese, who occupied Indochina during World War II. From 1942 Giáp led a small band of soldiers and gradually built a network of local support. By 1944 he had sufficient forces to launch serious assaults on Japanese outposts and could boast significant territorial gains by the time Japan surrendered to the allies in 1945. In August that year Giáp led his forces into Hanoi, paving the way for the creation of the Democratic Republic of Vietnam.

However, the allied "big three"—President Roosevelt, Winston Churchill, and Soviet leader Joseph Stalin—had already decided that Vietnam was to be divided in two, with the Nationalist Chinese in charge of the north and the British in the south. The British quickly seceded control to Vietnam's erstwhile colonial overlords, France, and the Chinese soon left the north after striking a deal with the French in return for the French giving up their territorial interests within China. A lengthy and gruelling war between the Vietminh and the French ensued, with Giáp evolving his ideas on guerrilla warfare into a philosophy of "people's war" that culminated in a decisive victory at Dien Bien Phu in 1954. The French were effectively expelled from the country, although Vietnam remained divided between Communist north and non-Communist south (which received support from the United States in its struggle against their common Communist foes).

▲ *General Giáp on a visit to Muong Phang in 1994. Forty years earlier, he planned the strategy for Dien Bien Phu whilst hiding in the forest here.*

So began Giáp's third great battle—to defeat the US-backed forces of south Vietnam and reunite the country under a Communist government. Again, he marshalled his humble military resources expertly to overcome the world's foremost military power through a crafted blend of guerrilla and conventional tactics. His military brilliance saw the establishment of a united Socialist Republic of Vietnam, and left the United States with a psychological scar that has never truly healed.

A RICH HERITAGE

The idea of a smaller force utilizing destabilizing attacks against a larger enemy is by no means a modern invention, as this very book attests. Ancient history is replete with tales of numerically smaller, often oppressed peoples having their day against imperial overlords grown tired of coping with debilitating, on-going, low-level attacks (see the American Revolution page 78).

Traditional guerrilla tactics include the use of ambush and sabotage, usually supported by espionage, intelligence gathering, and deception. Crucially, large set-piece encounters are avoided so as to deprive the enemy of the chance to overrun their

TIME LINE

1911
Giáp is born in Quảng Bình Province.

1938
He becomes a member of Hò Chí Minh's Indochinese Communist Party.

1941
He is a founder member of the Vietminh independence movement, headed by Hò Chí Minh.

1944
Giáp leads a guerrilla war against the occupying Japanese.

1945
Hò Chí Minh proclaims the Democratic Republic of Vietnam. Giáp is named interior minister.

1954
Giáp masterminds the defeat of French forces at Dien Bien Phu. French colonial rule is ended but Vietnam is left divided in two. War soon breaks out between the Communist north and anti-Communist south.

1962
Giáp publishes People's War, People's Army.

1965
The United States lands increasing numbers of troops in south Vietnam to counter the Vietcong. Giáp sends troops from the North to support his comrades.

1973
The battle-weary US government withdraws its troops.

1975
Communist forces take the south's capital, Saigon, and proclaim the united Socialist Republic of Vietnam. Giáp is named minister of defense and also serves as deputy prime minister.

1991
He retires from front-line politics.

2013
Giáp dies and is given a state funeral.

militarily weaker opponent. The aim of the guerrilla is to exhaust the enemy and diminish their will to fight on. Historically, it has proved most effective against foreign occupying forces and domestic regimes lacking local support. Often, the guerrilla forces' efficacy is bolstered by the local knowledge of their fighters, who can take advantage of their intimacy with the local terrain and their ability to rally indigenous support. The first theorist to expound on such strategies was Sun Tzu in his sixth-century *Art of War*. The word "guerrilla" derives from the Spanish for "little war" and gained popular usage during Spain's struggles with Napoleonic France. It was a tactic also used to great effect by the Boers against the British in South Africa, before Mao Zedong rewrote the rules in his *On Guerilla Warfare* to suit twentieth-century circumstances. Yet it was Giáp who was arguably the age's greatest guerrilla leader, seeing off three mighty enemies (the Japanese, the French, and the Americans) with a much inferior force.

GIÁP'S GUIDING PRINCIPLES

In his landmark 1962 work, *People's War, People's Army*, Giáp wrote what was in essence a manual for the late-twentieth century guerrilla fighter. He described war as a rebalancing of power comprising three stages. The first "defensive" stage is dominated by guerrilla activities designed to undermine the enemy's morale. A second phase, in which "equilibrium" is restored, sees guerrilla efforts bolstered by more conventional military units. This becomes possible as the enemy's resources and will are depleted, at the same time as the guerrilla force gains in confidence, expertise, and local support. The final third phase demands a full-scale counteroffensive in which

mobile conventional forces take on and defeat the enemy, with continued support from renegade guerrilla groups. Giáp emphasized the fluidity between these three phases: His troops might have to move back a phase under certain circumstances secure in the knowledge that they would win victory eventually.

Learning much from the experience of Mao in China, Giáp echoed Mao's belief that the guerrilla should cultivate local support in order to win the hearts and minds of the people. Indeed, Giáp came

▲ *Vietnamese soldiers shelter in a trench during the battle of Dien Bien Phu, 1954. This victory resulted in the expulsion of the French from Vietnam.*

to believe he was heading nothing less than a "people's war" in which "each inhabitant was a soldier, each village a fortress" The struggle in Vietnam thus came to be carried out on every available front—military, political, economic and diplomatic.

ADAPTING TO CIRCUMSTANCE

Giáp was also a great realist and recognized that his relatively under-resourced forces could not expect a quick victory against their stronger enemies. Instead he advocated a policy of "protracted warfare" in which the enemy is softened up by a series of debilitating small-scale reverses before succumbing to a full-scale counteroffensive. Crucially, he also demanded his forces be adaptive to whatever circumstances they might face. The ability to quickly change tack was one of the key advantages the Vietminh had against their various enemies, and Giáp extracted the full benefit. "In a time of war, you have to take your lead from the enemy..." he wrote in *People's War, People's Army*. "When the enemy changes his strategy or tactics, you have to do the same." Elsewhere, he summed it up even more succinctly: "Is the enemy strong? One avoids him. Is he weak? One attacks him."

"People's war, protracted war, guerrilla warfare developing step-by-step into mobile warfare," wrote Giáp, "such are the most valuable lessons of the war of liberation in Vietnam." As Douglas Pike, a leading scholar of the Vietnam War, put it, Giáp championed "a strategy for which there is no known counter strategy."

STRATEGY ANALYSIS

STRATEGY TYPE: *Strategy of attack*
KEY STRATEGY: *Prepared a small, motivated force for a prolonged battle to overcome a larger enemy*
OUTCOME: *The establishment of the Socialist Republic of Vietnam*
Also used by: *Mao Zedong in China, 1946-49, and Che Guevara in Cuba, 1950s.*

42 PREPARATION IS KEY

THE ALLIED FORCES EXECUTED A MASTERPIECE OF PLANNING AGAINST THE AXIS POWERS ON D-DAY

KEY PLAYER: *The Allied forces*
NATIONALITY: *British, French, Russian, and American*
STRATEGY IMPLEMENTED: *June 6 1944*
CONTEXT: *By 1943 Hitler's Germany was overstretched as it battled for control in Russia, western Europe, and northern Africa. With the Allies gaining the upper hand, plans were put in place to recapture France from the Nazis before launching an assault on Germany itself*

Operation Overlord was the name given to the Allied plan to reclaim France, weakening Germany's powerbase in Western Europe and setting the scene for an invasion of Germany itself, with Russian forces from the east moving in on Berlin at the same time. The task of landing hundreds of thousands of troops in occupied France was a monumental one but it was achieved with aplomb following months of meticulous planning on a scale unprecedented in the history of warfare.

That much-used adage, supposedly originated by Benjamin Franklin, that if you fail to plan, you plan to fail was certainly taken to heart by the leaders of the Allied forces in World War II. With Germany's forces straining by 1943, the Allies knew the time was ripe to strike at the Nazi heart. The result was Operation Overlord, which required the landing of a vast army in occupied France. A stunning example of careful preparation and strategic planning undertaken by the combined Allied forces, Overlord was to begin on D-Day, when tens of thousands of troops would enter France during an amphibious operation on the Normandy coast. Utilizing all the elements of the Nazis' own Blitzkrieg tactics (see page 166), the Allies hoped to quickly take back control of France and force Germany into retreat.

Yet the scheme was undoubtedly a risky one. Although the Allied forces had been bolstered by the entry of America into the war in 1941, even an over-stretched Germany remained a formidable foe. The defeat of the combined French and British forces in 1940, culminating in the traumatic Dunkirk evacuations, was still fresh in the mind. More pertinently, the logistical demands of landing an entire army from the sea into an occupied country boasting significant coastal defenses (though imperfect, Hitler's Atlantic Wall—a ribbon of fortifications stretching from Spain to Norway—had been under construction since 1942) were formidable.

The Allied commanders were all in agreement that if they were to succeed, the operation had to be thoroughly planned down to the last detail. It would be impossible to prepare for absolutely every eventuality, but they sought to leave as little to providence as possible. As the great war-chronicler Basil Liddell Hart put it: "The aim of strategy

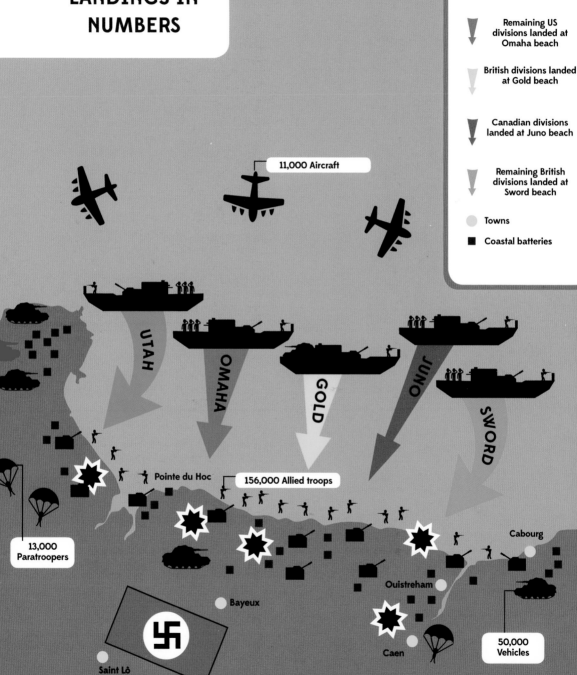

THE D-DAY LANDINGS IN NUMBERS

US divisions landed at Utah beach

Remaining US divisions landed at Omaha beach

British divisions landed at Gold beach

Canadian divisions landed at Juno beach

Remaining British divisions landed at Sword beach

Towns

Coastal batteries

11,000 Aircraft

UTAH

OMAHA

GOLD

JUNO

SWORD

Pointe du Hoc

156,000 Allied troops

13,000 Paratroopers

Cabourg

Ouistreham

Bayeux

Caen

Saint Lô

50,000 Vehicles

TIME LINE

1939
Britain and France declare war on Germany after Hitler invades Poland.

1940
France succumbs to Germany, with British forces in the country forced to evacuate via Dunkirk.

1941
The Nazis invade Russia. America enters the war after Japan bombs Pearl Harbor.

1943
An Anglo-American staff charged with planning D-Day is established at the Casablanca Conference in January. In August the initial plan for D-Day is agreed on by the Allies at the Quebec Conference.

December 1943
Field Marshal Erwin Rommel is charged by Hitler to improve Germany's Atlantic defences. US General, Dwight D. Eisenhower, is named Supreme Allied Commander in charge of Operation Overlord. Britain's General Bernard Montgomery is put in charge of the landings themselves.

1944
In January an amphibious exercise involving 16,000 American troops takes place in Devon as a dry-run of D-Day. In May, senior officers are given a final briefing.

June 1944
On 5th June the first troop convoys leave England. At 11 p.m., British and American airborne troops begin taking off. They begin landing a little after midnight on June 6. At around 5.30 a.m. Allied ships begin bombarding Germany's coastal defenses. An hour later, American troops begin landing on Omaha and Utah beaches. An hour after that, British forces land on the Gold, Juno, and Sword beaches. By 9 p.m. 140,000 Allied troops have landed, establishing a crucial foothold in Continental Europe.

1945
Allied forces reach Berlin. Hitler commits suicide and Germany surrenders on May 7.

must be to bring about this battle under the most advantageous circumstances."

DUE DILIGENCE

The D-Day preparations were influenced by a set of general principles authored by the American Brigadier General John W. Daniel in May 1943. These called for army, navy, and air personnel to be under a single command and that all operations should be planned on the basis of reliable and considered intelligence. He also demanded that no single vessel or landing craft carry either troops or equipment so essential to the success of an operation that its loss would prove critical. Furthermore, any amphibious invasion was to be executed under cover of dark, with the relevant landing beaches secured before dawn. In order to adhere to these guidelines, extensive coordination was essential, especially given the multinational nature of the endeavor. Rarely if ever was an international force (the D-Day assaults primarily comprised British, Canadian, and US troops) so well prepared as that which undertook the Normandy landings.

The first major task that the Allied strategists faced was to choose a suitable landing spot. Pas de Calais was the area in France closest to Britain. However, it was also the most obvious choice and one Hitler was intent on fortifying. The Normandy coast, by contrast, offered the Allies a broad landing area. But it lacked extensive port facilities, making the landing of essential provisions more hazardous. The answer was to prepare a provisional solution. So it was that the British developed the Mulberry Harbour, a prefabricated, portable, and temporary harbor that could be floated across the Channel and set up where required. In addition, tanks known as Hobart's Funnies were modified for the landings so as to be able to climb sea walls.

▲ *An aerial view of the D-Day landings reveals how air, sea, and land forces combined to reclaim France from the Nazis.*

No detail was left unconsidered. Planners looked for a date when there was a full moon to aid the fighter pilots who were to provide air cover and knock out essential German infrastructure. The hour of the attack was to be a little before dawn, in between high and low tides and with the tide coming in, so as to assist the troops landing on the beaches. In the months leading up to the launch of Operation Overlord, the Allied commanders met to tweak their plans and troops were given training to cope with the particular challenges with which they were to be confronted.

This was itself a complex and demanding task, requiring the coordination of personnel from the British, American, and Canadian armed forces, along with French underground fighters. It also called for a clear chain of command in which potential personal rivalries and differences of opinion were set aside for the greater good. Churchill and Roosevelt agreed that an American would be in supreme command, and the job fell to General Dwight D. Eisenhower. His chief of staff was another American, Lieutenant General Walter Bedell Smith, but Eisenhower oversaw a senior command team dominated by Britons, including most prominently General Sir Bernard Montgomery, who was in charge of the combined Allied Ground Forces. In addition, a team of air and naval commanders

A soldier's eye-view from an Allied landing craft, ▲ as US troops wade through the sea toward the Fox Green section of Omaha Beach.

MAKE A PLAN

D-Day set a benchmark for unstinting military planning, which nations have sought to emulate ever since. One such example was the liberation of Kuwait from Iraqi forces undertaken by a US-led coalition in 1991. Operation Desert Storm, as the action was known, was a much-admired set piece of planning that saw troops sweeping into the hostile, occupied country. Saddam Hussein's Iraqi troops were expelled in a little over a month. However, if that was a shining example of planning, the Second Gulf War that saw US-led forces topple the Saddam regime in Iraq in 2003 was less satisfying. While the initial invasion swiftly succeeded in its aim, the lack of preparation to deal with what would happen next proved disastrous. The US and her allies found themselves embroiled in a bloody civil war that fostered anti-Western feeling, the implications of which are still being felt around the world.

added their expertise, including Air Chief Marshalls Sir Arthur Tedder and Sir Trafford Leigh-Mallory plus Admiral Sir Bertram Ramsay. Meanwhile, provisions were stockpiled and equipment dutifully prepared. If the landings were to fail, no-one could say it was for want of planning.

SLEIGHT OF HAND

While it was crucial that the Allies were ready for what lay ahead, it was equally as important that the Germans were not. If Hitler got wind of when and where the invasion was to occur, he could simply move his defenses into place and pick off the enemy at will. So came about one of the most intriguing elements of the D-Day landings: The plot to deceive Hitler as to the Allies' real intentions. As the British Prime Minister Winston Churchill noted in 1943: "In wartime, truth is so precious that she should always be attended by a bodyguard of lies."

Thus from late 1943 the Allies put Operation Bodyguard into action (see entry on Arminius on page 42). The aim was to divert Hitler's attention away from Normandy as much as possible, a goal achieved by an array of tactics. The British employed German double-agents to feed misinformation to Berlin. Because the German Enigma code had already been cracked, Allied spymasters were able to gauge just what bait Hitler and his henchmen were taking. For instance, information was disseminated to give the impression that Pas de Calais was to be the point of invasion. Indeed, on D-Day itself, dummies were parachuted into the waters around Pas de Calais to maintain the ruse and Hitler remained convinced that the activities in Normandy were merely a diversion from the real assault planned there.

Word was also put out that 350,000

Allied troops were stationed in Scotland ahead of an invasion via Norway, to be led by the US's General Patton. Fake radio messages were sent with the intention that the Germans intercepted them, and plywood airplanes and inflatable tanks were stationed on the ground to fool Nazi reconnaissance planes. In the event, German troops who could have defended Normandy were either held back in Scandinavia or scattered throughout France, unsure of when and where the Allies would hit. Sun Tzu, author of the ancient Chinese text *The Art of War* wrote: "All war is based on deception." Never was that more the case than on D-Day.

REACTING TO CIRCUMSTANCE

Yet for all the diligent preparation, D-Day did not go without a hitch for the Allies. The weather was not favorable (something even they could not do much about) but it was considered impossible to delay the operation until conditions improved. There were other things too that simply could not be prepared for. These included failures of equipment (for instance, many of the so-called DD amphibious tanks especially designed for the mission became engulfed in the choppy waters and sank before reaching land) and human error (conditions were not conducive to easy navigation so several vessels missed their designated landing zones).

D-Day itself began in the early hours with paratroopers attacking behind enemy lines to knock out key targets and capture strategically important positions such as bridges. A little later, German defenses were bombarded from both the air and sea, while French resistance fighters knocked out communications. Finally, amid all this confusion, Allied troops began landing on the beaches themselves, which had been divided into five main sites: The Americans were to take the beaches code-named Utah and Omaha, the British were responsible for Gold and Sword, while the Canadians led the way on Juno.

By the end of the day, 4,000 Allied troops were dead and the plans to join the five landing beaches in a united front had failed. Nonetheless, the Allies achieved their overall strategic aims, they had successfully made inroads into German-occupied France and dealt Nazi Germany a major military blow. By the end of August, France was liberated and within a year Hitler was dead by his own hand as Allied forces converged on Berlin from both east and west to bring the war to a close. D-Day was crucial to breaking Hitler's grip in Western Europe and could not have succeeded without what historian Correlli Barnett called "a never surpassed masterpiece of planning."

STRATEGY ANALYSIS

STRATEGY TYPE: *Preparation*
KEY STRATEGY: *Launched a combined air, sea, and land assault after months of preparation*
OUTCOME: *Operation Overlord, one of the most ambitious military assaults the world has ever seen*
Also used by: *US forces at the Battle of Iwo Jima, 1945., and the US-led coalition during Operation Desert Storm, 1991.*

43 EMPIRE BUILDING

RUPERT MURDOCH BECOMES A GLOBAL MEDIA MAGNATE

KEY PLAYER: *Rupert Murdoch (1931–)*
NATIONALITY: *Australian*
Strategy implemented: *1954–*
CONTEXT: *Rupert Murdoch began as proprietor of a single newspaper in Australia but soon started to expand internationally and across media platforms*

Rupert Murdoch is respected by some and loathed by others. Whether he cares much either way is moot. In a career spanning seven decades, he has built a business that includes television, film, books, newspapers, the internet, and sport, and which transcends international boundaries. As founder of the News Corp. conglomerate, his decision-making has always been driven by the bottom line, at the expense—according to his critics—of cultural and social impact.

Australian by birth, Murdoch was educated at the University of Oxford in England before returning home to take over his father's newspaper company, News Ltd, in Adelaide. Within a couple of years, he was already expanding his domestic interests, buying Perth's *Sunday Times*, and by the end of the decade, he had added two Sydney titles, *The Daily Mirror* and *Sunday Mirror*. Not willing to stop there in 1964 he established a new title, a politically engaged national called *The Australian*. Within a few short years he had built up a nationwide presence that ranged from low- to high-brow. It was a strategy he would come to replicate around the world.

Always an internationalist by nature, it was natural that Murdoch, having established a firm base in his homeland, would next look to the United Kingdom, where he had studied. (There are those who suggest that his experiences at Oxford informed his subsequent anti-establishment sentiments.) In 1969 he wrestled for control of the mass-market Sunday paper, the *News of the World*, along with a struggling daily, the *Sun*. Characteristically, Murdoch was not afraid of the challenge. He was prepared, as he always has been, to write off short-term losses for long-term gains. He set about redefining both titles. He converted the *Sun* from a broadsheet to a tabloid and introduced a form of sensationalist journalism new to the United Kingdom. In due course, he would also add pictures of topless young women in a bid to increase circulation.

With this move Murdoch showed his disregard for what critics might think of him. His concern was to make the papers commercially successful. In the case of the *Sun*, he took an also-ran and turned it into the biggest daily paper in the country, with a circulation currently exceeding four million. Nor was he repentant about his hands-on approach to dictating what went within its covers. As he has argued: "As proprietor, I'm

MURDOCH'S GLOBAL EMPIRE

Real time net worth $13.3 billion

Murdoch publishes 175 newspapers

Satellites deliver programs in 5 continents

Listed 32nd most powerful person in the world

Listed 78th richest person in the world

TV channels

Cable TV networks

Satellite TV networks

Film studios

Book publishers

Newspapers/data

Online

Marketing

the one who in the end is responsible for the success or failure of my papers ... why shouldn't I interfere when I see a way to strengthen the approach." Murdoch was building an empire and there was to be no doubt as to who was emperor.

FROM SMALL ACORNS

Having gained a foothold internationally, Murdoch was unstinting in his desire for expansion. He moved into the American market in 1973 with the purchase of the *San Antonio Express* and the *San Antonio News*. With the United States the global cultural capital, he moved there permanently a year later and in the 1980s even took citizenship, which allowed him to bypass regulations concerning foreign ownership of media. He built quickly, amassing a stable of tabloids and more upmarket publications. Whatever the market demanded, he provided. In his own words: "I answer to no-one but the public. They tell me what they want, and I give it to them."

In 1985 he gave a new signal of intent when he moved away from newspapers to buy the movie giant, Twentieth Century Fox. Next came television channels and the creation of the Fox broadcasting network. Murdoch wanted to broaden his holdings across media platforms as well as internationally.

In 1987 he purchased book publishing giant Harper & Row, which later merged with two other companies to form HarperCollins. Meanwhile, he was among the first to realize the potential of cable and satellite television, establishing BSkyB in 1990 and buying up rights to broadcast sporting events at seemingly outrageous cost. It was money well

TIME LINE

1931
Rupert Murdoch is born on March 11 in Melbourne, Australia.

1954
He takes over the family business, News Ltd.

1969
He enters the British media scene, buying the News of the World and the Sun.

1973
He buys his first American newspapers.

1979
News Corporation is registered in Australia.

1985
He buys Twentieth Century Fox and becomes a naturalized citizen of the US.

1986
He establishes Fox Broadcasting.

1990
He forms BSkyB, a satellite broadcaster.

2004
News Corp. is incorporated in the US.

2011
He shuts the News of the World after it is implicated in a phone-hacking scandal.

2012
It is announced that News Corp. will split into a television and film company and a newspaper and book publishing company.

invested, though, as his sports offering came to drive subscriptions. He also extended his geographical reach yet again with acquisitions throughout Europe, Asia, and the Pacific Basin.

A STRATEGIC APPROACH

While his purchases often took commentators by surprise, they were part of an all-embracing strategy rooted in his sense of changing trends. Ever alert to emerging technologies, he recognized that owning a broad spectrum of media platforms would allow for cross-fertilization of his various interests. Where many doubted that his satellite TV offerings would be able to challenge the might of the terrestrial channels, he was convinced he could make his services profitable. Sure enough, by adding the latest-release films to his sporting roster, he succeeded in confounding his critics. Meanwhile his newspapers played a vital role in, for instance, creating the hunger for Premier League Football that for a while only BSkyB could sate. Similarly, his book publishing interests provided ample material for newspaper serialization. And so the wheel turned with each part of his vast empire informing and benefiting the others.

THE GRAND PRAGMATIST

Allied to his unquestionably acute instinct for what will work commercially, Murdoch has been the arch pragmatist. He is famously ruthless in his business dealings, rarely paying above the odds. (Even the vast sums shelled out for soccer rights seem like money well spent now.) In his earlier years he borrowed heavily to fund his empire building, while his success in later years has seen him reinvest company profits. By 2000 his conglomerate, News Corp., comprised over 800 companies in some 50 countries.

He has, controversially, also used his media power to leverage social influence. In the United Kingdom he fostered close relations with successive prime ministers, notably Margaret Thatcher and Tony Blair. In the United States Murdoch has wielded influence primarily because politicians want Fox on side. He also has powerful personal friends such as Rudy Giuliani, a key supporter in the wake of the hacking scandal. Meanwhile, he has exerted pressure for reform of media ownership laws unfavorable to his interests. But while he courts the great and the good wherever he operates, he remains a distinctly "outsider figure" with few people of influence crossing him willingly.

When his *News of the World* was caught up in a phone-hacking scandal in 2011 that put the spotlight on the journalistic ethics of his staff, Murdoch responded in typically sanguine fashion. The venerable title was shut down and News Corp. was split into two constituent parts. It was a move that in fact brought a windfall to the Murdoch coffers. In 2013 Forbes put his personal worth at US$13.4 billion. As a 1996 *Time* magazine article put it: "If Machiavelli were alive today, he would be reading Murdoch." Whatever criticisms may be leveled at him, he has utterly changed the global media landscape. In his own words: "For better or for worse, our company is a reflection of my thinking, my character, my values."

▲ *Rupert Murdoch grew one of the world's most formidable media empires, garnering a fearsome reputation for himself in the process.*

ADAPTABILITY

Murdoch is a thoroughly modern businessman. He has proved enormously adaptable to a rapidly changing media environment, establishing a multimedia base that has allowed him to seize the opportunities presented by, for instance, satellite broadcasting and the internet, while his rivals struggle to catch up. He may at heart be a newspaper man, but in an age when the printing presses have given way to the touchscreen, he has remained a giant.

STRATEGY ANALYSIS

STRATEGY TYPE: *Dominance*
KEY STRATEGY: *Astute acquisitions to expand his portfolio internationally and across media platforms*
OUTCOME: *One of the world's largest media empires*
ALSO USED BY: *Ted Turner since the 1960s, and Jeff Bezos, Amazon, 1994 .*

44 FRANCHISING KING

RAY KROC TURNS MCDONALD'S INTO A GLOBAL FAST-FOOD GIANT

KEY PLAYER: *Ray Kroc (1902-84)*
NATIONALITY: *American*
Strategy implemented: *1955-84*
CONTEXT: *In the mid-1950s, Ray Kroc was a milkshake-mixer salesman in his 50s when he stumbled upon a burger restaurant in San Bernardino, California, run by the McDonald brothers. Recognizing the potential, he persuaded them to take their business nationwide*

Ray Kroc was closer to the end of his career than its beginning when he encountered the McDonald Brothers's self-service restaurant. He talked them into letting him sell their method coast-to-coast via a franchise model. Focusing on efficiency and consistent quality, he took a successful and popular restaurant and replicated it time and again until McDonald's came to dominate the fast-food market across the globe.

Ray Kroc was 52 years old and making a comfortable living selling multi-mixers in 1954. However, he noticed that sales were stalling as neighborhood soda fountains closed in rapidly accelerating numbers. That is why he was so interested when a small restaurant in San Bernardino, California, ordered eight of the mixers—enough to make some 40 milkshakes in one go. What sort of place needed to cater in those numbers, he wondered? His curiosity piqued, he paid the restaurant a visit.

What he saw made an immediate impact. Run by two brothers, Dick and Mac McDonald, it was a self-service, no-frills, take-away joint that offered a low-price menu restricted to burgers, fries, and drinks. The food was produced by a team working on an assembly line in the kitchen, so customers never had to wait more than a minute to receive their orders. This was, he realized, dining out to suit modern American tastes. And he wanted a piece of the action.

He could see that the restaurant was raking in a lot of cash and contemplated the riches to be made from a chain of them. So he approached the McDonalds about the possibility of going into business together. They, however, were happy with their lot and had no great desire to expand the business themselves. But they had recently lost their franchise agent and so were prepared to let Kroc sell their name and catering methods to other operators. In 1955 Kroc formed the McDonald's System Inc. to issue McDonald's franchises under license from the McDonald brothers. Nonetheless, he always saw the business as a partnership, likening it to a three-legged stool: franchisees as one leg, suppliers as the second leg, and McDonald's corporation as a third. "In business for yourself, but not by yourself," he proclaimed as he gathered together an army of motivated franchise-holders. By the end of his life, the enterprise would earn him half a billion dollars.

Sells more than **75** hamburgers every second

36,000 restaurants in over **100** countries

1 in 8 American workers have been employed by McDonald's and the company hires **1 million** workers in the United States every year

Big Mac went on sale in **1967** for **45** cents. **2.5 million** are sold per day (**900 million** per year)

McDonald's restaurants feed **69 million** people every day

20% of all sales at McDonald's include a toy

OPEN

MCDONALD'S IN NUMBERS

ASSEMBLY LINE DINNER

Kroc himself opened the first link in the McDonald's chain, in Des Plaines, Illinois, a Chicago suburb. Here he would perfect the McDonald's method and use the outlet as a showcase from which to sell more franchises. His motto for the company was "Quality, Service, Cleanliness, and Value." No matter who owned a franchise or where, he wanted each restaurant bearing the McDonald's name to offer the same levels of quality in product and service. With this aim in mind, and using the San Bernardino restaurant as a template, he demanded rigorous discipline in all areas of the business.

For a start, food preparation methods were to be uniform. Like a fast-food Henry Ford (see page 137) he insisted the kitchens used an assembly line to put together and deliver customer orders. In his kitchens, the making of a burger was to be as precise as the construction of a car. His system was documented in the 'McDonald's Method', a manual that ran to some 75 pages and which was composed by the company's then operations vice president, Fred Turner. Burgers were to consist of patties weighing precisely 1.6 ounces, a quarter-ounce of onion, a tablespoon of tomato ketchup, and a teaspoon of mustard. Fries, meanwhile, were to be cut to minutely precise dimensions. Ultimately, he opened a Hamburger University in Illinois to ensure staff were trained to the highest level. If the brand was going to be a success, precision and uniformity were essential.

Despite almost immediate success in selling franchises, the terms of his deal with the McDonalds meant Kroc made very little money. So he changed approach, buying up land which he then leased to franchisees, who paid him either a regular rent or a proportion of their profits—whichever was higher. In the blink of an eye, Kroc had become not only a fast-food operator but a property tycoon to boot. This guaranteed revenue stream proved key to further growing the brand.

TIME LINE

1902
Raymond Kroc is born on October 5 in Illinois.

1940
Richard and Mac McDonald open a restaurant in San Bernardino, California.

1948
They remodel it as a fast-food burger joint.

1954
Kroc visits the McDonald's restaurant on a sales trip and becomes the brothers' franchising agent.

1955
Kroc founds McDonald's Systems, Inc. (renamed the McDonald's Corporation in 1960).

1961
He buys out the McDonald brothers for US$2.7 million.

1963
McDonald's sells its billionth burger and opens its 500th branch.

1965
McDonald's is listed on the stock exchange.

1967
The first McDonald's restaurant outside the US opens in Canada.

1970
A branch opens in Costa Rica.

1971
McDonald's restaurants appear in Asia, Australia, and Europe.

1984
Kroc dies on January 14 in San Diego, California.

A GLOBAL BRAND

As an international icon of American culture, McDonald's has been at the forefront of globalization since the 1970s. To some, it offers a story of unparalleled success: A small, hometown brand grows to captivate a worldwide market. To others, it represents all that is wrong with globalization, from aggressive commercial practices to cultural homogeneity. Yet Kroc's magic has continued even after his death, with his company consistently registering among the top ten most recognizable brands in the world. In 2014 Interbrand, a brand management consultancy, valued it at US$42 billion, putting it second only to Coca-Cola in the food and beverages industry. Whatever the company's critics might feel, Kroc created a company that continues to lead the way in global growth.

THE COMFORT OF THE FAMILIAR

Within three years, McDonald's had sold its 100 millionth burger. In 1961 Kroc bought out the McDonald brothers, with whom relations had long been tricky, and in 1963 his chain notched up its billionth burger sale and 500th store opening. He had created a dining experience and a brand (epitomized by the famous "golden arches" logo) that made people feel comfortable. It might not offer the most glamorous surroundings or most sumptuous fare, but people knew what to expect from a McDonald's meal and they loved it. As Kroc once wryly observed: "The definition of salesmanship is the gentle art of letting the customer have it your way."

A GLOBAL BRAND

Even so, he was still not ready to sit back and enjoy the rewards of his success. Another of his maxims was that a laurel rested upon soon wilts. McDonald's had conquered America, keeping at bay rivals including Kentucky Fried Chicken and Burger King. Now he became intent upon world domination. A promotional character—a clown called Ronald McDonald—was introduced in 1963 and became as familiar to children around the world as prime ministers, presidents, and even Disney characters (see page 161). In 1965 the company went public, providing funds for international expansion.

Kroc encouraged franchisees to be creative, leading to the emergence of products including the Egg McMuffin and the Big Mac. As ever, their production was standardized so diners in any branch enjoyed precisely the same experience. In 1974, McDonald's symbolically surpassed US Steel in market value. Meanwhile, the "McDonald's System" was sold with astonishing success abroad, give or take a few concessions to local tastes and circumstances. In Japan, for instance, the company renamed itself Makudonaldo to assist with pronunciation, while German franchises sold beer and Indian McDonald's restaurants took beef and pork products off the menu. Nonetheless, a McDonald's restaurant remains recognizably a McDonald's restaurant wherever you go. That is why countless travelers head to a branch as a first port of call in a new land where they remain suspicious of the indigenous cuisine.

Kroc carried on working until his death in 1984 and his philosophy of efficiency and consistency endures. Today, 36,000 branches in over 100 countries serve approximately 69 million customers each day. Proof that Kroc got his recipe just right.

▲ Famous "Golden Arches": A portrait of Ray Kroc eating a burger outside the restaurant he introduced to the world.

STRATEGY ANALYSIS

STRATEGY TYPE: *Innovation*
KEY STRATEGY: *Bringing the assembly line into the kitchen*
OUTCOME: *One of the world's most recognizable and successful brands*
ALSO USED BY: *Harland Sanders, Kentucky Fried Chicken, 1952, and Fernando Duarte and Robert Brozin, Nando's, 1987.*

PREACHING A NEW VISION

MARTIN LUTHER KING ADVOCATED CIVIL DISOBEDIENCE TO GALVANIZE THE US CIVIL RIGHTS MOVEMENT

KEY PLAYER: *Martin Luther King (1929-68)*
NATIONALITY: *American*
STRATEGY IMPLEMENTED: *1955-68*
CONTEXT: *In an America in which segregation and anti-black legislation were still rife, Martin Luther King emerged as unofficial leader of the black civil rights movement*

Martin Luther King was a pastor whose skills as an orator and advocacy of nonviolent protest saw him rise to national and international prominence. He adapted the nonviolent strategies used by Gandhi in India to work in the context of the United States. His commitment to force change by peaceful means earned him the Nobel Peace Prize and succeeded in bringing about significant changes in the law.

In 1954 King became a pastor in Montgomery, Alabama. A year later, it was here that an African-American woman by the name of Rosa Parks was arrested for refusing to give up her seat on a bus to a white man. The episode became notorious around the world and proved the jumping-off point for King's career as a civil rights campaigner after he organized a high-profile boycott of the city's buses. In 1957 he co-founded the Southern Christian Leadership Conference and was given responsibility for coordinating the civil rights movement in the region.

America in the 1950s was a hotbed of racial discrimination. Many states operated a system of segregation so that black children could not attend school with white children, eat at the same restaurants, or sit on a bus in place of a white person. Such prejudice was enshrined in state laws, while there was also unlegislated racism that saw black people overlooked for jobs and left at serious economic and social disadvantage. Up until this point, the National Association for the Advancement of Colored People had dominated the black civil rights campaign. However, it worked within the existing legal and political systems (for instance fighting landmark court cases) but was not an organization of mass action. The Montgomery bus boycott transformed the civil rights landscape.

To a large extent, King found himself thrust into the limelight, having never sought a leadership role for himself. However, he was a natural leader able to command great authority and once he found himself in a position of responsibility, he refined and elucidated a new approach to winning civil rights reform.

LEARNING FROM A MASTER
King's philosophy was deeply anchored in his Christian beliefs, so that violence was instinctively anathema to him. However, he did not set out committed to nonviolence.

Martin Luther King waves to the crowd from Washington's Lincoln Memorial in 1968 on the day he delivered his "have a dream" address.

His interest in Mahatma Gandhi and his theory of nonviolent protest as a powerful means to effect change, was first piqued by a lecture he attended in the early 1950s and was consolidated by Bayard Rustin, a leading advisor to King in the 1950s who familiarized himself with the Indian's teachings. As King would come to describe it:

TIME LINE

1929
Martin Luther King, Jr. is born in Atlanta, Georgia, on January 15.

1954
He becomes pastor at Dexter Avenue Baptist Church in Montgomery, Alabama.

1955
Rosa Parks is arrested for refusing to give her bus seat to a white man. King coordinates a bus boycott in protest at her treatment.

1956
The United States Supreme Court rules that bus segregation is unconstitutional, marking a moral victory for King and the civil rights movement.

1957
King becomes president of the Southern Christian Leadership Conference.

1959
He travels to India to study Gandhi's nonviolent strategies.

1963
He leads protestors in a high-profile campaign in Birmingham, Alabama. In August he delivers his "I have a dream" speech.

1964
Time magazine names him "Man of the Year." In July the Civil Rights Act is passed. In December he is awarded the Nobel Peace Prize.

1965
He increasingly speaks out against the Vietnam War.

1967
He initiates a Poor Peoples' Campaign that transcends race.

1968
On April 4, King is shot dead on a hotel balcony in Memphis, Tennessee.

1983
King's birthday is designated a national holiday.

"Christ gave us the goals and Mahatma Gandhi the tactics."

In 1959 he made a visit to India so that he could better understand how the philosophy had been employed practically. "Since being in India," King commented, "I am more convinced than ever before that the method of nonviolent resistance is the most potent weapon available to oppressed people in their struggle for justice and human dignity."

For King, nonviolence was vital to "avoiding the internal violence of spirit" that would otherwise compromise his movement's desired goals, arguing that the "... means we use must be as pure as the ends we seek." While violence might force social change, he wanted it to be achieved by consensus. His nonviolence aimed for nothing less than to win the friendship and understanding of the oppressor in order to facilitate a lasting and complete change.

TAILORING THE PHILOSOPHY

Yet King was not so naïve as to believe that what worked in India's quest for independence would suit America, so he set about fashioning Gandhi's philosophy for his own purposes. For instance, while Gandhi led a major political party (Congress), King worked hard to maintain political neutrality. He argued that both the Democrats and Republicans had let down the black population in different ways throughout their history and that by maintaining nonalignment he could ensure he became neither servant nor master of either. He also made the bold demand that the government ought to make financial recompense for its historic crimes through payments to disadvantaged groups.

King understood the power of media and employed his tremendous skills as a public speaker. His personal charisma was arguably his greatest strength, enabling him to spread his message across boundaries of race, age, religion, and social class. By 1963—a year in which some 20,000 people were arrested for their involvement in the civil rights movement—he was at the peak of his powers. Leading sit-ins and rallies, he was also the figurehead of protests in Birmingham, Alabama, where police used water cannons, dogs, and batons against protesting students and children. His eloquence captivated not only his core supporters but also white liberals up and down the nation. Like Gandhi before him, he was starting to change the way the oppressor thought about itself.

▲ Demonstrators outside the White House in 1965. Martin Luther King galvanised the civil rights movement in the United States.

DELIVERING A VISION OF THE FUTURE

He delivered his most famous speech on August 28 that year in Washington, D.C., in front of a quarter of a million protestors. Standing before the Lincoln Memorial, King delivered his seminal "I have a dream" speech. Poetic in its content, it expressed "a dream deeply rooted in the American dream—one day this nation will rise up and live up to its creed, 'We hold these truths to be self-evident: that all men are created equal.'" With a single address, he captured the essence of his movement, inspiring the converted and winning over countless new followers. It was difficult to find fault with the intent of his words, which invoked the founding principles of the nation itself. It was, in fact, a defining moment in the construction of the national psyche.

Nonetheless, King still had his critics. Militant movements such as the Nation of Islam and the Black Panthers spoke out against his equanimity. Malcolm X, perhaps the other most prominent figure in black civil rights in this period, argued: "I believe it's a crime for anyone being brutalized to continue to accept that brutality without doing something to defend himself." But King was determined that his middle way was the

PROTEST FOR CHANGE

Martin Luther King's assassination in 1968 brought his life to a tragic end but immortalized him for future generations, who continue to venerate him and adopt his principles. His commitment to civil disobedience as a form of peaceful protest has been reflected in recent years in, for instance, the Occupy movement against the excesses of global capitalism, and even in aspects of the Arab Spring. Furthermore, while racism continues to raise its ugly head in American society, it is self-evident that the country has come a long way in the half-century or so since "I have a dream." Most notably, a black man came to power in the White House. In 2009 Barack Obama acknowledged his debt to both Gandhi and King, whose ethics "changed the world."

King met Malcolm X just once, in 1964. Where King preached peace, Malcolm X's approach was more aggressively confrontational. ▲

most effective route to achieve genuine change. Sure enough, a year after the Lincoln Memorial address, the government passed the Civil Rights Act, outlawing discrimination on grounds of race.

WINNING HEARTS AND MINDS

King's philosophy is neatly summed up in his 1958 work *Stride Toward Freedom*: "We will match your capacity to inflict suffering with our capacity to endure suffering ... And in winning our freedom we will so appeal to your heart and conscience that we will win you in the process."

King's passive resistance was never the manifestation of a weak spirit, but the fruits of a boundlessly strong one. It imbued him with an enormous moral authority, which played well with many who might have instinctively opposed his politics and was crucial to drawing key figures to the negotiating table. Here was a man with whom Middle America could do business, but more than that, here was a man who persuaded Middle America to take a look into its own soul.

While America is still dealing with its racial demons (it is a fact that a black American is still more likely to be poorer, less educated and in prison that their white counterpart), much progress has undeniably been made in terms of social mobility. No longer can black Americans be deprived of the right to vote, to go to school, or to live in the neighbourhood of their choice. Fundamentally, racism has been sidelined, a sorry anachronism no longer acceptable within civil society. No-one else did more to move the issue forward than King, whose selfless philosophy commanded such wide appeal. Furthermore, his ideals have fueled the passions of other civil rights movements around the world, from South America to the Eastern Bloc and Tiananmen Square.

STRATEGY ANALYSIS

STRATEGY TYPE: *Leadership*
KEY STRATEGY: *Advocating civil disobedience and galvanizing the American civil rights movement with impassioned oration*
OUTCOME: *Legislation to outlaw racial discrimination*
ALSO USED BY: *Mohandas Gandhi, and the Occupy movement, founded in 2011.*

46 ATTENTION TO DETAIL

OSCAR NIEMEYER AND LÚCIO COSTA MERGED ARTISTRY AND FUNCTIONALITY IN A NEW CAPITAL FOR BRAZIL

KEY PLAYERS: *Oscar Niemeyer (1907-2012) and Lúcio Costa (1902-98)*
NATIONALITY: *Brazilian*
STRATEGY IMPLEMENTED:
1956-60
CONTEXT: *It had been the plan since the nineteenth century to transfer Brazil's capital from Rio de Janeiro but it was only in 1956 that President Juscelino Kubitschek pushed the project through. Niemeyer and Costa were chosen as its chief architects*

Rio de Janeiro is undeniably one of the world's great cities but its location on the coast means that it is vulnerable to attack. This was the original motivation for moving Brazil's capital, a decision taken as far back as the 1820s, though it would take another 130 years before the project got underway. By then, it was hoped that a new, visionary metropolis would help revitalize the moribund Brazilian interior. With careful planning and fastidious attention to detail, Niemeyer and Costa turned the dream into a reality.

Numerous Brazilian governments had long considered that an inland location for the capital city would offer greater security and that it could spur economic and social development too. In 1891 a new constitution even included provision for the new city to be built on the Planato Central. Yet the weeks and months rolled into years and decades without anything being done. Successive governments lacked either the political will or economic muscle to get things moving.

That all changed in 1955 when presidential hopeful Juscelino Kubitschek promised, if elected, to build a new capital on the interior plateau. After he took office, he stayed true to his promise and in April 1956 pushed through a bill establishing an agency to oversee construction of the metropolis, which was to be called Brasília. Kubitschek wanted a city that was not merely functional, but encapsulated something of the spirit of the nation and which would prompt large-scale regeneration.

Such a project was not without precedent. Washington, D.C. and Russia's St Petersburg were both "planned" capitals, but such schemes had a heritage of running vastly over-budget and over-schedule. If it was to work, Brasília needed a team of effective visionaries to see the job through. They would need to marry artistic vision with the practical considerations of creating a viable capital city for Brazil.

A BLANK SHEET OF PAPER
In 1957 an open competition was held to become chief urban planner. Costa won with proposals for a city "born of a primary gesture of one who marks or takes possession of

TIME LINE

1902
Lúcio Costa is born on February 27 in France.

1907
Oscar Niemeyer is born on December 15 in Rio de Janeiro.

1930s
Niemeyer and Costa begin their professional partnership, both working with Le Corbusier.

1956
Niemeyer is approached by President Juscelino Kubitschek to work on a new capital city.

1957
Costa wins a public competition to be its urban planner. Niemeyer is to be chief architect of its civic buildings. Construction begins.

1960
Brasília is inaugurated on April 21. Its population is around 140,000 people. The Palácio do Planalto (the seat of government) is completed.

1961
The University of Brasília is established.

1964
A military dictatorship takes over in Brazil and holds power for 21 years. Niemeyer is forced into exile abroad.

1970
Work finishes on the Cathedral of Brasília and the Itamaraty Palace. The population reaches 500,000.

1985
Niemeyer returns to Brazil.

1987
Brasília gains UNESCO World Heritage status.

1992
Niemeyer becomes leader of Brazil's Communist Party.

1998
Costa dies on June 13 in Rio.

2012
Niemeyer dies on December 5 in Rio.

a place, two axes crossing at right angles, the very sign of the Cross." Viewed from above, Costa's city looks rather like an aeroplane or a dragonfly. His vision was clear: "The city should be planned for orderly and efficient work, but, at the same time, should be both vital and pleasing, suitable for reverie and intellectual speculation, it should be such a city that, with time, could become not only the seat of government and administration, but also one of the more lucid and distinguished cultural centers in the country."

By this time, Costa was already a well-established star of the Brazilian

TIME AND MONEY

It has traditionally taken centuries, even millennia, for mega-cities to emerge. However there have been exceptions where a government has decided to build a metropolis out of the dust, from Pi-Ramesses in ancient Egypt to St Petersburg and Washington, D.C. In recent decades, there has been a growing trend towards creating brand new capitals, especially in the developing world. We have seen the emergence, for instance, of Belmopan in Belize, Naypyidaw in Burma, Putrajaya in Malaysia, and Abuja in Nigeria. More often than not, such vast projects have taken decades to complete, often financially crippling the nation into the bargain. Few, it must be said, are regarded with great warmth by their populations. These relative failures only go to highlight the achievement of Niemeyer and Costa in creating a city in under four years that truly does hold its own on the global stage.

> ▲ The spectacular interior of Brasilia's cathedral, one of the modernist landmarks that Niemeyer and Costa raised from the soil.

architectural firmament. He had championed modernism since the 1920s, working with the European master of modernist architecture, Le Corbusier. He had taken Le Corbusier's style and adapted it to Brazil's specific needs, working on several occasions in tandem with Oscar Niemeyer, who had initially been his intern in the 1930s. Together they had created the Brazilian pavilion for the 1939 New York World's Fair and joined forces on a landmark building in Rio for the Ministry of Health and Education. Niemeyer was also a favorite of Kubitschek, so it was perhaps little surprise that Niemeyer was brought on board to be the chief designer of Brasília's civic buildings. This was to be a project guided by personal vision, not one governed by committee—a method that so often stifles large public infrastructure projects as organizers attempt to provide all things to all men.

FUNCTIONAL AND BEAUTIFUL

Instead, Niemeyer and Costa were given their wings to create. Niemeyer was a socialist by political inclination (he would lead Brazil's Communist Party in the 1990s) and designed buildings that strove to be egalitarian as well as functional. Apartment blocks were designed to house government employees of all ranks next to each other. Reinforced concrete was one of his materials of choice but he played with the

A satellite image of the Brazilian capital. The location was chosen in part to economically revitalize the country's moribund interior.

often rather utilitarian lines of modernism to give them a Brazilian twist. "What attract me are free and sensual curves," he once said. "The curves we find in mountains, in the waves of the sea, in the body of the woman we love."

It was an aesthetic he brought to fruition in such constructions as the presidential headquarters, the national congress complex, the main city thoroughfare and the sumptuous Metropolitan Cathedral. These were buildings designed to fulfill a job while pleasing the eye and raising the spirit. The future, he seemed to suggest, could be functional and just, but elegant and playful too. Costa, meanwhile, kept close control of all aspects of the urban planning, down to the color of the hats the bus drivers were to wear (gray, to convey respect). While Niemeyer unleashed his imagination, Costa ensured a unity of purpose across the city.

FROM DREAM TO REALITY

Brasília was formally dedicated and the capital transferred there on April 21 1960. A capital city had emerged out of nothing in just four years—an unprecedented achievement. Nonetheless, a project of such scale had, and has, its critics. Because they prized open space so much, Costa and Niemeyer created a city that is difficult to traverse other than in a car, which does not perhaps fit the twenty-first-century environmental ideal. It was also designed to be zonal, incorporating residential, civic, commercial, and cultural areas. As such, some judge it to be rather clinical, missing the appealing "messiness" of a city that grows organically and has mixed-use neighborhoods. So it may not qualify as a utopia, but which city does? For all its flaws, it is a metropolis in which many aspects of Niemeyer and Costa's combined vision came to fruition. Its buildings are playful and memorable, its planning well-intentioned and ambitious.

Niemeyer spoke of their aim to "build a new capital to bring progress to the interior of Brazil" and it has indeed succeeded in inspiring long-term economic growth in the region. While the construction phase almost inevitably went over budget, it has indeed succeeded in inspiring long-term economic growth in the region. And as the city population expands naturally, it may yet take on some of the "messiness" that marks out the great world cities like Rio, New York, and London. For all its imperfections (and even because of them), Brasília is highly successful as a manifestation of personal vision, embodying socialist politics, modernist aesthetics, and an understanding of the needs of those who live there. Furthermore, its lead architects succeeded in creating

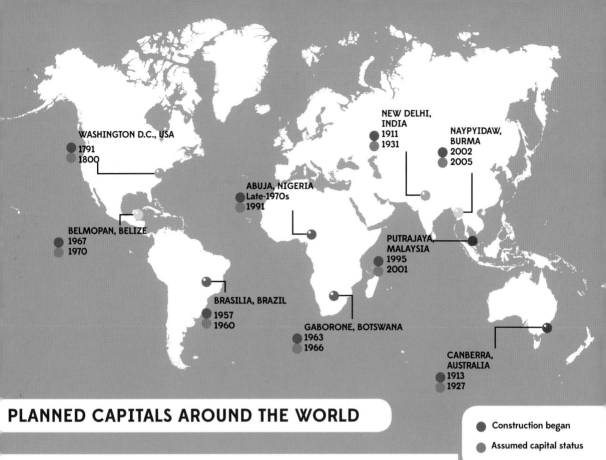

WASHINGTON D.C., USA
1791
1800

NEW DELHI, INDIA
1911
1931

NAYPYIDAW, BURMA
2002
2005

ABUJA, NIGERIA
Late-1970s
1991

BELMOPAN, BELIZE
1967
1970

PUTRAJAYA, MALAYSIA
1995
2001

BRASILIA, BRAZIL
1957
1960

GABORONE, BOTSWANA
1963
1966

CANBERRA, AUSTRALIA
1913
1927

PLANNED CAPITALS AROUND THE WORLD

● Construction began
● Assumed capital status

that distinctly Brazilian twist that roots the city in a specific place and culture. Brasília is no "build by numbers" city. The result of a careful balancing of practical considerations and artistic vision, it is a functional city that was delivered on schedule (even if the construction phase inevitably went a little over budget) and is testament to its creators' ability to combine grand scope with an eye for detail. Instead, Niemeyer and Costa created a bold template for designing our cities of the future.

STRATEGY ANALYSIS

STRATEGY TYPE: *Preparation*
KEY STRATEGY: *Combining civic planning with modernist architecture to create a modern city.*
OUTCOME: *The creation of a hugely ambitious and visionary capital in under four years*
ALSO USED BY: *The American government at Washington, D.C., 1791, and Canberra, Australia, 1915-27.*

BE A BIG FISH

BILL GATES PROVIDED THE SOFTWARE THAT RUNS THE WORLD

KEY PLAYER: *Bill Gates (1955-)*
NATIONALITY: *American*
STRATEGY IMPLEMENTED: *1980-*
CONTEXT: *The 1970s saw the birth of the modern computer age. Bill Gates, head of Microsoft, was one of Silicon Valley's hottest young properties when, in 1980, he agreed a deal with industry giant IBM that allowed his company's products to dominate the global market*

As head of Microsoft, Bill Gates has become one of the richest men on the planet. By focusing first on business customers and then personal users, he has seen his company's software (and in particular, Microsoft Windows) become the most widely used in the world. He paved the way for this success by repeatedly being first to market in the burgeoning software sector and by agreeing astute deals that ensured the rapid spread of his products.

As a schoolboy, Gates was an exceptional software coder, providing money-making programs to commercial firms while still a teen and negotiating time to hone his skills on his school's computers in return for digitizing his teacher's schedules. There was never much doubt about which industry he would go in to.

In 1975, Gates—then a student at Harvard—and his old school friend, Paul Allen, were keen to take their passion for computer programming to the next level. Hungry for progress, Gates made an audacious move that epitomizes his approach to business. At the time a company called MITS had released one of the first microcomputers, the Altair 8800. Such machines were very expensive but Gates had come to believe that the price would soon fall so that eventually it would be profitable to produce accompanying software. This was something of a grand assumption, but one that proved to be right. The gutsy Gates was determined to become a leading figure in an industry that hardly even existed.

So he rang up the head of MITS, Ed Roberts, and told him he was developing a modified version of the BASIC programming language for use with the Altair 8800. Intrigued, Roberts told Gates he'd love to see a demonstration and set up a meeting for a few weeks later. In reality, Gates and Allen had produced no such software but were simply sounding out whether it would have potential interest. Now they found themselves up against the tightest of deadlines to come up with something to impress Roberts. Remarkably, they succeeded and entered into a deal with MITS. A short while afterward, Gates and Allen established Micro-soft (jettisoning the hyphen later on). Backing his ability to deliver, Gates had chanced his arm and it had paid off.

MICROSOFT IN NUMBERS

1 By the early 1990s had sold more than **100 million** copies of the program MS-DOS

2 In the 1990s **90%** of the world's PCs ran on Microsoft operating system

3 1996: Topped **$2 billion** in net income for first time. Grew to **$14 billion** in 2009

4 In 2010 the Xbox 360 was the most-used games console in the United States

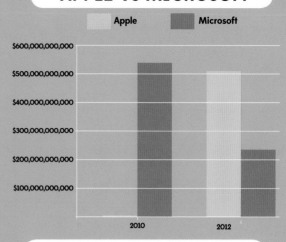

APPLE VS MICROSOFT

Apple | Microsoft

In December 2000, Microsoft had a market capitalization of $510 billion, dwarfing Apple's $4.8 billion. As of June 2012 Microsoft had dropped to a market cap of $249 billion, while Apple boasted a market cap of $541 billion.

AUDACIOUS DEAL-MAKER

The company went from strength to strength in the next few years, developing software for a number of different companies. By the end of the decade Microsoft had annual revenues of some US$2.5 million per year. For some, that would have been success enough, but Gates always dreamed bigger and in 1980 he made the deal that would change everything.

IBM was the undisputed giant of the computing world and it was preparing to market its first personal computer. However, word got out that the company was struggling to perfect its operating system, which would run everything the computer did. So in July 1980, Gates made an approach, offering to create an operating system on their behalf. They readily agreed and Gates took a typically pragmatic approach to fulfilling the brief. He bought the rights to an existing operating system from a Seattle company,

APPLE VS MICROSOFT

The personal rivalry between Gates and Steve Jobs at Apple helped drive the progress of the technological revolution that began in the 1970s. While Jobs saw the computer as a means of expressing individual creativity, Gates saw it as a driver of commerce. The two fell out over the release of Windows, with Jobs accusing Microsoft of ripping off Apple's interface but by the mid-1990s Microsoft seemed to have won the battle of the tech firms. That all changed after the turn of the century, when Apple creations such as the iPad, iPod, and iPhone saw the company outstrip Microsoft in terms of value. But the world has proved big enough for both, and tech consumers have reaped the benefits.

TIME LINE

1955
Bill Gates is born in Seattle on October 28.

1968
He writes his first computer program.

1975
Gates and his school friend, Paul Allen, form Microsoft after selling a software program to MITS.

1980
Gates reaches a deal with IBM to provide an operating system for the industry giant's forthcoming personal computer.

1985
Microsoft launches Windows.

1986
Microsoft goes public, earning Gates over a quarter of a billion dollars in a day.

1989
Microsoft Office launches.

1990
The launch of Windows 3 sees Microsoft achieve sales of US$1 billion per year.

1995
Windows 95 is released, featuring the Internet Explorer browser.

1998
The US Department of Justice launches an anti-trust investigation against Microsoft.

2000
Steve Ballmer replaces Gates as chief executive. A judge rules that Microsoft should be split into new companies—one producing operating systems, and the other software. The ruling is later overturned. The Bill and Melinda Gates Foundation begins operating.

2008
Microsoft receives a record fine from the European Commission for noncompliance with previous anti-trust rulings. Gates ends his full-time post with Microsoft to concentrate on his Foundation's work.

paying them a modest one-off figure. He then reconfigured it to the needs of IBM, presenting them with MS-DOS (the Microsoft Disk Operating System). IBM accepted it, marketing it as PC-DOS.

The IBM PC came with a choice of three software packages, including PC-DOS. Gates knew that his long-term fortunes lay in being number one of the three. So Microsoft took a relatively low one-time fee for the product, which meant it was sold much cheaper than the competing packages. Crucially, Microsoft also retained copyright in PC-DOS. This meant that they could license the system to other companies manufacturing PCs on the IBM model, as Gates predicted (again correctly) would happen.

It was another calculated risk. However, PC-DOS was by far the most popular of IBM's packages and as sales of the IBM computers escalated, so too did Microsoft's reputation. Furthermore, they were soon providing MS-DOS to other manufacturers and making serious money on the back of it. Sales increased from US$7 million to US$16 million between 1980 and 1981. Within a few years Microsoft was by far and away the biggest name in the booming software business. A less astute operator than Gates might have seen dollar signs in his eyes when he partnered with IBM. Instead, Gates made only a little profit from that deal but used it as a springboard to much bigger things.

READING THE MARKET
In spite of his success with PC-DOS, Gates was not prepared to rest on his laurels. As he explained many years later, in a sector as rapidly evolving as the technology business, "Any company that stays the same will be passed by very quickly." Indeed, he was already well aware that the "next big thing" on the software

horizon—a graphical user interface (GUI)—could sweep MS-DOS away. Gates was determined that Microsoft should remain ahead of the game.

By now, the industry was becoming less about the giants of old, like IBM, and more about the agile young guns, of whom Microsoft was only truly rivaled by Steve Jobs and Steve Wozniak's Apple. Gates knew that Apple was preparing to release the Macintosh personal computer in 1984, complete with an elegant user interface that users could navigate with a mouse. Gates's response was to announce in late 1983 the impending arrival of his own GUI, Microsoft Windows.

▲ *Bill Gates at the 2013 Clinton Global Initiative Annual Meeting. He has evolved from global technology king into philanthropist.*

In the end the GUI Microsoft Windows did not appear on the market until 1985, a year after the Macintosh. Although it was not an immediate smash hit, it gradually gained traction in the market and was soon outselling the second-generation operating system it had developed for IBM. Although Apple had its devotees and Windows its critics, after several reboots Windows was utterly dominating the market by the 1990s (notably after the release of the Microsoft Office suite), with its software running somewhere in the region of 90 percent of the world's personal computers. As of 2014, Microsoft had revenues in excess of US$86 billion and employed almost 130,000 people around the world. Gates had proved himself not only a talented coder but also a brilliant market strategist.

STRATEGY ANALYSIS

STRATEGY TYPE: *Innovation*
KEY STRATEGY: *Offering deals to secure dominant market share*
OUTCOME: *Microsoft Windows, the world's most widely used software*
ALSO USED BY: *John D. Rockefeller, 1870–1911, and Apple and the launch of the iTunes Store, opened in 2003.*

TAKING SHOPPING ONLINE

JEFF BEZOS CREATED THE WORLD'S LEADING INTERNET RETAILER

KEY PLAYER: *Jeff Bezos (1964-)*
NATIONALITY: *American*
STRATEGY IMPLEMENTED: *1994-*
CONTEXT: *Jeff Bezos was a successful hedge-fund manager when he read a report on the rapid acceleration of internet commerce. Determined not to miss the boat, he set to work on a business model ideally suited to the new technology*

Bezos created Amazon after reading a report that internet commerce was growing by some 2,300 percent per year in the early 1990s. Recognizing a once-in-a-lifetime opportunity, he coolly devised a list of 20 products he believed were most suitable for online retail. Deciding to initially focus on books, he established Amazon as the world biggest online bookstore. Since then it has turned into a general retailer unrivaled in its global reach.

Fearful of the regret he would feel if he didn't try to win a piece of the cyber Wild West that was emerging in the 1990s, Bezos gave up his lucrative hedge-fund career. However, he retained the same steely approach in his new business. He settled on books as his key commodity because they attract global demand, there is an almost endless supply of titles to sell, and they come with a low price-point perfect to reel in punters.

He first called his business cadabra.com but changed the name for fear that it sounded too much like cadaver. He opted instead for Amazon as a name redolent of exoticism and grandness. Furthermore, it conveniently guarantees an early entry in any alphabetical listing. Bezos was conscious that in the online world—even more than in its bricks-and-mortar equivalent—branding is essential. With no storefront to bring customers in, it is almost all you have.

He launched the company from his garage, using his own funds. The enormous personal risk involved indicates the faith he had in his business plan and his ability to make it work. Just like Mark Zuckerberg (see page 210), Bezos was looking to play the long game in a fast-moving online environment where many players were looking only at the short term. Amazon sold its first book in 1995 and within a few months it was recording sales of US$20,000 each week from customers in every state of the United States and from more than 40 countries around the world. It was a promising start but brought little profit. But Bezos wasn't interested in turning a quick buck.

ALL IN THE NUMBERS

He knew it would be years before Amazon was a truly profitable company and he was entirely comfortable with that. Indeed, Amazon famously did not turn a profit until the end

AMAZON'S DIVERSIFICATION

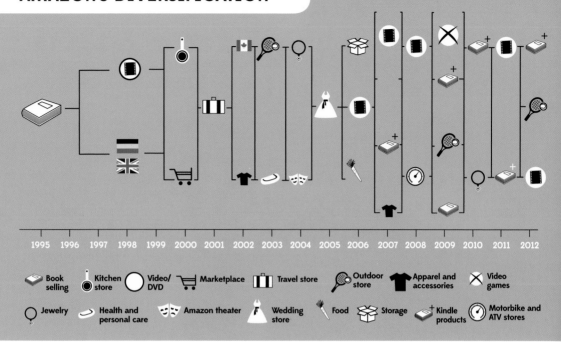

1995	1996	1997	1998	1999	2000	2001	2002	2003	2004	2005	2006	2007	2008	2009	2010	2011	2012

Book selling · **Kitchen store** · **Video/DVD** · **Marketplace** · **Travel store** · **Outdoor store** · **Apparel and accessories** · **Video games**

Jewelry · **Health and personal care** · **Amazon theater** · **Wedding store** · **Food** · **Storage** · **Kindle products** · **Motorbike and ATV stores**

of 2001, when it recorded a US$5 million surplus on revenues in excess of a billion dollars. Far more important than a quick profit, Bezos knew, was to keep growing the business in these early years. The internet was changing so quickly that to stand still would prove fatal. So he ploughed income back into the company and secured significant private investment before going public in 1997. In so doing, Amazon evolved from online book retailer to dealer in everything from DVDs to clothes, DIY products, and diapers. His openness that Amazon did not expect to make a profit for years put off many investors but plenty of others saw the potential. By a process of self-selection, they shared Bezos's willingness to be in for the long haul. As he noted: "We're trying to build something lasting."

Given his Wall Street background, it is little surprise that he has always kept his eye on the bottom line. He can be a notoriously spiky boss, often accused of paying little heed to an individual's personal circumstances if they are not adding value to the business. Such an attitude might not make him a great humanitarian but it has only been to the benefit of the business. In addition, he places unstinting reliance on metrics to guide the business: What can be measured is, and that raw data is used to determine the development of everything from the company's customer service provision to the pricing of individual products. Data, after all, does not lie.

That is not always good news for suppliers and partners, many of whom have accused the company of squeezing them into near oblivion in Amazon's quest for ever-lower prices for the customer and greater profit margins. For instance, Dennis Johnson, the co-owner of the small publishing company Melville House, has reported that in 2004 Amazon requested a payment from his company but refused to yield details of how many of the firm's books it had sold. When Johnson refused to pay, he found all his book listings on the site were stripped of their "Buy" button. Cowed, he duly paid the amount

1964
Jeffrey Bezos is born in New Mexico, on January 12.

1994
He gives up his career in hedge funds to found Amazon.

1995
Amazon launches.

1997
The company goes public.

1998
The site starts to sell videos and DVDs as well as books. Amazon launches in the UK and Germany.

2000
Amazon begins operating in France and Japan.

2002
The company records a quarterly profit for the first time. Canada gets its own Amazon site and Amazon Web Services launches.

2004
Amazon enters the Chinese market.

2007
Amazon introduces the Kindle, an electronic reading device that revolutionizes the publishing industry.

2009
Amazon Publishing begins trading.

2010
Amazon starts operating in Italy.

2012
Amazon begins trading in Brazil and launches Amazon Games Studio.

2013
Bezos buys the Washington Post. Amazon launches in India and Mexico. Amazon Art also begins trading.

2014
Amazon enters the Spanish and Dutch markets. Bezos's personal wealth is estimated at over US$30 billion.

demanded and his books became available for purchase again. The "bottom line" approach has not made Amazon popular in many quarters but it has undoubtedly been a commercially astute move.

HARD BOTTOM LINE
Amazon has also employed analytics to see what the opposition is doing well and where Amazon might catch up. This has led to an aggressive expansionism that has seen the company buy dozens of rivals over the years, so that Bezos at times comes across like a latter-day Rockefeller (see page 116). For example, in 2010 Amazon bought Quidsi—a young start-up company retailing products to stretched new parents—having effectively made an offer its owners could not refuse. Wal-Mart was also bidding for Quidsi but were too slow off the mark, while Bezos

CLICK AND COLLECT

Bezos realized that the internet could connect a retailer to consumers like never before. It allowed him to create a store that could supply anything to anybody. So started a retail revolution that continues to evolve, with no major retailer now daring to do without an online presence. The same year that Amazon launched, so did eBay, an auction site that arguably marked the ultimate democratization of the market place as buyers established the true going rate of everything from luxury yachts to stuffed stoats to items of food nibbled by celebrities. In 2013 global e-commerce was valued at around US$1.2 trillion. And Bezos had not missed the boat.

made it clear he would drive Quidsi from the market by slashing diaper prices if they would not sell to him.

OUR MASTER, THE CUSTOMER
If suppliers and rivals have grounds for complaint, Bezos has always striven to give the customer the best deal. His philosophy is that everything should stem from what the consumer wants. Indeed, the company's "14 principles of leadership" begin with the assertion that "leaders start with the customer and work backward." The focus is always on lowering prices where possible, expanding the range of goods and services available and offering fast and reliable customer care. While data drives the business, Bezos has a personal email open to the public so that he can maintain direct contact with his end-users. When an employee once demanded to know why whole teams of people were directed away from their day-to-day business to deal with seemingly trivial customer complaints, Bezos asserted that they represented nothing less than "an audit ... We treat them as precious sources of information."

The "principles of leadership" further elucidate the company ethos that always keeps the customer at its center. The company's managers, for instance, are urged to think long-term, be inventive, and search for elegantly simple solutions. They are also expected to "look round corners for ways to serve customers."

Bezos regards the internet as an evolving hinterland, constantly changing and throwing up shocks and challenges. By a combination of rigorous attention to the bottom line and relentless customer focus, he has created a store that aims to give everybody everything—an achievement only possible in the internet age and unparalleled in the history of commerce.

▲ Bezos's pragmatic approach toward retailing has made Amazon a global force but has also drawn criticism from those who believe suppliers suffer.

STRATEGY ANALYSIS

STRATEGY TYPE: *Dominance*
KEY STRATEGY: *Offering online consumers the widest range of products at the lowest prices*
OUTCOME: *An online "everything store"*
ALSO USED BY: *Ebay, founded 1995, and Alibaba, founded in China in 1999.*

49 CONNECT THE WORLD

MARK ZUCKERBERG CONQUERED THE CYBER-WORLD OF SOCIAL NETWORKING

KEY PLAYER: *Mark Zuckerburg (1984-)*

NATIONALITY: *American*

STRATEGY IMPLEMENTED: *2004-*

CONTEXT: *As internet usage rocketed in the new millennium, a Harvard student Mark Zuckerberg spotted a gap in the market. He developed a platform devoted to social networking, where mutually acknowledged "friends" can share news, personal information, and media*

In 2004 Mark Zuckerberg was a twenty-year-old student at Harvard with a passionate interest in computer coding. Taking inspiration from college yearbooks in which students' information (including brief biographical sketches and contact details) are included, he decided to set up a website for his fellow university alumni. As his innovation rapidly gained in popularity, he realized his real mission was nothing less than to "help people become more open" in the internet age.

From a young age, Zuckerberg showed a talent for programming, creating software in his senior year at school that brought him to the attention of both AOL and Microsoft. However, he gave up the opportunity of a job in Silicon Valley to take a place at Harvard in 2002. It was not long before his extraordinary IT skills got him a reputation around campus. Firstly, he created Facemash, a light-hearted site that used hacked photos of students, which their contemporaries were invited to judge in the style of the established "Hot or Not" website. For his unauthorized use of images, Zuckerberg earned himself a college reprimand. It was, though, symbolic of Zuckerberg's belief that the rules of privacy were changing in the online era.

In February 2004 he led a small posse of friends in launching thefacebook.com from his dorm room. In years to come, exactly who made what contribution in this launch phase would prompt several expensive lawsuits. Clearly, though, Zuckerberg was at the forefront of the code-creation, taking inspiration from extant social networking sites like Friendster and Myspace. thefacebook.com launched small, serving only Harvard's student body. Within a few weeks, half of the faculty had an account. But while several of Zuckerberg's partners in crime were happy to have achieved such notable local success, Zuckerberg himself was already dreaming bigger. Much bigger.

OPENING UP THE WORLD

After the website was rolled out to other colleges and universities throughout the United States over the next few months, Zuckerberg decided to put his money where his mouth

FACEBOOK BY NUMBERS

Gender breakdown:

53% female

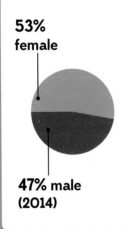

47% male (2014)

 Over **1.39 billion** monthly active Facebook users

 9,199 Facebook employees

 Most common age demographic: **25 to 34 (30% of users)**

 890 million daily active users

Statistics as of December 2014

was. He turned his back on his studies to concentrate full-time on the business, moving operations to Palo Alto in California (the heart of Silicon Valley) and in 2005 changing the company name to the neater "Facebook." By August 2005, he had raised close to US$13 million in capital for development and in 2006 anyone with an email could join up to the network. That year he turned down the opportunity to sell the business to search engine giant Yahoo! for US$1 billion. In short order, Facebook had gone from college hobby to serious business.

His rejection of the Yahoo! offer illustrates one of Zuckerberg's strategic strengths: His ability to look very long-term. That is a potent weapon when set against his skill at analyzing the latest technical developments, envisaging new applications, and perceiving trends. So it was that Facebook soon overtook older social networking giants like MySpace.

Zuckerberg has always been very clear about what Facebook offers its users: The ability to share information quickly and widely. In 2010 he wrote an article for the *Washington Post* that neatly encapsulates what he considers makes Facebook not only

1984
Mark Zuckerberg is born in White Plains, New York, on May 14.

2003
While a student at Harvard, he releases a website called Facemash, a forerunner of Facebook.

2004
Facebook launches, but for Harvard students only. It soon spreads to other educational institutions and Facebook is incorporated as a company, moving operations to Palo Alto. It has a million users by the end of the year.

2006
Yahoo! tries to buy Facebook for US$1 billion.

2008
The site gets its hundred-millionth user.

2012
Facebook is listed on the stock exchange, with an initial valuation of US$104 billion. Meanwhile, the site gets its billionth user.

2014
Facebook buys the messaging app WhatsApp for US$19 billion.

great but important too: "If people share more, the world will become more open and connected. And a world that's more open and connected is a better world." This is the dream of a man raised on the internet, with its potential to breach traditional borders, whether geographical, social, or temporal. The internet makes it possible for people to connect with someone they might never expect to encounter in their everyday "real world," perhaps living on a different continent and inhabiting an entirely different time zone and social class. So Zuckerberg desires to become the ultimate social facilitator, allowing previously unthinkable connections to be made. It is a vision that has proved compelling for hundreds of million users, with Facebook becoming not merely a web service but an essential cornerstone of social lives conducted without boundaries.

MIXING BUSINESS AND PLEASURE
Nonetheless, the Zuckerberg vision is not without controversy since, as openness increases, privacy inevitably correspondingly diminishes. Furthermore, given that Facebook generates most of its revenues from advertising that relies on the harvesting of personal information, large numbers of commentators have become seriously nervous about the company's position on privacy. They claim that many users simply do not understand how their information is stored and how it can be shared. Zuckerberg, though, is unrepentant, stating that people do own their personal information and have complete control over whom they share it with. Facebook, he once told the *New York Times*, "has always tried to push the envelope. And at times that means stretching people and getting them to be comfortable with things they aren't yet comfortable with. A lot of this is just social norms catching up with what technology is capable of."

CONTINUAL DEVELOPMENT
Certainly, Facebook has continued to go from strength to strength, notching up its billionth user in 2012 and going public the same year. In 2014 the company was valued at over US$200 billion. While Zuckerberg has kept faith with his original aims, he has maintained user interest by encouraging constant innovation. He considers the site to be permanently a work in progress, regularly introducing new features and functionality.

A billionaire in 2007 at the age of 23 and worth an estimated US$33 billion by his thirtieth birthday, he has shown no desire to take his foot off the gas. In 2010 he told *Wired* magazine: "The thing I really care about is the mission, making the world open." Zuckerberg's business strategy thus remains underpinned by a truly grand objective.

As well as allowing friends and acquaintances to organize social events, the company has added features to the website—from the era-defining "like" button to the ability to make video calls or send someone a "virtual gift"—that allow individuals and groups to advance political causes, promote goods and services, track down missing people, and even reunite distressed children with their lost teddy bears. As you would hope, Facebook is considered a pretty sociable place to work too, with 93 percent of employees polled in 2014 stating that they would recommend the company to a friend. Its headquarters, meanwhile, boasts free dining facilities, a gym, shuttle busses for the journey to and from San Francisco, and even the opportunity to undertake a woodworking course in a specially designed centre (a perk management hopes will encourage staff to "think outside the box").

CHANGING THE WORLD
In 2011 Zuckerberg claimed he wanted his company to "make a really big change in the

TWEET POWER

288 MILLION MONTHLY ACTIVE USERS

500 MILLION TWEETS ARE SENT PER DAY

world." Steve Jobs, another technological giant of the modern age, had a similar ethos, urging his colleagues to put a "dent in the universe." Zuckerberg has certainly done that, creating an internet phenomenon as attractive to big businesses, celebrities, and politicians intent on raising their profiles as it is to private individuals who see it as an essential tool in administering their social lives. By combining a desire for ever-greater openness alongside brilliant programming skills and business acumen, Zuckerberg has helped ensure the world is better connected now than ever before.

#INFLUENCE

While it was not quite the first to market, Facebook propelled the evolution of social networking, so that today it is instrumental even in the election of presidents and the overthrow of governments (see entry on Barack Obama on page 215). While Facebook maintains its status as the world's number one social networking site, it also created the space in which another giant has been able to grow. Established in 2006, Twitter offered a unique service allowing users to communicate in messages of not more than 140 characters. By mid-2014 it boasted 500 million users. Its influence has been pervasive, helping to create stars like Justin Bieber and Kim Kardashian, changing the way that news is delivered and allowing for instant mass mobilizations of people. Such has been its impact that it is almost unimaginable to think just a few short years ago we lived in a world without social media.

STRATEGY ANALYSIS

STRATEGY TYPE: *Innovation*
KEY STRATEGY: *Changing the way people communicate*
OUTCOME: *The world's leading social networking site, boasting in excess of one billion users*
ALSO USED BY: *Jack Dorsey, Evan Williams, Biz Stone, and Noah Glass, who founded Twitter in 2006.*

MOBILIZE SUPPORT

BARACK OBAMA USED SOCIAL MEDIA TO SPREAD HIS MESSAGE OF CHANGE AND WIN THE PRESIDENTIAL ELECTION

Barack Obama swept into the White House in 2008 on a tide of optimism. The senator who two years previously barely registered in the public consciousness had become the first African-American to win the presidency—an achievement many suspected was still years off. Fueling his meteoric rise in popularity was his engagement with social media, which brought an additional benefit of generating unprecedented campaign funds.

KEY PLAYER: *Barack Obama (1961-)*

NATIONALITY: *American*

STRATEGY IMPLEMENTED: *2008*

CONTEXT: *In 2007 Barack Obama was not even favorite to secure the Democratic presidential candidacy, let alone the White House itself. Yet by dedicated and inspired use of emerging technologies, he built unstoppable momentum*

Democrat candidate Barack Obama came out of left-field to win the presidency. Not only did he have to defeat his Republican rival, John McCain, but he first had to displace the one-time favorite for the Democratic nomination, Hillary Clinton (wife of the former president, Bill Clinton, and subsequently a New York senator). Compared to both his rivals, Obama lacked any real public profile. A lawyer, academic, and community organizer, Obama had only been voted a senator in 2004, during which election he had garnered modest attention for a keynote address he delivered at the Democratic convention. A few people began to whisper that he had the makings of a president but most of America would have struggled to pick him out in a crowd. It was a problem he knew he needed to address.

When Obama announced his desire to be the Democratic presidential candidate in February 2007, he was one of a number of names in the hat. However, before long it had turned into a two-horse race between himself and Clinton. She was already a household name and a member of Democratic royalty, having served two terms as First Lady. Republicans who despised Bill Clinton may have reviled her, but the Clinton name was still a widespread vote-winner. In addition, she had spent her post-First Lady years establishing herself as a respected political mover in her own right. The question most commentators were asking was whether America was ready for its first female president? Few were predicting that the real question was, would America elect a black president? Obama knew that any chance he had of success relied on an upswing in his public profile. While the political classes were just about coming to terms with the idea that the internet could be useful as an analytical and fund-raising tool, Obama was awake to the emergence of social networking. Could this, he wondered, be his secret weapon?

1961
Barack Hussain Obama is born on August 4 in Hawaii.

1982
He graduates from Columbia University in New York and begins working for the Chicago-based Developing Communities Project.

1991
He graduates from Harvard Law School.

1992
He directs the Illinois Project Vote, registering minority voters.

1996
He is elected to the Illinois State Senate for the Democratic Party.

1999
He fails to win election to Congress.

2004
In July, Obama makes a well-received keynote speech at the Democratic National Convention. In November he is elected to the US Senate.

2007
In February Obama formally announces his candidacy. In November media celebrity Oprah Winfrey endorses him and agrees to campaign for him.

2008
On "Super Tuesday," Obama wins 13 of 23 primaries against 10 for Hillary Clinton. Will.i.am releases a pro-Obama song on YouTube that goes viral. In March Obama makes his "A More Perfect Union" address in Philadelphia. Clinton concedes the Democratic race in June and gives her support to Obama.

November 2006
On the fourth, election day, Obama wins 53 percent of the popular vote against John McCain.

2009
He is inaugurated on January 20.

2012
Obama wins a second term in the White House.

TWEET POWER

If the 2008 election was the first US presidential poll won through the internet, the Arab Spring of 2011 was the first revolution coordinated by social media. A wave of popular uprisings spread throughout the Arab world, from North Africa and across the Middle East. The governments of Tunisia, Egypt, Libya, and Yemen fell, while Syria descended into civil war and several other administrations were forced into making democratic concessions. Time and again, it was reported that protestors relied for information on text messages, Facebook, and Twitter feeds, giving them an instant communications networks that the authorities could not contain. In many of the affected countries, social media use doubled during the protests. Furthermore, camera phones, instant messaging, and Twitter allowed for real-time news of events to be sent around the world. Gil Scott-Heron once sang that "the revolution will not be televised." It will, however, be tweeted and Facebooked.

MAKING CONNECTIONS

In early 2007 Obama started making informal approaches to some of the rising stars of Silicon Valley. He wanted an honest appraisal of how the internet and new media might help his campaign, following in a proud lineage of presidential candidates who had sought to take advantage of new methods of mass communication. Thomas Jefferson, for instance, had realized the power that newspapers could wield, while Franklin D.

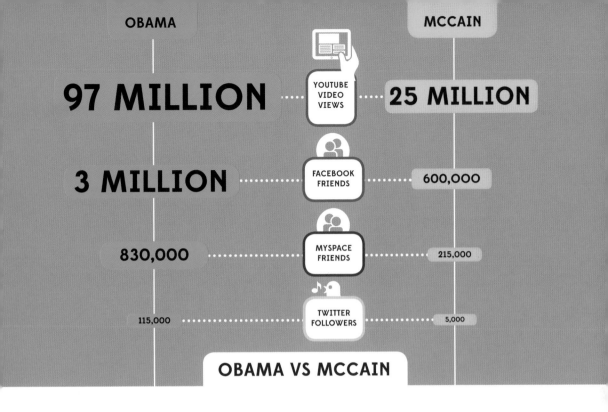

OBAMA

MCCAIN

97 MILLION

YOUTUBE VIDEO VIEWS

25 MILLION

3 MILLION

FACEBOOK FRIENDS

600,000

830,000

MYSPACE FRIENDS

215,000

115,000

TWITTER FOLLOWERS

5,000

OBAMA VS MCCAIN

Roosevelt embraced the radio, and John F. Kennedy leveraged the reach of television. Difficult as it is to imagine today, back in the dark ages of 2007, such now-familiar names as Facebook and Twitter were in their infancy.

Nonetheless, Obama was persuaded of their potential. With relative youth on his side and a recent background in community action and academic life, he was open to the idea of new technologies in a way that his older rivals were perhaps not. By August 2008 Clinton had withdrawn from the race for the Democratic nomination, having seen Obama gain ascendancy in the primaries. In November 2008 he fairly swept aside McCain in the presidential vote, winning by 200 electoral college votes and some 8.5 million popular votes. The media soon started talking of the "Facebook Election," and for good reason.

The raw statistics regarding Obama's engagement with the internet and social media are remarkable. He boasted some five million "friends" across a range of social networking sights, including three million on Facebook alone (McCain's Facebook account, by comparison, counted only 600,000 "friends," while Clinton's had racked up a measly 3,200 by the time Obama was at the quarter-million mark). On Twitter, which had been founded only in 2006 offering the opportunity of instant connection with supporters, Obama had 115,000 followers, fully 23 times more than McCain. On YouTube, 50 million people spent a combined 14 million hours watching videos uploaded by the Obama camp, while his opponent could claim only a quarter as many viewers. Obama also built up an email list comprising a colossal 13 million people, who together received 7,000 variations of over one billion emails. A further three million signed up for text messages, receiving on average between five and 20 per month. Numbers to make the head spin indeed.

CROWD FUNDING

Then there was the finance element. In June 2008 Obama became the first serious presidential candidate to turn down public financing since the 1970s. In choosing to accept public financing, candidates restrict their opportunity to privately fund raise. Obama, however, knew that he could raise far more by going down the private route. Sure enough, 6.5 million online donations brought him over US$500 million in funding. Crucially, six million of these donations were for less than US$100. In previous elections, candidates have tended to rely on a few large donations. Obama and the internet turned this strategy on its head.

CHANGING THE LANDSCAPE

If the money was important (and there is no doubt it was), the real impact of Obama's embracing of social media was to show how emerging technologies could mobilize support and create momentum. Obama won an overwhelming majority of the young vote, largely because he and his election team went to the places where young people hang out: On their computers and mobile phones. For relatively little expense (the cost of texting and posting on Facebook was negligible compared with the price of prime-time TV advertising, for instance) Obama connected to a large part of the electorate who

Obama and family on the 2008 campaign trail in Denver, Colorado. Obama was hailed for his oratory but social media was vital to his success.

had come to feel cut off from traditional politics. He created an environment in which mostly young, largely disenchanted people felt like they had joined a community of like-minded souls.

They bought into Obama's message of hope and then did the job of disseminating it for him. The pop star will.i.am posted a video clip, "Yes We Can," that went viral, notching up millions of views within days of release. Money simply cannot buy you that sort of attention. Where people had grown tired of being told what to think by politicians, newspapers, and broadcasters, they were much more receptive to messages passed on through friends and peers. Politics had become dreadfully impersonal, but receiving a text or email direct to your account made it feel quite the opposite.

▲ *Obama has changed the campaigning landscape. Candidates can no longer ignore the opportunities technology offers for communication.*

And if all that weren't enough, Obama found himself with an enormous database of useful personal information. He had the contact details of millions of people who gave them willingly in return for being "kept in the loop" via texts and emails. Furthermore, data-harvesting tools meant that the Obama team could more accurately model behavior, tailor particular messages to certain recipients, and even prioritize who to call in order to mobilize the vote in swing states. Because he created a sense of community among his supporters, Obama was able to rely on an extraordinary level of enthusiastic and well-coordinated volunteer activity. So it was that Obama used emerging technologies not merely to win votes but to create a movement. In so doing, he changed the nature of electioneering forever.

STRATEGY ANALYSIS

STRATEGY TYPE: *Communication*
KEY STRATEGY: *Generating grassroots support and securing huge funding via social media*
OUTCOME: *Obama becomes president of the United States.*
ALSO USED BY: *The Arab Spring protest leaders, 2011, and Beppe Grillo, leader of the Italian Five Star Movement.*

INDEX

Figures in bold type indicate
illustrations.

ACKNOWLEDGMENTS

The author would like to dedicate this book to Rosie and Lottie.

Quantum Books would like to thank the following for supplying images for inclusion in this book:

Alamy
Peter Horree 19; Interfoto 45

Corbis
Leemage 41; Leemage 99; English Heritage/Arcaid 107; Hulton-Deutsch Collection 125

Getty
SuperStock 11; Merry Joseph Blondel 47; DEA Picture Library 73; Science & Society Picture Library/contributor 83; Time Life Pictures/contributor 143; Sovfoto/contributor 155

Library of Congress, Prints & Photographs:
LC-DIG-ppmsca-37245 2; LC-USZ62-39587 79; LC-DIG-det-4a26438 94; LC-USZ62-117450 103; LC-USzC4-10261 115; LC-DIG-npcc-01382 117; LC-USF34-081966-E 123; LC-B2-499-3A 135; LC-USZ62-19261 140; LC-USZ62-118659 141; LC-USZ62-69229 149; LC-USZ62-31831 157; LC-DIG-ggbain-37131 159; LC-USZ62-111201 181; LC_DIG-highsm-12949 191; LC-DIG-ds-05267 195; LC-DIG-highsm-03848 218

Shutterstock.com
AISA - Everett 15; mountainpix 25; saiko3p 27; AISA - Everett 65; Everett Historical 77; Jule_Berlin 111; s_bukley 187; JStone 205; Featureflash 214; Action Sports Photography 219

Wikimedia
By Sébastien Slodtz, Loicwood (2006), CC BY-SA 2.5 33; By Jakub Hałun, CC BY-SA 3.0 37; RIA Novosti archive, image #324, Boris Kudoyarov, CC-BY-SA 3.0 49; By Miniwark, CC BY-SA 3.0 53; Bronzino, Public domain, The Yorck Project 61; By Pasquale Cati, CC BY 2.0 67; Jean-Pierre Houël, Public domain 87; Imperial War Museum, Q 81486, Public domain 133; Bundesarchiv, Bild 183-2004-0430-501, CC-BY-SA 151; Bundesarchiv, Bild 146-1976-071-36, CC-BY-SA 169; Bundesarchiv, Bild 152-50-10, Friedrich Franz Bauer, CC-BY-SA 3.0 173; By Chief Photographer's Mate (CPHoM) Robert F. Sargent, Public domain 182; US military employee, Public domain 193; By Marion S. Trikosko, U.S. News & World Report Magazine, Public domain 196; By Cayambe, CC BY-SA 3.0 199; Brian Solis, www.briansolis.com and bub.blicio.us, CC, 213

Other
Garden Cities of Tomorrow, Ebenezer Howard 129; NASA Earth Observatory image created by Jesse Allen, using EO-1 ALI data provided courtesy of the NASA EO-1 team and the United States Geological Survey 200; Amazon.com, Amazon Media Room: Images & Videos 209

All infographics have been created for Quantum Books, information sources
Buisness Insider.com, "The 10 Greatest Empires in the History of the World" 55; Encyclopedia Britannica, "The Three Branches of the Medici Family" 59; The Richest.com, "10 Richest People Who Have Ever Lived" 75; American dead and wounded: Shy, pp. 249–50, necrometrics.com, "Statistics of Wars, Oppressions and Atrocities of the Eighteenth Century" 81; La Guillotine en 1793 by H. Fleischmann (1908), page 269 90; Map Collection, Napoleon's Empire, 1810 97; Figure for people living in modern slavery according to the Walk Free Foundation's 2014 Global Slavery Index 101; CNN.com, "25 of Mankind's Greatest Engineering Achievements" 105; "The Communist Manifesto in Perspective" by Eric Hobsbawm 108-109; Notes on Matters Affecting the Health, Efficiency, and Hospital Administration of the British Army by Florence Nightingale, "Diagram of the causes of mortality in the army in the East" 113; Autoevolution.com, "Ford Cars and Brand History" 139; BBC, Inside Out: South West, "Decoy Q-Boats" 147; History.com, "6 Famous WWI Fighter Aces" 153; The Numbers.com 162–163; Museum of Tolerance, Multimedia Learning Center, "36 Questions About the Holocaust" 171; The Guardian, "Rupert Murdoch, his New Corp empire and the BSkyB takeover," 14th March 2011 185; Vanity Fair.com, "Microsoft's Lost Decade," August 2012 203; Amazon Genius.com, "Timeline History Amazon.com" 207

While every effort has been made to credit contributors, Quantum Books would like to apologize should there have been any omissions or errors and would be pleased to make the appropriate correction to future editions of the book.